AA

# BIG ROAD ATLAS BRITAIN

## CONTENTS

| | |
|---|---|
| ■ Road Signs | |
| ■ Route Planning Map | II–III |
| ■ Central London | IV–V |
| ■ Key and Legend | VI |
| ■ Road Maps | 1–67 |
| ■ Road Map and Index of Ireland | 68–69 |
| ■ Index | 70–82 |

6th Edition October 1986
Reprinted December 1986
5th Edition September 1985
Reprinted December 1985
4th Edition September 1984
Reprinted February 1985
June 1985
3rd Edition May 1983
Reprinted January 1984
2nd Edition May 1982
Reprinted September 1982
1st Edition May 1981
Reprinted June 1981

Produced by the Cartographic Department, Publishing Division of the Automobile Association.

Based on the Ordnance Survey maps, with the permission of the Controller of Her Majesty's Stationery Office.
Crown Copyright Reserved.

Printed Web Offset in England by Petty and Sons Ltd., Leeds, member of the BPCC Group.

Published by the Automobile Association, Fanum House, Basing View, Basingstoke, Hampshire RG21 2EA.

**SCALE 4 miles to 1 inch 1:250,000 Approximately**

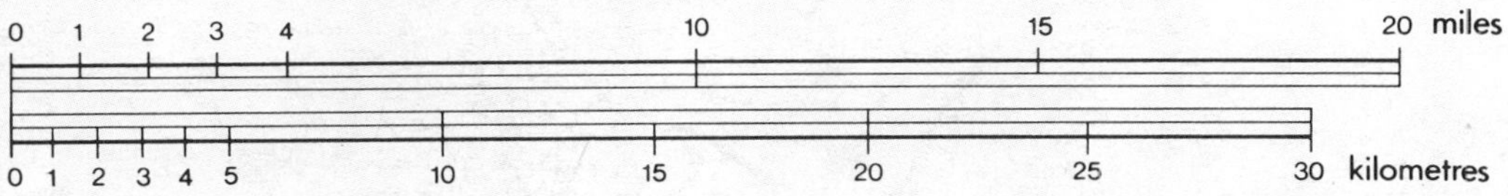

Published by The Automobile Association

# Route Planning Map

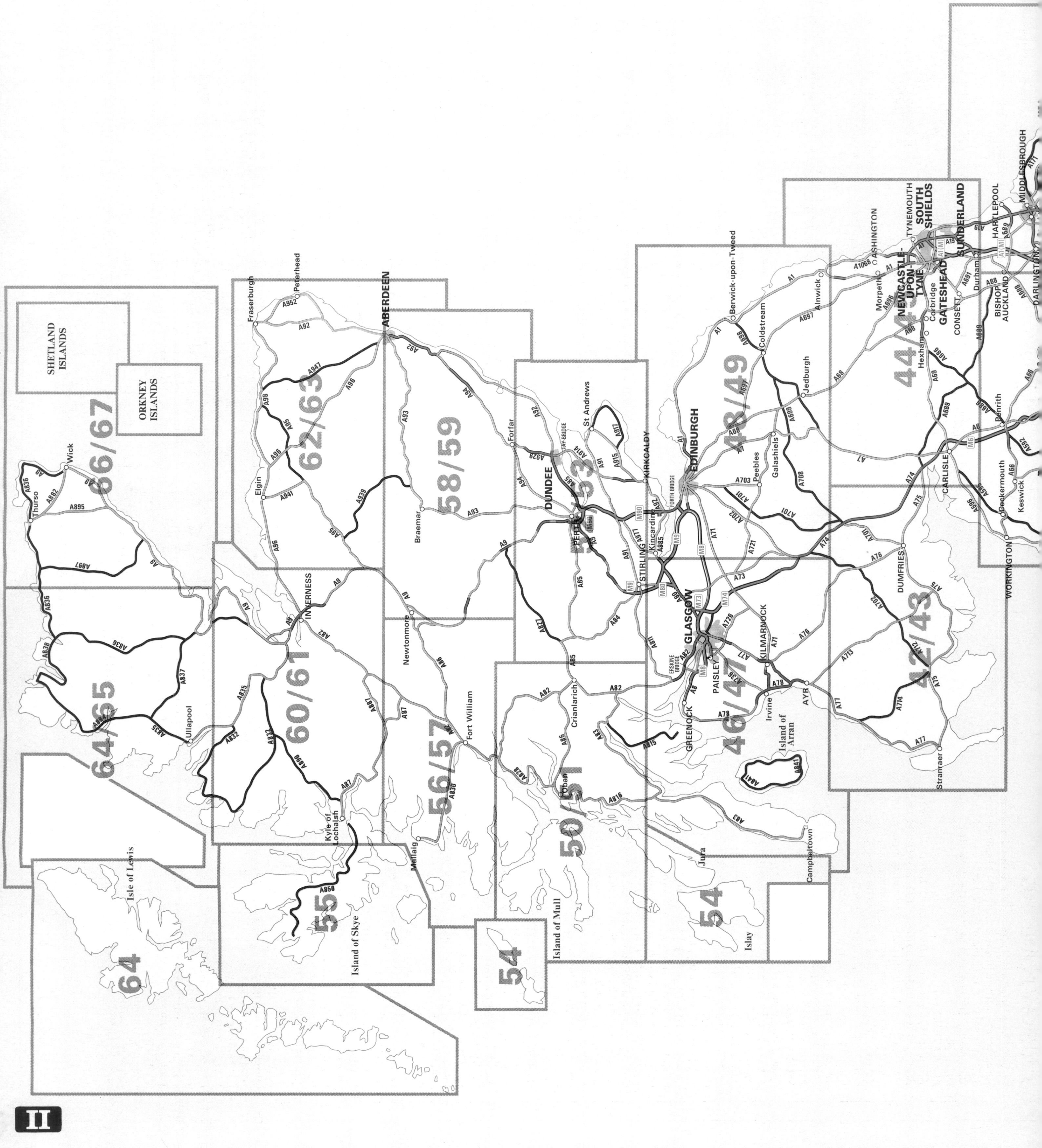

# JOURNEY PLANNING

This atlas of Great Britain and Ireland combines superb maps with accurate and practical routefinding aids. These aids are designed to help the motorist complete a journey as quickly and with as little stress as possible.

## ALERTNESS

Whether a journey is undertaken for business or pleasure, it is essential that the driver should set out feeling alert and confident, and that he should remain so until his destination is reached. A tired, frustrated driver is a potential danger to himself, to his passengers, and to other road users. The driver will feel more confident, and will certainly have a less troublesome journey, if he has planned his journey in advance. It is not wise to undertake a long journey without making regular stops for fresh air and exercise.

## ROUTE PLANNING

Once an indication of the journey length and time has been ascertained it is necessary to decide on a general route, and for this the route planning map on these pages is an invaluable guide. It depicts principal routes throughout the country, and pinpoints the large conurbations on those routes. Detailed routes can be worked out from the maps in the main atlas section of this book. The driver may find it useful to make a note of road numbers and route directions before setting out, as this can reduce his need to stop and consult the atlas. The driver is advised, where possible, to avoid driving through towns and built-up areas, even if such routes appear to be more direct from the map. Delays caused by traffic lights, one-way systems, pedestrians, etc will almost certainly be encountered in such areas.

## RADIO

Frequent radio bulletins are issued by the BBC and Independent Local Radio stations on road conditions, possible hold-ups, etc, and these can be of great assistance to the driver. By tuning in to the local stations of areas being passed through, it may be possible to avoid delays, and be prepared to make running changes to the route.

## MOTORWAYS

When planning routes, many drivers will consider using motorways. They have several advantages over other types of road; not only are they faster, but they are also very easy to follow and allow a more consistent speed to be maintained. Drivers should, however, be fully conversant with the special rules for motorway driving, which are contained in the Highway Code. Perhaps the most ignored of these is that the outside lanes of a motorway should be used for overtaking only; there is no such thing as a 'fastlane'.

For many drivers, one of the worst motoring obstacles until recently was the journey around London's perimeter. With the opening of the complete Orbital Motorway (M25) this has become much easier and quicker.

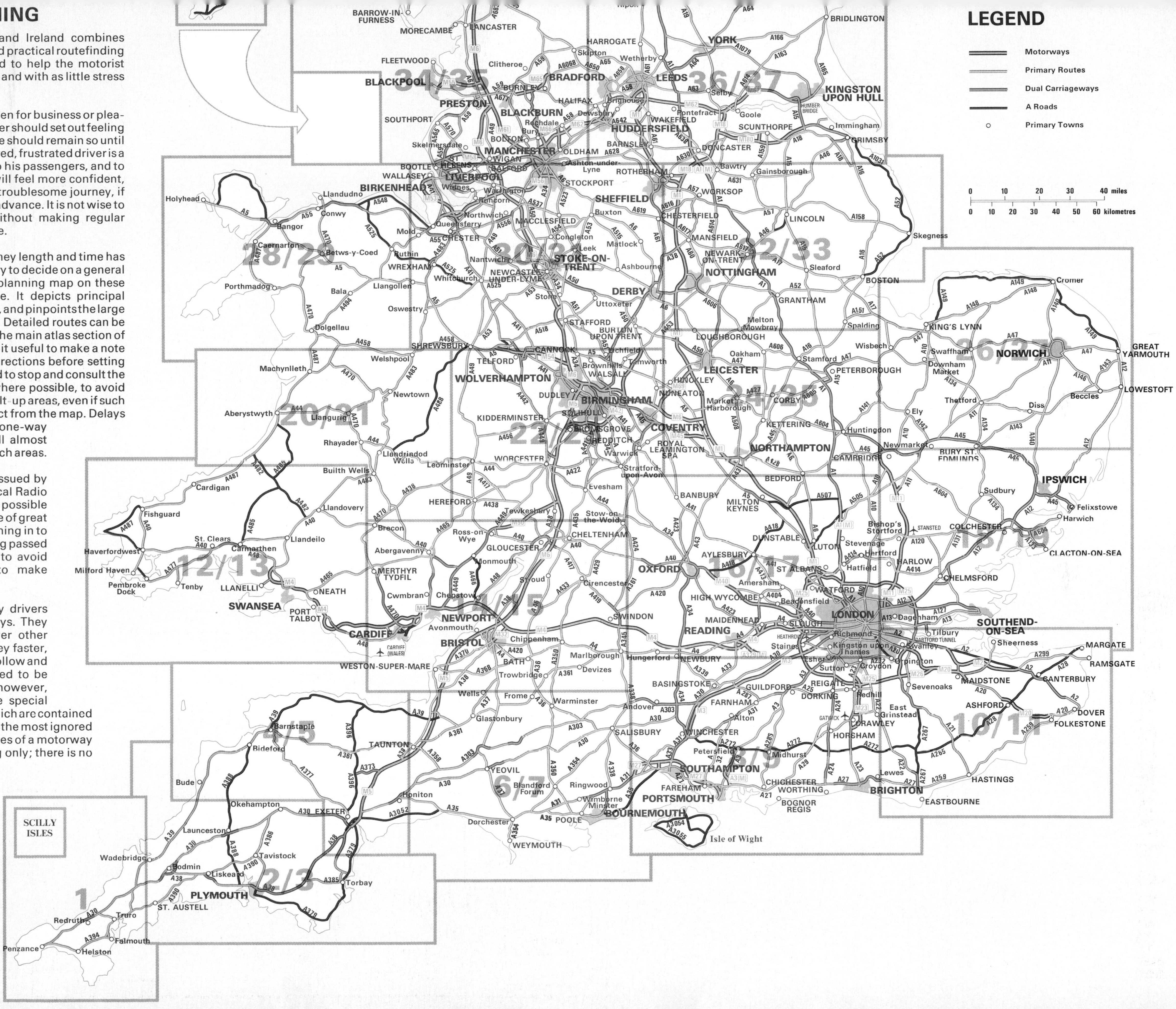

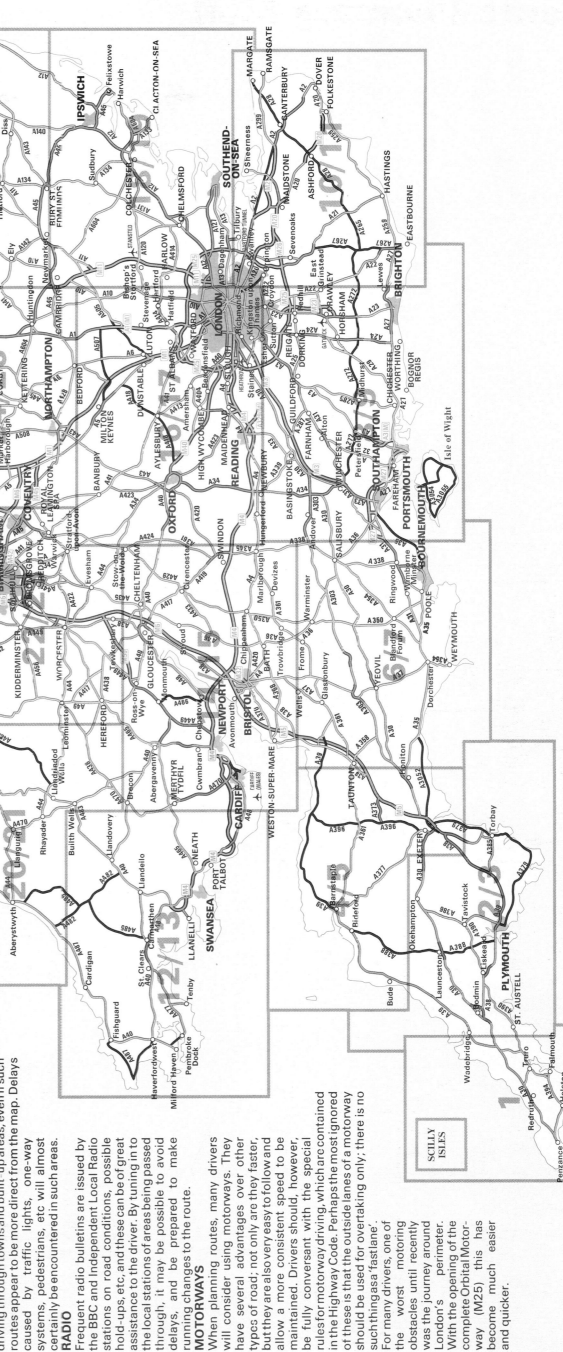

# Central London

CLERKENWELL
BLOOMSBURY
HOLBORN
SOHO
ST GILES
STRAND
ST JAMES'S
LAMBETH
WESTMINSTER
NEWINGTON
University College
University of London
British Museum
Russell Square
Coram's Fields Playground
Brunswick Housing & Shopping Centre
Dickens House
Hospital for Sick Children
Gray's Inn
Lincoln's Inn Fields
Lincoln's Inn
Royal Courts of Justice
London School of Economics
Inns of Court and Chancery
Middle Temple Hall
Inner Temple
Somerset House
Bush House
Charterhouse
Central Markets (Smithfield)
St Bartholomew's Hospital
St Bartholomew the Great
National Postal Museum
Holborn Viaduct Station
Central Criminal Court
St Paul's Cathedral
Blackfriars Station
Covent Garden
Seven Dials
Leicester Square
Piccadilly Circus
National Gallery
National Portrait Gallery
St Martin-in-the-Fields
Trafalgar Square
Nelson Column
Admiralty Arch
Admiralty
Horse Guards
Government Offices
Banqueting House
Cenotaph
Norman Shaw Building (MP's Offices)
Cleopatra's Needle
Charing Cross Sta
Embankment
Hungerford Bridge (Foot)
Royal Festival Hall
Queen Elizabeth Hall
National Film Theatre (Club)
Hayward Gallery
National Theatre
Jubilee Gardens
County Hall
Waterloo Station
Old Vic Theatre
Young Vic Th
St James's Park
St James's Park Lake
Duck Island
Cabinet War Rooms
Queen Elizabeth II Conf Centre
Westminster Abbey
Houses of Parliament
Big Ben
Westminster Hall
Jewel Tower
Dean's Yard
Westminster Pier
Westminster Br
Lambeth Bridge
Lambeth Palace
Archbishop's Park
St Thomas's Hospital
Imperial War Museum
St George's Cathedral
St George's Circus
Elephant & Castle
Metropolitan Tabernacle
London College of Printing
Westminster Hospital
Westminster Children's Hosp
Millbank Tower
Tate Gallery
Victoria Tower Gardens
Ethelred Estate
Cotton Gardens Estate
Restricted to light vehicles max. height 12ft
Closed to traffic on Sundays
RIVER THAMES
V

# Key & Legend

## TOURIST INFORMATION

- Abbey or Cathedral
- Ruined Abbey or Cathedral
- Castle
- House and Garden
- House
- Garden
- Industrial Interest
- Museum or Collection
- Prehistoric Monument
- Famous Battle Site
- Preserved Railway or Steam Centre
- Windmill
- Sea Angling
- Coastal-Launching Site
- Surfing
- Climbing School
- County Cricket Ground
- Gliding Centre
- Artificial Ski Slope
- Golf Course
- Horse Racing
- Show Jumping/Equestrian Centre
- Motor Racing Circuit
- Cave
- Country Park
- Dolphinarium or Aquarium
- Nature Trail
- Wildlife Park (mammals)
- Wildlife Park (birds)
- Zoo
- Forest Drive
- Lighthouse
- Tourist Information Centre
- Tourist Information Centre (Summer only)
- Long Distance Footpath
- AA Viewpoint
- Other Place of Interest
- Boxed symbols indicate tourist attractions in towns

## MOTORING INFORMATIO

- M25 Motorway with number
- 6 Junctions with and without numbers
- 3 Junctions with limited entries or exits
- S Service area
- Motorway & junction under construction
- A4 Primary route
- A340 Other A roads
- B4353 B roads
- Unclassified roads
- A33 Dual Carriageway
- Road with limited entries or exits
- Under construction
- Scotland: narrow roads with passing place
- AA 24 hour AA Centre (24 hours ☎)
- AA AA Centre (normal office hours)
- AA info AA Motorway Information Centre
- AA Road Service Centre
- AA Port Service Centre
- AA & RAC telephones
- BT telephones in isolated areas
- PS Picnic site
- Steep gradient (arrows point downhill)
- Toll LC Road toll Level crossing
- V Vehicle ferry (Gt. Britain)
- V CALAIS Vehicle ferry (continental)
- Hovercraft ferry
- Airport
- Urban area Village
- National boundary
- County boundary
- 5 Distance in miles between symbols
- 2331 Spot height in feet
- River and Lake
- Sandy beaches
- 12 Overlaps and numbers of continuing pages
- Little Chef (7am-10pm)
- Little Chef Lodge (accomodation)

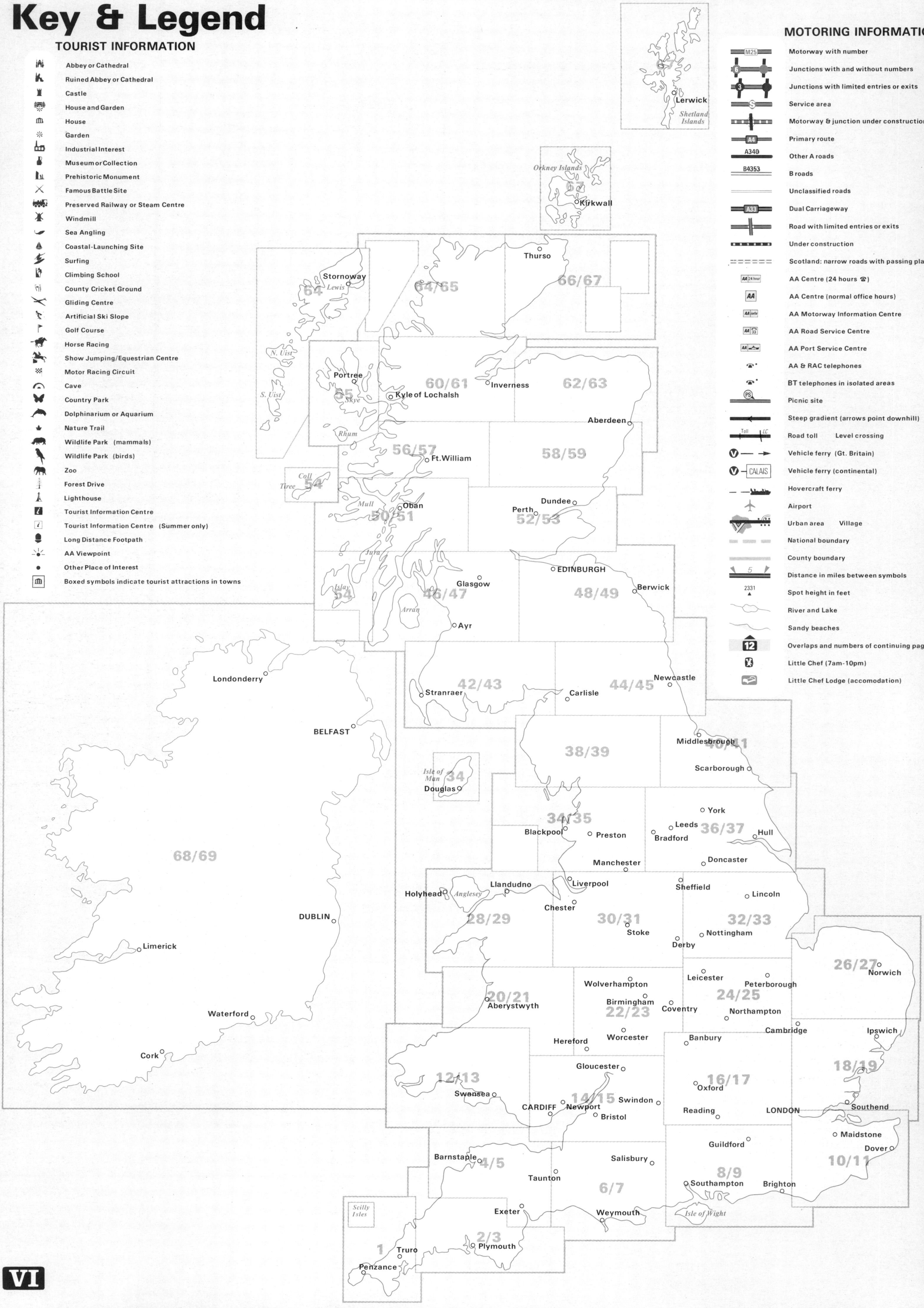

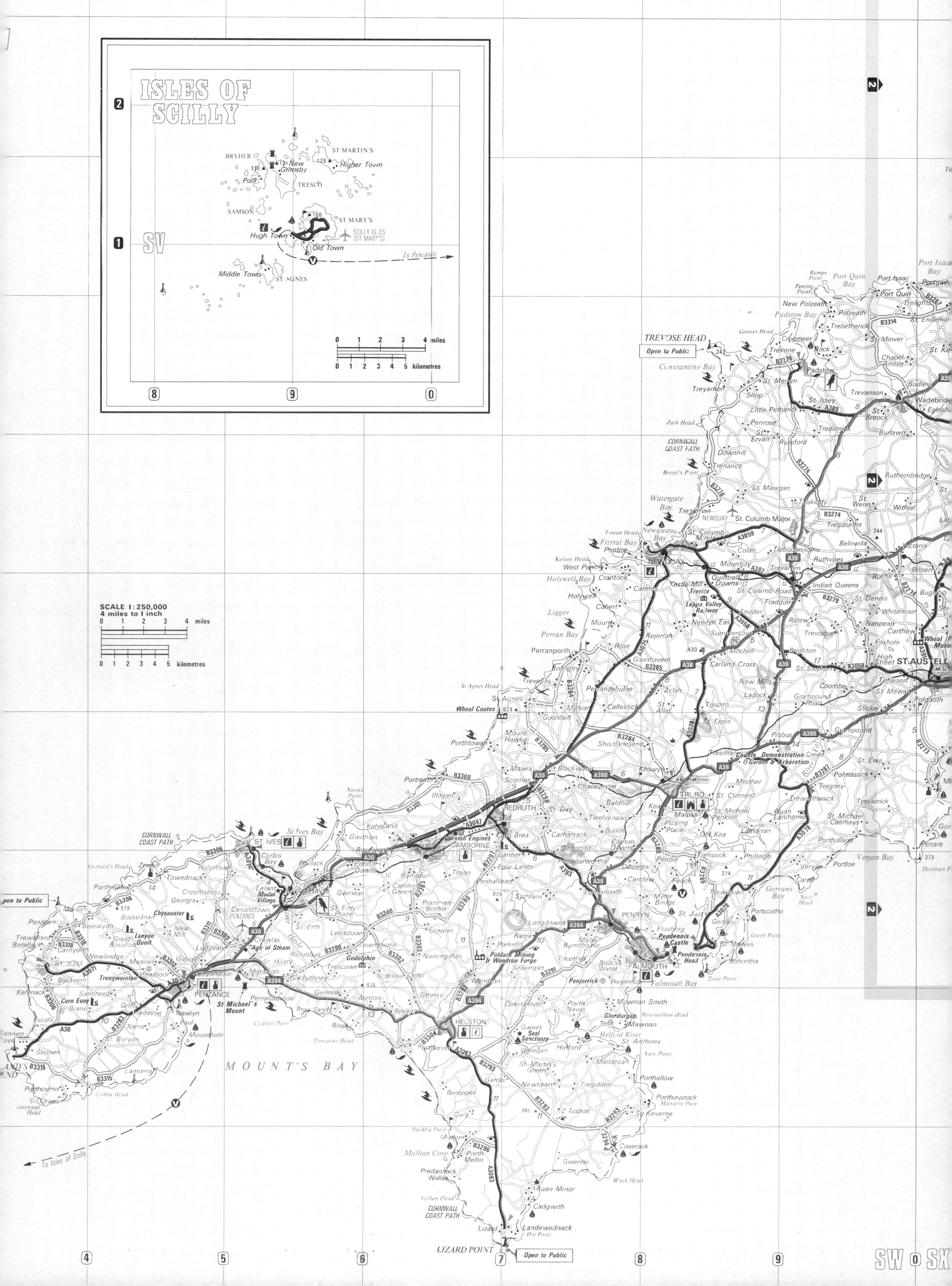
ISLES OF SCILLY
BRYHER
ST MARTIN'S
New Grimsby
Higher Town
Poor
TRESCO
SAMSON
ST MARY'S
Hugh Town
SCILLY ISLES (ST MARY'S)
Old Town
To Penzance
Middle Town
ST AGNES
SV
0 1 2 3 4 miles
0 1 2 3 4 5 kilometres
SCALE 1:250,000
4 miles to 1 inch
0 1 2 3 4 miles
0 1 2 3 4 5 kilometres
TREVOSE HEAD
Open to Public
Constantine Bay
Trevone
Padstow
Padstow Bay
New Polzeath
Polzeath
Port Quin Bay
Port Isaac
Port Isaac Bay
St. Minver
Rock
Trebetherick
St. Merryn
Treyarnon
St. Issey
Wadebridge
Little Petherick
St. Breock
Park Head
CORNWALL COAST PATH
St. Ervan
Rumford
Burlawn
Tredinnick
Trevanson
Ruthernbridge
Downhill
Trenance
Berryl's Point
Watergate Bay
St. Mawgan
Tregaswith
NEWQUAY
St. Columb Major
St. Wenn
Withiel
Towan Head
Newquay Bay
St. Columb Minor
Fistral Bay
Pentire
Colan
Mountjoy
Belowda
Victoria
Kelsey Head
West Pentire
Crantock
Holywell Bay
Holywell
Quintrell Downs
Trerice
Kestle Mill
St. Columb Road
Indian Queens
Roche
Ruthvoes
Lappa Valley Railway
Fraddon
St. Dennis
Whitemoor
Bugle
Ligger
Cubert
Mount
Newlyn East
Enoder
Retew
Nanpean
Carthew
Foxhole
Perran Bay
Rejerrah
Summercourt
Trevisco
Perranporth
Rose
Goonhavern
Mitchell
Carland Cross
Brighton
St. Stephen
High Street
ST. AUSTELL
Bolingey
Trevellas
St Agnes Head
St. Agnes
Wheal Coates
Perranzabuloe
Zelah
St. Allen
New Mills
Ladock
Trewoon
St. Mewan
Coombe
Grampound Road
Sticker
Polgooth
Callestick
Goonbell
Mithian
Trispen
Mount Hawke
Shortlanesend
Probus
Grampound
Porthtowan
County Demonstration Garden & Arboretum
Tresillian
Creed
St. Ewe
Polmassick
Portreath
Mawla
Scorrier
Blackwater
Chacewater
Kenwyn
TRURO
Merther
Tregony
St. Clement
Illogan
REDRUTH
St. Day
Baldhu
Kea
Malpas
St. Michael Penkivil
Ruan Lanihorne
Trewarthenick
Trevarrick
St. Michael Caerhays
Navax Point
St Ives Bay
ST. IVES
CORNWALL COAST PATH
Gwithian
Cornish Engines
CAMBORNE
Carn Brea
Carharrack
Twelveheads
Bissoe
Playing Place
Old Kea
Lamorran
Portholland
Veryan Bay
Veryan
Dodman Point
Portloe
Gurnard's Head
Zennor
Towednack
Halsetown
Carbis Bay
Phillack
Hayle
Lelant
Model Village
Connor Downs
Roseworthy
Barripper
Troon
Lanner
Four Lanes
Penhalvean
Gwennap
Perranarworthal
Carnon Downs
Devoran
Penpol
Trelissick
Philleigh
Carne
Gerrans Bay
Nare Head
Porthmeor
Cripplesease
Georgia
Chysauster
Canonstown
Gwinear
Carnhell Green
Praze-an-Beeble
St. Erth Praze
St. Erth
Stithians
Ponsanooth
Carclew
Mylor Bridge
Feock
St. Just
Gerrans
Portscatho
Pendeen
Morvah
Boskednan
Bojewyan
Trewellard
Botallack
Carnyorth
Great Bosullow
Lanyon Quoit
New Mill
Ludgvan
Crowlas
Age of Steam
Leedstown
Crowan
Longdowns
PENRYN
Flushing
Pendennis Castle
Pendennis Head
St. Mawes
Bohortha
Zone Point
Newbridge
Madron
Heamoor
Gulval
Chyandour
PENZANCE
Marazion
St. Hilary
Relubbus
Godolphin
Townshend
Nancegollan
Porkellis
Rame
Burnthouse
Mabe
Treverva
Budock Water
FALMOUTH
Falmouth Bay
Poldark Mining & Wendron Forge
Seworgan
Wendron
Pennance
Trengwainton
Kelynack
Bosavern
Sancreed
Carn Euny
Brane
Drift
Tredavoe
Newlyn
Paul
Mousehole
Kerris
St. Buryan
Sennen
Sennen Cove
LAND'S END
St Michael's Mount
Perranuthnoe
Praa Sands
Germoe
Goldsithney
Trescowe
Godolphin Cross
Ashton
Breage
Rinsey
Cudden Point
Trewavas Head
Sithney
HELSTON
Constantine
Porth Navas
Mawnan Smith
Glendurgan
Mawnan
Rosemullion Head
Gweek
Seal Sanctuary
Helford River
Helford
St. Anthony
Nare Point
Manaccan
Porthleven
MOUNT'S BAY
Lamorna
Penberth
Porthcurno
St. Levan
Gwennap Head
Cribba Head
Garras
St. Martin's Green
Newtown
Tregidden
Porthallow
Porthoustock
Manacle Point
St. Keverne
Trelowarren
Traboe
Berepper
Cury
Poldhu Point
Mullion
Mullion Cove
Porth Mellin
Coverack
Gwenter
Predannack Wollas
Black Head
Ruan Minor
Vellan Head
CORNWALL COAST PATH
Cadgwith
Lizard
Landewednack
Hot Point
LIZARD POINT
Open to Public
To Isles of Scilly
4
5
6
7
8
9
SW 0 SX

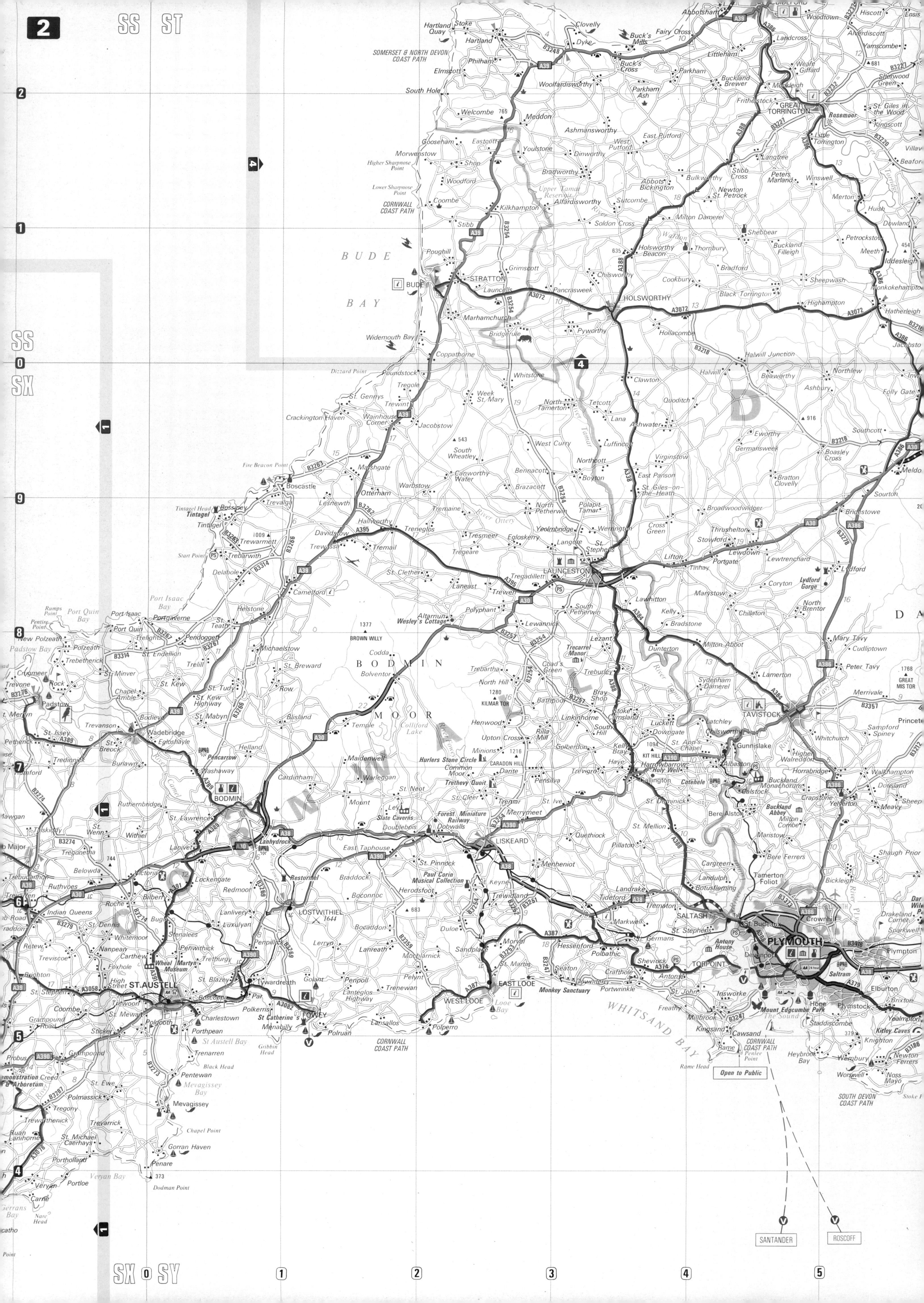
SS ST
SS
SX
SX 0 SY
1
2
3
4
5
Hartland Quay
Stoke
Hartland
Clovelly
Dyke
Buck's Mills
Fairy Cross
Abbotsham
BIDEFORD
Woodtown
Hiscott
Alverdiscott
Yarnscombe
Landcross
Weare Giffard
Littleham
SOMERSET & NORTH DEVON COAST PATH
Philham
Elmscott
Buck's Cross
Parkham
Buckland Brewer
Woolfardisworthy
Parkham Ash
South Hole
Welcombe
Meddon
Ashmansworthy
Monkleigh
Frithelstock
GREAT TORRINGTON
Rosemoor
St. Giles in the Wood
Kingscott
Sherwood Green
Little Torrington
East Putford
West Putford
Gooseham
Eastcott
Youlstone
Dinworthy
Morwenstow
Higher Sharpnose Point
Shop
Woodford
Bradworthy
Lower Sharpnose Point
Upper Tamar Reservoir
Alfardisworthy
Abbots Bickington
Langtree
Stibb Cross
Peters Marland
Winswell
Newton St. Petrock
Coombe
CORNWALL COAST PATH
Kilkhampton
Sutcombe
Merton
Huish
Soldon Cross
Milton Damerel
Dowland
Stibb
Shebbear
Buckland Filleigh
Petrockstow
Meeth
Iddesleigh
Poughill
BUDE
BAY
Grimscott
Holsworthy Beacon
Thornbury
Bradford
Cookbury
Sheepwash
BUDE
STRATTON
Launcells
Pancrasweek
Chilsworthy
HOLSWORTHY
Black Torrington
Highampton
Monkokehampton
Hatherleigh
Marhamchurch
Bridgerule
Pyworthy
Hollacombe
Widemouth Bay
Coppathorne
Halwill Junction
Jacobstow
Dizzard Point
Poundstock
Whitstone
Clawton
Halwill
Beaworthy
Northlew
Ashbury
Folly Gate
Tregole
St. Gennys
Week St. Mary
North Tamerton
Tetcott
Quoditch
Trewint
Crackington Haven
Wainhouse Corner
Jacobstow
Lana
Ashwater
D
Southcott
South Wheatley
West Curry
Luffincott
Ewarthy
Germansweek
Boasley Cross
Fire Beacon Point
Marshgate
Canworthy Water
Northcott
Virginstow
Boscastle
Otterham
Warbstow
Bennacott
Boyton
East Panson
St. Giles-on-the-Heath
Bratton Clovelly
Meldon
Sourton
Tintagel Head
Tintagel
Bossiney
Trevalga
Lesnewth
Brazacott
Tremaine
North Petherwin
Polapit Tamar
River Ottery
Broadwoodwidger
Bridestowe
Hallworthy
Davidstow
Treneglos
Tresmeer
Egloskerry
Yeolmbridge
Werrington
Cross Green
Thrushelton
Trewarmett
Trewassa
Tremail
Tregeare
Langore
St. Stephens
Stowford
Lewdown
Start Point
Trebarwith
Delabole
St. Clether
LAUNCESTON
Lifton
Tinhay
Portgate
Lewtrenchard
Lydford
Laneast
Tregadillett
Camelford
Trewen
Coryton
Lydford Gorge
Port Isaac Bay
Port Quin Bay
Rumps Point
Pentire Point
Port Isaac
Portgaverne
Port Quin
Helstone
Altarnun
Wesley's Cottage
Polyphant
South Petherwin
Lawhitton
Marystow
North Brentor
Kelly
Chillaton
Bradstone
Lewannick
St. Teath
New Polzeath
Polzeath
Trelights
Pendoggett
Michaelstow
BROWN WILLY
Lezant
Dunterton
Milton Abbot
Mary Tavy
Cudliptown
Padstow Bay
Trebetherick
St. Endellion
Codda
Trecarrel Manor
Treburley
Peter Tavy
GREAT MIS TOR
St. Minver
Trelill
St. Breward
BODMIN
Bolventor
Trebartha
Coad's Green
Sydenham Damerel
Lamerton
Crugmeer
Rock
Chapel Amble
St. Kew
North Hill
Trevone
St. Tudy
St. Kew Highway
Row
KILMAR TOR
Bathpool
Bray Shop
Merrivale
Padstow
St. Mabyn
MOOR
Stoke Climsland
Latchley
TAVISTOCK
Bodieve
St. Merryn
Blisland
Linkinhorne
South Hill
Luckett
Downgate
Chilsworthy
Princetown
Trevanson
Wadebridge
Egloshayle
Temple
Colliford Lake
Henwood
Rilla Mill
Sampford Spiney
St. Issey
St. Breock
Upton Cross
Golberdon
KIT HILL
St. Ann's Chapel
Gunnislake
Whitchurch
Helland
Minions
CARADON HILL
Kelly Bray
Higher Walreddon
Petherick
Tredinnick
Pencarrow
Hurlers Stone Circle
Haye
Albaston
Horrabridge
Burlawn
Maidenwell
Common Moor
Darite
Harrowbarrow
Holy Well
Walkhampton
Washaway
Cardinham
Warleggan
Trethevy Quoit
Pensilva
Trevigro
Callington
Cotehele
Calstock
Buckland Monachorum
Dousland
Rumford
BODMIN
St. Neot
Tremar
Merrymeet
St. Ive
St. Dominick
Crapstone
Yelverton
Meavy
Ruthernbridge
Mount
Ley
Slate Caverns
Buckland Abbey
Milton Combe
St. Lawrence
Doublebois
Forest Miniature Railway
Dobwalls
LISKEARD
Quethiock
St. Mellion
Bere Alston
Mawgan
St. Wenn
Talskiddy
Lanivet
Lanhydrock
East Taphouse
St. Pinnock
Pillaton
Maristow
Shaugh Prior
Withiel
Tregonetha
Paul Corin Musical Collection
Menheniot
Bere Ferrers
Belowda
Victoria
Lockengate
Restormel
Braddock
Cargreen
Tamerton Foliot
Trebudannon
Ruthvoes
Redmoor
Herodsfoot
St. Keyne
Landulph
Bickleigh
Roche
Bilberry
Trewidland
Botusfleming
Indian Queens
Lanlivery
LOSTWITHIEL
Boconnoc
Tideford
Landrake
Trematon
SALTASH
St. Budeaux
Crownhill
Drakeland Corner
Sparkwell
St. Dennis
Bugle
Luxulyan
Bocaddon
Duloe
Markwell
St. Germans
St. Stephens
Whitemoor
Stenalees
Lerryn
Sandplace
Morval
Hessenford
Antony House
PLYMOUTH
Plympton
Retew
Nanpean
Penwithick
Penpillick
Lanreath
Muchlarnick
Polbathic
Sheviock
TORPOINT
Devonport
Treviscoe
Carthew
Treburgy
Wheal Martyn Museum
Pelynt
St. Martin
Crafthole
Saltram
Foxhole
Seaton
Downderry
Antony
Elburton
High Street
ST. AUSTELL
St. Blazey
Tywardreath
Golant
Penpoll
Trenewan
EAST LOOE
Monkey Sanctuary
Portwrinkle
St. John
Insworke
Hooe
Plymstock
Brixton
Yealmpton
Coombe
Trewoon
Boscoppa
Par
Polkerris
St Catherine's
FOWEY
Lanteglos Highway
WEST LOOE
Looe Bay
WHITSAND BAY
Freathy
Mount Edgcumbe Park
The Sound
Staddiscombe
Grampound Road
St. Mewan
Charlestown
Menabilly
Lansallos
Polperro
Millbrook
Kingsand
Cawsand
Kitley Caves
Knighton
Sticker
Polgooth
Porthpean
Polruan
CORNWALL COAST PATH
Rame
Penlee Point
Heybrook Bay
Wembury
Newton Ferrers
Gribbin Head
St Austell Bay
Rame Head
Open to Public
Noss Mayo
Worswell
Probus
Grampound
Trenarren
Black Head
SOUTH DEVON COAST PATH
Creed
Pentewan
St. Ewe
Mevagissey Bay
Polmassick
Tregony
Mevagissey
Trewarthenick
Trevarrick
Chapel Point
Ruan Lanihorne
St. Michael Caerhays
Gorran Haven
Portholland
Penare
Veryan Bay
Dodman Point
Veryan
Portloe
Carne
Gerrans Bay
Nare Head
SANTANDER
ROSCOFF
A39
A30
A38
A386
A388
A3072
A395
A390
A384
A387
A374
A3082
A3058
A391
A389
A379
B3248
B3254
B3218
B3263
B3266
B3314
B3267
B3257
B3269
B3359
B3253
B3247
B3274
B3279
B3287
B3273
B3276
B3227
B3220
B3216
B3278
B3357
B3212
B3373
B3416
B3186

3
SCALE 1:250,000
4 miles to 1 inch
0 1 2 3 4 miles
0 1 2 3 4 5 kilometres
TAUNTON
WELLINGTON
TIVERTON
CREDITON
EXETER
HONITON
OTTERY ST. MARY
SIDMOUTH
SEATON
EXMOUTH
BUDLEIGH SALTERTON
DAWLISH
TEIGNMOUTH
NEWTON ABBOT
ASHBURTON
BUCKFASTLEIGH
TORBAY
TOTNES
DARTMOUTH
KINGSBRIDGE
SALCOMBE
SOUTH MOLTON
BABBACOMBE BAY
TOR BAY
START BAY
SOUTH DEVON COAST PATH
To Alderney and Guernsey (Summer only)
Dartmouth Castle
Torbay and Dartmouth Railway
Dart Valley Railway
Dartington Hall
Buckfast Abbey
Killerton
Knightshayes Court
Powderham
A la Ronde
Devon & Exeter
Compton
Start Point
Prawle Point
Bolt Head
Bolt Tail
Berry Head
Hope's Nose
Beer Head
Loughwood Meeting House
Wellington Monument
BLACKDOWN HILLS
7
8
9
SY 0 SZ
1
2
3

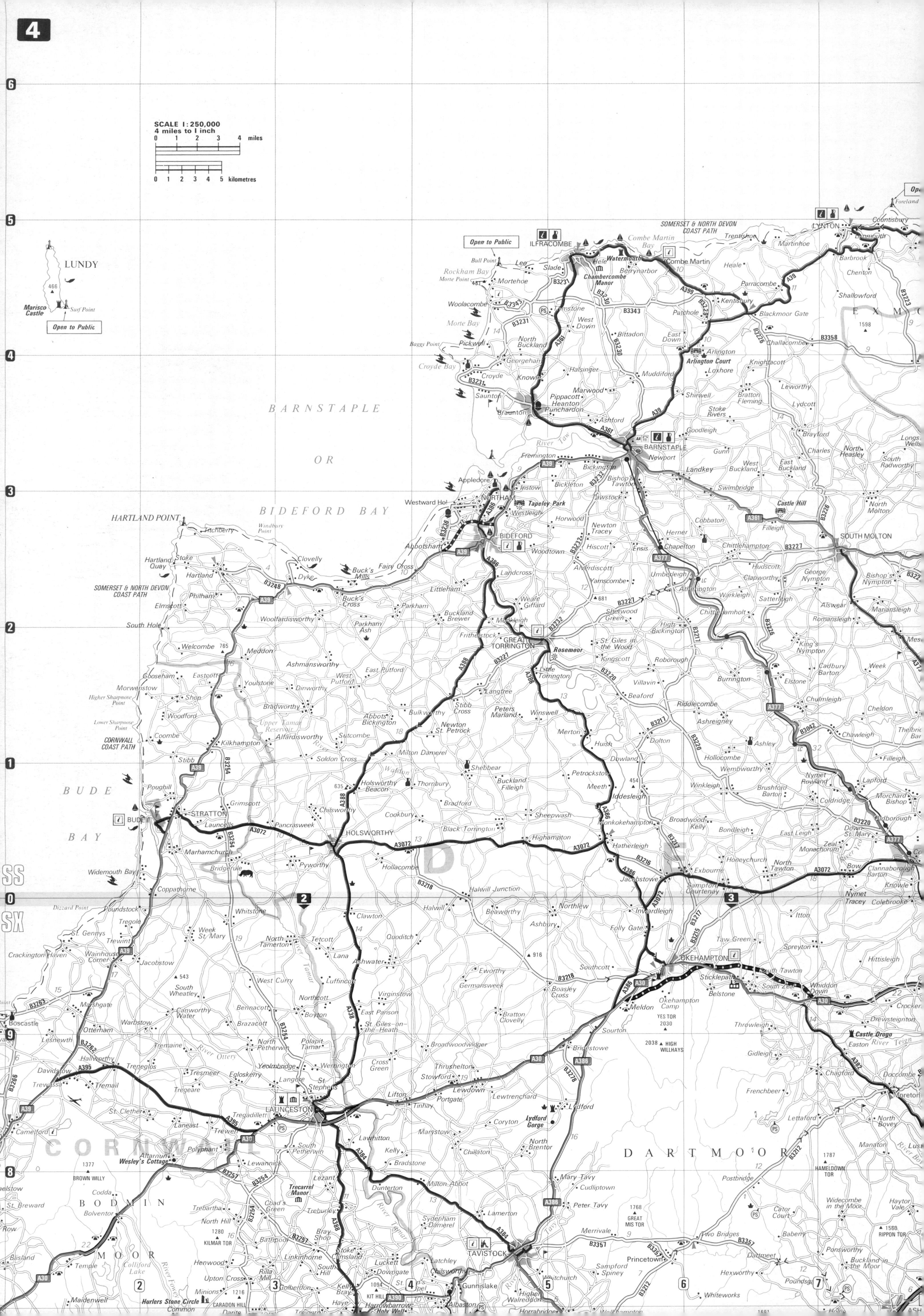
SCALE 1:250,000
4 miles to 1 inch
0 1 2 3 4 miles
0 1 2 3 4 5 kilometres
LUNDY
Marisco Castle
Surf Point
Open to Public
BARNSTAPLE
OR
BIDEFORD BAY
HARTLAND POINT
BUDE
BAY
SOMERSET & NORTH DEVON COAST PATH
CORNWALL COAST PATH
ILFRACOMBE
Combe Martin
Combe Martin Bay
Watermouth
Chambercombe Manor
Berrynarbor
Bull Point
Lee
Slade
Rockham Bay
Morte Point
Mortehoe
Woolacombe
Morte Bay
Baggy Point
Pickwell
Croyde Bay
Croyde
Georgeham
Saunton
Braunton
Knowle
Pippacott
Heanton Punchardon
Ashford
Marwood
Halsinger
Muddiford
North Buckland
West Down
Bittadon
East Down
Arlington
Arlington Court
Loxhore
Shirwell
Patchole
Kentisbury
Blackmoor Gate
Parracombe
Trentishoe
Martinhoe
LYNTON
Lynmouth
Countisbury
Foreland
Barbrook
Cheriton
Shallowford
Challacombe
EXMOOR
Heale
BARNSTAPLE
Newport
Landkey
Goodleigh
Gunn
Swimbridge
West Buckland
East Buckland
Stoke Rivers
Bratton Fleming
Knightacott
Leworthy
Lydcott
Brayford
Charles
North Heasley
South Radworthy
Castle Hill
Filleigh
North Molton
SOUTH MOLTON
Fremington
Bickington
Instow
Appledore
Westward Ho!
NORTHAM
Tapeley Park
Westleigh
Bishop's Tawton
Tawstock
Horwood
Newton Tracey
Bickleton
BIDEFORD
Abbotsham
Woodtown
Hiscott
Ensis
Chapelton
Herner
Cobbaton
Chittlehampton
Umberleigh
Atherington
Hudscott
Clapworthy
George Nympton
Bishop's Nympton
Landcross
Alverdiscott
Yarnscombe
Weare Giffard
Monkleigh
Frithelstock
GREAT TORRINGTON
Rosemoor
Little Torrington
St. Giles in the Wood
Kingscott
Sherwood Green
High Bickington
Roborough
Chittlehamholt
Warkleigh
Satterleigh
Alswear
Mariansleigh
Romansleigh
King's Nympton
Cadbury Barton
Burrington
Week
Elstone
Chulmleigh
Cheldon
Chawleigh
Villavin
Beaford
Riddlecombe
Ashreigney
Ashley
Dolton
Dowland
Hollocombe
Wembworthy
Winkleigh
Brushford Barton
Nymet Rowland
Lapford
Coldridge
Morchard Bishop
Iddesleigh
Monkokehampton
Broadwood Kelly
Bondleigh
East Leigh
Zeal Monachorum
Down St. Mary
Clannaborough Barton
Knowle
Bow
Nymet Tracey
Colebrooke
North Tawton
Honeychurch
Exbourne
Sampford Courtenay
Jacobstowe
Hatherleigh
Highampton
Black Torrington
Sheepwash
Petrockstow
Meeth
Huish
Merton
Buckland Filleigh
Winswell
Peters Marland
Langtree
Stibb Cross
Newton St. Petrock
Bulkworthy
Abbots Bickington
Milton Damerel
Shebbear
Thornbury
Bradford
Cookbury
Holsworthy Beacon
Chilsworthy
Pancrasweek
HOLSWORTHY
Pyworthy
Hollacombe
Bridgerule
Marhamchurch
Launcells
STRATTON
BUDE
Poughill
Grimscott
Kilkhampton
Stibb
Coombe
Woodford
Shop
Morwenstow
Gooseham
Eastcott
Welcombe
Meddon
South Hole
Elmscott
Philham
Hartland
Hartland Quay
Stoke
Titchberry
Windbury Point
Clovelly
Dyke
Buck's Mills
Fairy Cross
Buck's Cross
Littleham
Parkham
Parkham Ash
Buckland Brewer
Woolfardisworthy
Ashmansworthy
East Putford
West Putford
Dinworthy
Youlstone
Bradworthy
Upper Tamar Reservoir
Alfardisworthy
Sutcombe
Soldon Cross
Higher Sharpnose Point
Lower Sharpnose Point
Widemouth Bay
Coppathorne
Dizzard Point
Poundstock
Whitstone
Tregole
St. Gennys
Trewint
Week St. Mary
Crackington Haven
Wainhouse Corner
Jacobstow
North Tamerton
Tetcott
Clawton
Quoditch
Halwill
Halwill Junction
Beaworthy
Northlew
Ashbury
Inwardleigh
Folly Gate
OKEHAMPTON
Taw Green
Spreyton
Itton
Hittisleigh
South Tawton
Sticklepath
Belstone
South Zeal
Whiddon Down
Crockernwell
Drewsteignton
Castle Drogo
Easton
River Teign
Chagford
Gidleigh
Throwleigh
Okehampton Camp
Meldon
Sourton
YES TOR
HIGH WILLHAYS
Bridestowe
Southcott
Germansweek
Eworthy
Boasley Cross
Bratton Clovelly
Ashwater
Lana
Luffincott
West Curry
South Wheatley
Canworthy Water
Warbstow
Otterham
Marshgate
Boscastle
Lesnewth
Bennacott
Brazacott
Northcott
Boyton
Virginstow
East Panson
St. Giles-on-the-Heath
North Petherwin
Polapit Tamar
Tremaine
River Ottery
Tresmeer
Egloskerry
Yeolmbridge
Werrington
Langore
St. Stephens
Hallworthy
Davidstow
Trewassa
Tremail
Treneglos
Tregeare
St. Clether
Laneast
Tregadillett
Trewen
LAUNCESTON
Camelford
Polyphant
Altarnun
Wesley's Cottage
Lewannick
South Petherwin
Lawhitton
Lifton
Tinhay
Cross Green
Broadwoodwidger
Thrushelton
Stowford
Lewdown
Portgate
Lewtrenchard
Coryton
Lydford
Lydford Gorge
Marystow
Chillaton
North Brentor
Kelly
Bradstone
Milton Abbot
Dunterton
Lezant
Trecarrel Manor
Treburley
Cad's Green
Trebartha
North Hill
KILMAR TOR
BROWN WILLY
Codda
BODMIN
MOOR
St. Breward
Bolventor
Temple
Colliford Lake
Blisland
Henwood
Upton Cross
Minions
Hurlers Stone Circle
CARADON HILL
Maidenwell
Bathpool
Linkinhorne
Rilla Mill
South Hill
Golberdon
Kelly Bray
Stoke Climsland
Bray Shop
Luckett
Downgate
KIT HILL
Harrowbarrow
Latchley
Chilsworthy
Gunnislake
Albaston
Sydenham Damerel
Lamerton
TAVISTOCK
Mary Tavy
Cudliptown
Peter Tavy
GREAT MIS TOR
Merrivale
Whitchurch
Sampford Spiney
Higher Walreddon
Princetown
Two Bridges
Dartmeet
Hexworthy
Poundsgate
Whiteworks
DARTMOOR
Postbridge
Widecombe in the Moor
Cator Court
Babeny
Ponsworthy
Buckland in the Moor
RIPPON TOR
Haytor Vale
HAMELDOWN TOR
Manaton
North Bovey
Lettaford
Frenchbeer
Moretonhampstead
Doccombe
CORNWALL
DEVON

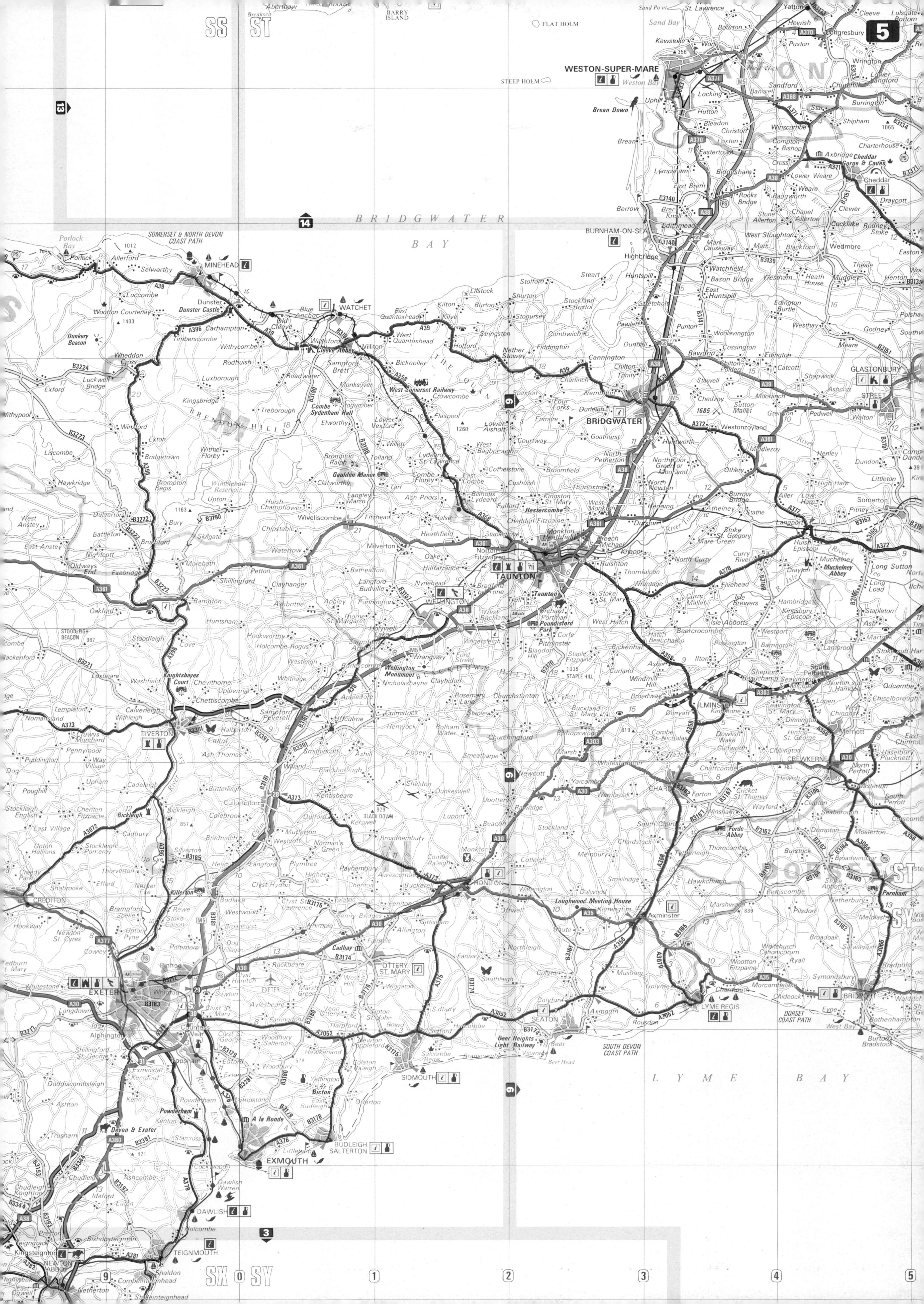
5
SS
ST
BARRY ISLAND
FLAT HOLM
STEEP HOLM
WESTON-SUPER-MARE
Weston Bay
Brean Down
AVON
BRIDGWATER BAY
SOMERSET & NORTH DEVON COAST PATH
Porlock Bay
Porlock
Allerford
Selworthy
MINEHEAD
Dunster
Dunster Castle
Luccombe
Wootton Courtenay
Dunkery Beacon
Blue Anchor
Old Cleeve
WATCHET
Washford
Cleeve Abbey
Williton
East Quantoxhead
West Quantoxhead
Kilve
Kilton
Lilstock
Stogursey
Stolford
Steart
BURNHAM-ON-SEA
Highbridge
Huntspill
Cannington
Nether Stowey
Combwich
West Somerset Railway
Combe Sydenham Hall
Stogumber
Crowcombe
BRENDON HILLS
Wheddon Cross
Exford
Withypool
Luxborough
Winsford
Exton
Bridgetown
Wimbleball Reservoir
Dulverton
Gaulden Manor
Wiveliscombe
Milverton
Bishops Lydeard
Hestercombe
BRIDGWATER
North Petherton
Othery
Langport
Somerton
STREET
GLASTONBURY
Wedmore
Cheddar
Cheddar Gorge & Caves
Axbridge
Congresbury
Yatton
Muchelney Abbey
TAUNTON
Taunton
Monkton Heathfield
Creech St. Michael
WELLINGTON
Wellington Monument
Poundisford Park
Bampton
Oakford
Tiverton
TIVERTON
Knightshayes Court
Stoodleigh Beacon
Crediton
CREDITON
Cullompton
Bickleigh
Killerton
Uffculme
Hemyock
Dunkeswell
Black Down
HONITON
Loughwood Meeting House
Axminster
CHARD
Forde Abbey
ILMINSTER
CREWKERNE
Barrington
Beaminster
Parnham
BRIDPORT
LYME REGIS
DORSET COAST PATH
SEATON
Beer Heights Light Railway
Beer Head
SOUTH DEVON COAST PATH
SIDMOUTH
OTTERY ST. MARY
Cadhay
BUDLEIGH SALTERTON
Bicton
A la Ronde
EXMOUTH
Powderham
Devon & Exeter
Dawlish Warren
DAWLISH
TEIGNMOUTH
NEWTON ABBOT
Kingsteignton
EXETER
Topsham
LYME BAY
SX
SY
0
1
2
3
4
5
9
13
14
3
6

SS ST
BRIDGWATER BAY
SOMERSET & NORTH DEVON COAST PATH
MINEHEAD
WATCHET
BURNHAM-ON-SEA
BRIDGWATER
GLASTONBURY
STREET
WELLS
Cheddar
TAUNTON
WELLINGTON
YEOVIL
ILMINSTER
CREWKERNE
CHARD
HONITON
TIVERTON
OTTERY ST. MARY
SIDMOUTH
BUDLEIGH SALTERTON
EXMOUTH
DAWLISH
TEIGNMOUTH
SEATON
AXMINSTER
LYME REGIS
BRIDPORT
LYME BAY
SOUTH DEVON COAST PATH
DORSET COAST PATH
BABBACOMBE BAY
Torquay
BRENDON HILLS
BLACKDOWN HILLS
SOMERSET
DEVON
Dunster Castle
Cleeve Abbey
West Somerset Railway
Combe Sydenham Hall
Gaulden Manor
Wellington Monument
Hestercombe
Poundisford Park
Muchelney Abbey
Fleet Air Arm Museum
Lytes Cary
Montacute
Brympton d'Evercy
Forde Abbey
Cricket St. Thomas
Parnham
Loughwood Meeting House
Cadhay
Bicton
A la Ronde
Powderham
Knightshayes Court
Killerton
Beer Heights Light Railway
SX 0 SY
1 2 3 4 5 6

SALISBURY PLAIN
WILTSHIRE
DORSET
HAMPSHIRE
NEW FOREST
SALISBURY
WARMINSTER
WESTBURY
FROME
SHAFTESBURY
WILTON
BLANDFORD FORUM
WIMBORNE MINSTER
POOLE
BOURNEMOUTH
CHRISTCHURCH
WAREHAM
SWANAGE
WEYMOUTH
FORTUNESWELL
POOLE BAY
WEYMOUTH BAY
HENGISTBURY HEAD
DURLSTON HEAD
ST ALDHELM'S OR ST ALBAN'S HEAD
THE NEEDLES
ISLE OF PURBECK
DORSET COAST PATH
Stonehenge
Old Sarum
Lulworth Cove
Kimmeridge
Corfe
Studland Bay
Christchurch Bay
Milford on Sea
Lymington
Ringwood
Fordingbridge
Amesbury
Gillingham
Wincanton
Mere
Open to Public
CHERBOURG Summer only
To Guernsey and Jersey
SCALE 1:250,000
4 miles to 1 inch
miles
kilometres

NEWBURY
WILTSHIRE
ANDOVER
BASINGSTOKE
FARNHAM
FLEET
ALTON
WINCHESTER
EASTLEIGH
ROMSEY
SOUTHAMPTON
NEW FOREST
LYMINGTON
FAREHAM
GOSPORT
PORTSMOUTH
HAVANT
HAYLING ISLAND
PETERSFIELD
THE SOLENT
COWES
RYDE
NEWPORT
SANDOWN
SHANKLIN
VENTNOR
Yarmouth
THE NEEDLES
HENGISTBURY HEAD
Christchurch Bay
SELSEY BILL
FORELAND
DUNNOSE
ST CATHERINE'S POINT
Open to Public
LE HAVRE
ST MALO CHERBOURG CAEN LE HAVRE
To Jersey and Guernsey
MICHELDEVER FOREST
Portsmouth Harbour
Langstone Harbour
Chichester Harbour
Stokes Bay
Hayling Bay
Brighstone Bay
Freshwater Bay

SU
TQ
CHERTSEY
WALTON-ON-THAMES
ESHER
EWELL
EPSOM
SUTTON
CROYDON
BROMLEY
BANSTEAD
WOKING
LEATHERHEAD
CATERHAM
SEVENOAKS
GUILDFORD
DORKING
REIGATE
GODALMING
CRAWLEY
EAST GRINSTEAD
HORSHAM
ST LEONARDS FOREST
ASHDOWN FOREST
CUCKFIELD
HAYWARDS HEATH
BURGESS HILL
SOUTH DOWNS WAY
DITCHLING BEACON
MOUNT HARRY
LEWES
ARUNDEL
SHOREHAM-BY-SEA
BRIGHTON
HOVE
PORTSLADE-BY-SEA
WORTHING
LITTLEHAMPTON
BOGNOR REGIS
NEWHAVEN
SEAFORD
DIEPPE
BEACHY HEAD
TV
SCALE 1:250,000
4 miles to 1 inch
1 2 3 4 miles
1 2 3 4 5 kilometres
SZ 0 TV
1
2
3
4
5

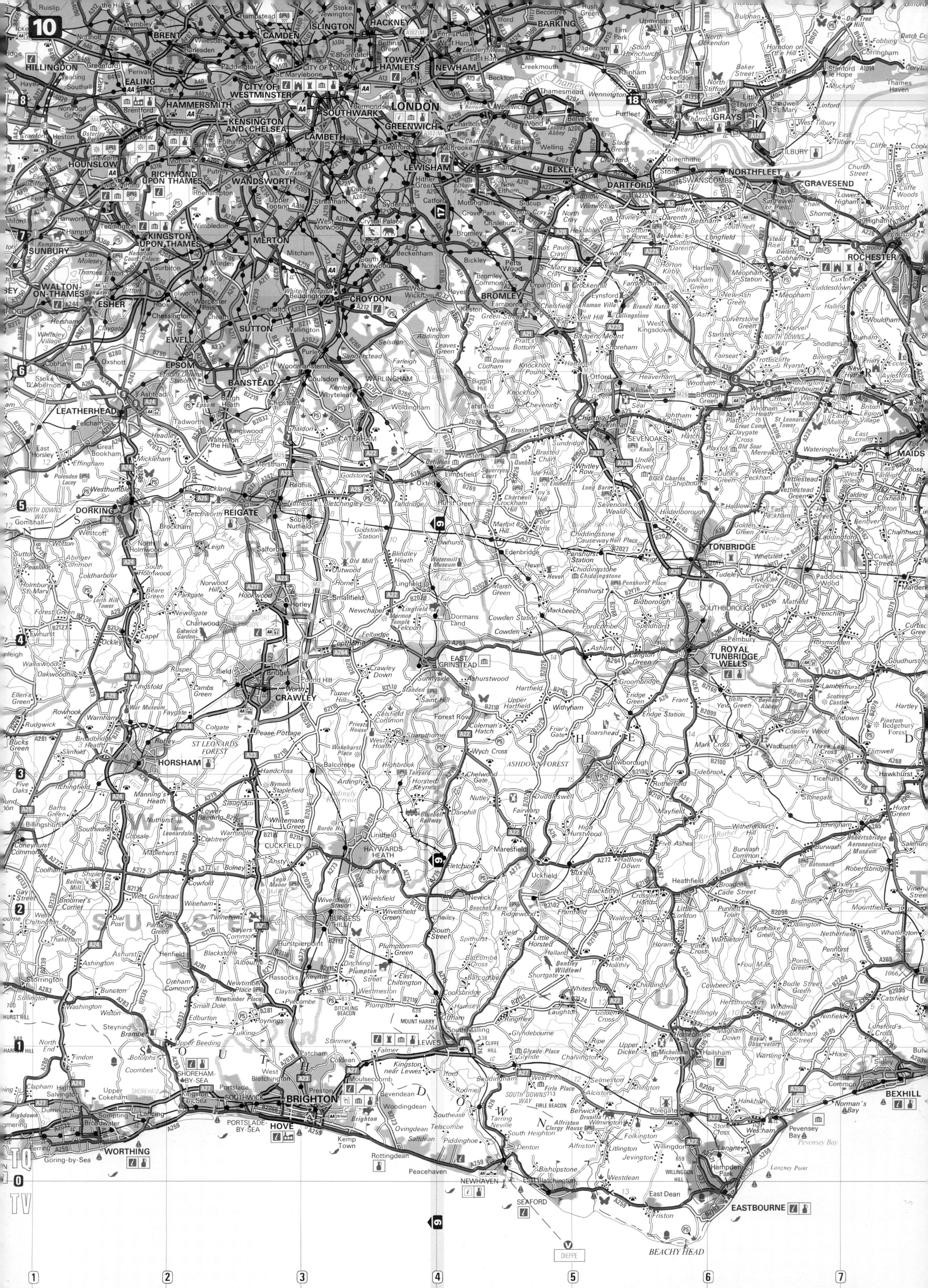

10
HILLINGDON
BRENT
CAMDEN
ISLINGTON
HACKNEY
BARKING
EALING
HAMMERSMITH
CITY OF WESTMINSTER
CITY OF LONDON
TOWER HAMLETS
NEWHAM
LONDON
SOUTHWARK
KENSINGTON AND CHELSEA
GREENWICH
LAMBETH
HOUNSLOW
RICHMOND UPON THAMES
WANDSWORTH
LEWISHAM
BEXLEY
DARTFORD
NORTHFLEET
GRAVESEND
GRAYS
KINGSTON UPON THAMES
MERTON
SUNBURY
WALTON-ON-THAMES
ESHER
CROYDON
BROMLEY
ROCHESTER
SUTTON
EWELL
EPSOM
BANSTEAD
LEATHERHEAD
WARLINGHAM
CATERHAM
SEVENOAKS
DORKING
REIGATE
TONBRIDGE
SOUTHBOROUGH
ROYAL TUNBRIDGE WELLS
EAST GRINSTEAD
CRAWLEY
HORSHAM
ASHDOWN FOREST
CUCKFIELD
HAYWARDS HEATH
BURGESS HILL
LEWES
BRIGHTON
HOVE
WORTHING
NEWHAVEN
SEAFORD
EASTBOURNE
BEXHILL
BEACHY HEAD
DIEPPE
SURREY
WEST SUSSEX
EAST SUSSEX
SOUTH DOWNS
NORTH DOWNS
River Thames
TQ
TV
1
2
3
4
5
6
7

TQ
TR
Great Wakering
North Shoebury
Southchurch
Westcliff-on-Sea
Shoeburyness
SOUTHEND-ON-SEA
Leigh Beck
19
VLISSINGEN (FLUSHING)
Allhallows
ISLE OF GRAIN
Grain
Stoke
Wallend
SHEERNESS
Minster
Halfway Houses
Queenborough
Warden Point
Warden
Eastchurch
Leysdown on Sea
ISLE OF SHEPPEY
ELMLEY ISLAND
ISLE OF HARTY
Shell Ness
The Swale
Iwade
Upchurch
Lower Halstow
Bobbing
Milton Regis
SITTINGBOURNE
Conyer
Rainham
Farthing Corner
Newington
Bapchild
Teynham
Hartlip
Borden
Tunstall
Rodmersham
FAVERSHAM
Oare
Uplees
Graveney
Goodnestone
Stockbury
Oad Street
Bredgar
Highsted
Lynsted
Ospringe
Preston
Hucking
Bicknor
Milsted
Doddington
Newnham
Thurnham
Wormshill
Frinsted
Eastling
Throwley
Hollingbourne
Eyhorne Street
Wichling
Leaveland
Harrietsham
West Street
Stalisfield Green
Leeds
Lenham
Warren Street
Broomfield
Kingswood
Boughton Malherbe
Lenham Heath
Charing
Challock Lees
Sutton Valence
Ulcombe
Grafty Green
Charing Heath
Westwell Leacon
Westwell
Egerton
Little Chart
Hothfield
The Forstal
Pluckley
Pluckley Station
Headcorn
Smarden
Maltman's Hill
Godinton Park
ASHFORD
Intelligence Corps Museum
Great Chart
Haffenden Quarter
Bethersden
Frittenden
Standen
Kingsnorth
High Halden
Biddenden
Shadoxhurst
Redbrook Street
St. Michaels
East End
TENTERDEN
Woodchurch
Orlestone
Leigh Green
Benenden
Kenardington
Warehorne
Hamstreet
Rolvenden
Kent & East Sussex Railway
Great Maytham Hall
Small Hythe
Smallhythe Place
Reading Street
Rolvenden Layne
ISLE OF OXNEY
Appledore
Newenden
Wittersham
Stone
Snargate
Brenzett
Brookland
Northiam
Great Dixter
Four Oaks
Peasmarsh
Iden
Beckley
Rye Foreign
Playden
East Guldeford
RYE
Udimore
Camber
Rye Harbour
Rye Bay
Brede
River Brede
Winchelsea
Winchelsea Beach
Icklesham
Guestling Green
Pett
Cliff End
Ore
Fairlight
HASTINGS
WALLAND MARSH
Old Romney
LYDD
Denge Marsh
Lydd-on-Sea
DUNGENESS
NEW ROMNEY
Littlestone-on-Sea
Greatstone-on-Sea
Romney Hythe & Dymchurch Light Railway
St. Mary's Bay
St. Mary in the Marsh
Ivychurch
Dymchurch
Martello Tower
ROMNEY MARSH
Newchurch
Burmarsh
Snave
Ruckinge
Bilsington
Port Lympne Sanctuary
Lympne
Aldington
Bonnington
Mersham
Sevington
Willesborough
Hinxhill
Kennington
Brabourne Lees
Brabourne
Smeeth
Sellindge
Stanford
Postling
Lyminge
Etchinghill
Newington
Beachborough
Saltwood
HYTHE
Sandgate
FOLKESTONE
BOULOGNE
East Wear Bay
Capel le Ferne
Hawkinge
Paddlesworth
Acrise Place
Elham
Rhodes Minnis
Lyminge Forest
Elmsted Court
Stowting
Lymbridge Green
Hastingleigh
Wye
Brook
Hassell Street
NORTH DOWNS WAY
Crundale
Boughton Lees
Boughton Aluph
Godmersham
Bilting
Molash
Chilham
Shottenden
Badlesmere
Selling
Sheldwich
Old Wives Lees
Chartham Hatch
Chartham
Harbledown
Thanington
CANTERBURY
Howletts
Bekesbourne
Patrixbourne
Bridge
Bishopsbourne
Nackington
Lower Hardres
Upper Hardres Court
Petham
Sole Street
Waltham
Bossingham
Stelling Minnis
Denton
Barham
Kingston
Aylesham
Derringstone
Wootton
Lydden
Swingfield Minnis
Densole
Alkham
St. Radigund's Abbey
West Hougham
DOVER
CALAIS BOULOGNE
ZEEBRUGGE OOSTENDE DUNKERQUE OUEST CALAIS BOULOGNE
Buckland
Temple Ewell
Ewell Minnis
River
Guston
West Cliffe
SOUTH FORELAND
St. Margaret's at Cliffe
St Margarets Bay
East Langdon
West Langdon
Whitfield
Coldred
Shepherdswell or Sibertswold
Eythorne
Woolage Green
Barfreston
Womenswold
Elvington
Tilmanstone
Easole Street
Nonington
Chillenden
Goodnestone
Adisham
Wingham
Ash
Knowlton
Eastry
Betteshanger
Northbourne
East Studdal
NORTH DOWNS WAY
Sutton
Ripple
Ringwould
Kingsdown
Walmer
DEAL
Great Mongeham
Sholden
Ham
Worth
Woodnesborough
Staple
SANDWICH
Marshborough
Sandwich Bay
Stonar
Richborough Roman Fort
Pegwell Bay
DUNKERQUE OUEST
RAMSGATE
Cliffsend
Minster
Monkton
East Stourmouth
West Stourmouth
Westmarsh
Elmstone
Hoaden
Preston
Wickhambreaux
Ickham
Littlebourne
Stodmarsh
Fordwich
Old Town Hall
Westbere
Grove
Upstreet
Chislet
Hersden
Sturry
Hales Place
Tyler Hill
Broad Oak
Blean
Honey Hill
Dunkirk
Boughton Street
Hernhill
Dargate
Yorkletts
Seasalter
WHITSTABLE
Chestfield
Swalecliffe
HERNE BAY
Reculver Roman Fort
Herne
Broomfield
Hillborough
Hoath
Boyden Gate
Sarre
St. Nicholas at Wade
Powell-Cotton Museum
Birchington
Westgate on Sea
MARGATE
Salmestone Grange
Acol
Manston
St. Peters
BROADSTAIRS
NORTH FORELAND
Open to Public
Foreness Point
White Ness
Long Nose Spit
A2
A20
A28
A249
A252
A256
A257
A258
A259
A299
M2
M20
SCALE 1:250,000
4 miles to 1 inch
0 1 2 3 4 miles
0 1 2 3 4 5 kilometres
TV
TW
9
0
1
2
3
4

SM
SN
20
Nanternis
Llangranog
Llwyndafydd
Penbryn
Aberporth
Parcllyn
Tresaith
Tan-y-groes
Sarnau
Brynhoffnant
Cemaes Head
Gwbert-on-Sea
Verwig
Blaenannerch
Tremain
Blaenporth
Glynarthen
Rhydlewis
PEMBROKESHIRE COAST PATH
St. Dogmaels
CARDIGAN
Llangoedmor
Penparc
Pantgwyn
Beulah
Troedyraur
Penrhiwpal
Ponthirwaun
Maesllyn
Moylgrove
Monington
Cilgerran
Llechryd
Llandygwydd
Felin-Geri Mill
Cwmcoy
Glanrhyd
Abercych
Llandyfriog
Bridell
Cenarth
Henllan
ROSSLARE
STRUMBLE HEAD
DINAS HEAD
Newport Bay
Open to Public
Pen Brush
Llanwnda
Fishguard Bay
Bryn-henllan
Parrog
Nevern
Velindre
Llanfair-Nant-Gwyn
Newchapel
NEWCASTLE EMLYN
Drefach
Goodwick
FISHGUARD
Dinas
Newport
Eglwyswrw
Boncath
Penrherber
Velindre
Penbwchdy
St. Nicholas
Manorowen
Llanychaer Bridge
MYNYDD CAREGOG
Pentre Ifan
Crosswell
Whitechurch
Blaenffos
Clydey
Capel Iwan
MOELFRE
Cwmpengraig
Bwlch-y-groes
Star
Ynysdeullyn
Scleddau
Pontfaen
Brynberian
Cilrhedyn
Trevine
Porthgain
Llanrian
Mathry
Trecwn
Foel Eryr
MYNYDD PRESELI
Mynachlog-ddu
Crymmych
Tegryn
Hermon
Llanfyrnach
Trelech
Croesgoch
Castle Morris
FOEL-CWMCERWYN
Puncheston
Little Newcastle
Castlebythe
Glandwr
Dinas
Berea
Tretio
Treglemais
Treddiog
Letterston
Maenclochog
Blaenwaun
Trelech a'r Betws
St David's Head
Treleddyd-fawr
Rhodiad
Treffynnon
Welsh Hook
St. Dogwells
Llanglydwen
Llangolman
Llanwinio
Talog
Rhosson
Whitchurch
Llandeloy
Wolf's Castle
Ambleston
New Moat
DYFED
St David's
Hayscastle
Hayscastle Cross
Rinaston
Wallis
Cwmfelin Mynach
Cwmbach
Solva
Treffgarne
Rosebush Resr
Llys-y-fran
Cefn-y-pant
Llanycefn
Ramsey Island
Mountain Water
Spittal
Maesgwynne
DUDWELL MT
Walton East
Login
Abernant
Gellywen
Newgale
Roch
Leweston
Pen-ffordd
Llanboidy
Meidrim
Scolton
Llandissilio
Wolfsdale
Clarbeston
Bletherston
Merthyr
Camrose
Clarbeston Road
Llanfalteg
Henllan Amgoed
Llangynin
CARMARTHEN
Keeston
Gelly
Sarnau
ST BRIDES BAY
Rickets Head
Wiston
Clynderwen
Cwmfelin Boeth
Whitland Abbey
Nolton
Crundale
Bethesda
Llanfallteg West
Whitland
Bancyfelin
Druidston
Lambston
Llawhaden
HAVERFORDWEST
Robeston Wathen
Llanddewi Velfrey
St. Clears
Llangynog
Llangain
Haroldston West
Portfield Gate
Merlin's Bridge
Uzmaston
NARBERTH
Crinow
Lampeter Velfrey
Llanddowror
Broad Haven
Little Haven
Walton West
Picton Castle
Minwear
Templeton
Tavernspite
Red Roses
Llanybri
Tower Point
Talbenny
Walwyn's Castle
Tiers Cross
Hook
Landshipping
Llandawke
Llanstephan
St. Brides
Robeston Cross
Johnston
Martletwy
Ludchurch
Crunwear
Llansadurnen
Laugharne
Ferry
SKOMER ISLAND
Hasguard
Rosemarket
Llangwm
Yerbeston
Reynalton
Thomas Chapel
Marros
Marloes
Herbrandston
Steynton
Newton Mountain
Loveston
Begelly
Pendine
Ginst Point
Llansaint
BROAD SOUND
Dale
St. Ishmael's
MILFORD HAVEN
Waterston
Houghton
Honeyborough
Lawrenny
Jeffreyston
Kilgetty
Amroth
Cresswell
Cresselly
NEYLAND
Burton
PEMBROKESHIRE COAST PATH
Dale Point
Llanstadwell
Carew Newton
East Williamston
Saundersfoot
SKOKHOLM ISLAND
Open to Public
MILFORD HAVEN
Cosheston
Carew
Redberth
Monkstone Point
Angle
Pwllcrochan
Pembroke Dock
Toll
St Ann's Head
ROSSLARE
Rhoscrowther
PEMBROKE
Carew Cheriton
New Hedges
Hundleton
Lamphey
St. Florence
Gumfreston
TENBY
CARMARTHEN BAY
Lamphey Palace
Penally
Castlemartin
Warren
St. Twynnells
Hodgeston
Jameston
St. Petrox
Trewent Point
Manorbier
Lydstep
CALDEY ISLAND
Linney Head
Stackpole
Bosherston
Stackpole Head
St Govan's Head
WORMS HEAD
SCALE 1:250,000
4 miles to 1 inch
0 1 2 3 4 miles
0 1 2 3 4 5 kilometres
SR
SS
8
9
0
1
2
3
5
4
3
2
1
0
9
8
7

13
SN SO
SS ST
Lampeter
Llandovery
Llandeilo
Ammanford
Llanelli
Burry Port
Swansea
Swansea Bay
The Mumbles
Mumbles Head
Gorseinon
Pontarddulais
Neath
Port Talbot
Maesteg
Bridgend
Porthcawl
Cowbridge
Llantwit Major
Pontypridd
Aberdare
Merthyr Tydfil
Mountain Ash
Treorchy
Treherbert
Brecon
Builth Wells
Llanwrtyd Wells
Black Mountain
Fforest Fawr
Brecon Beacons
Mynydd Eppynt
Dan-yr-Ogof Caves
Carreg Cennen
Talley Abbey
Margam Abbey
Garwnant Forest Centre
Penscynor Wild Life Park
Usk Reservoir
Talybont Reservoir
Pentwyn Reservoir
Pontsticill Reservoir
Ystradfellte Resr
Crai Resr
Llwyn-on Resr
Oxwich Bay
Port-Eynon Point
Nash Point
Glyncorrwg
Pontycymer
Ystradgynlais
Glanaman
Brynamman
Llandybie
Kidwelly
Pen-y-Fan
Fan Fawr
Fan Gihirych
Trichrug
Bryn Crwn
Bryn Brawd
Pen y Gurnos
Mynydd Trawsnant
Open to Public
5
6
7
8
9
1

SN
SO
SS
ST
BRECON
BRECON
BEACONS
PEN-Y-FAN
FAN FAWR
BLACK
MOUNTAINS
PEN ALLT-MAWR
WAUN FACH
HAY BLUFF
Sugar Loaf
SUGAR LOAF
GARN CAWS
HEREFORD
ABERGAVENNY
MONMOUTH
Chepstow
CHEPSTOW
MERTHYR
TYDFIL
ABERDARE
TREHERBERT
TREORCHY
MOUNTAIN
ASH
PONTYPRIDD
EBBW
VALE
BRYNMAWR
NANTYGLO
BLAINA
BLAENAVON
ABERTILLERY
ABRSYCHAN
PONTYPOOL
CWMBRAN
NEWBRIDGE
BLACKWOOD
BARGOED
TREDEGAR
RHYMNEY
YSTRAD
MYNACH
ABERCYNON
CAERPHILLY
BEDWAS
MACHEN
RISCA
ABERCARN
CAERLEON
NEWPORT
USK
BRIDGEND
COWBRIDGE
CARDIFF
PENARTH
BARRY
BARRY
ISLAND
FLAT HOLM
STEEP HOLM
PORTISHEAD
CLEVEDON
WESTON-SUPER-MARE
BURNHAM-ON-SEA
BRISTOL
Cheddar
Gorge & Caves
MOUTH OF THE SEVERN
BRIDGWATER
BAY
SOMERSET & NORTH DEVON
COAST PATH
Open to Public
SCALE 1:250,000
4 miles to 1 inch
0 1 2 3 4 miles
0 1 2 3 4 5 kilometres

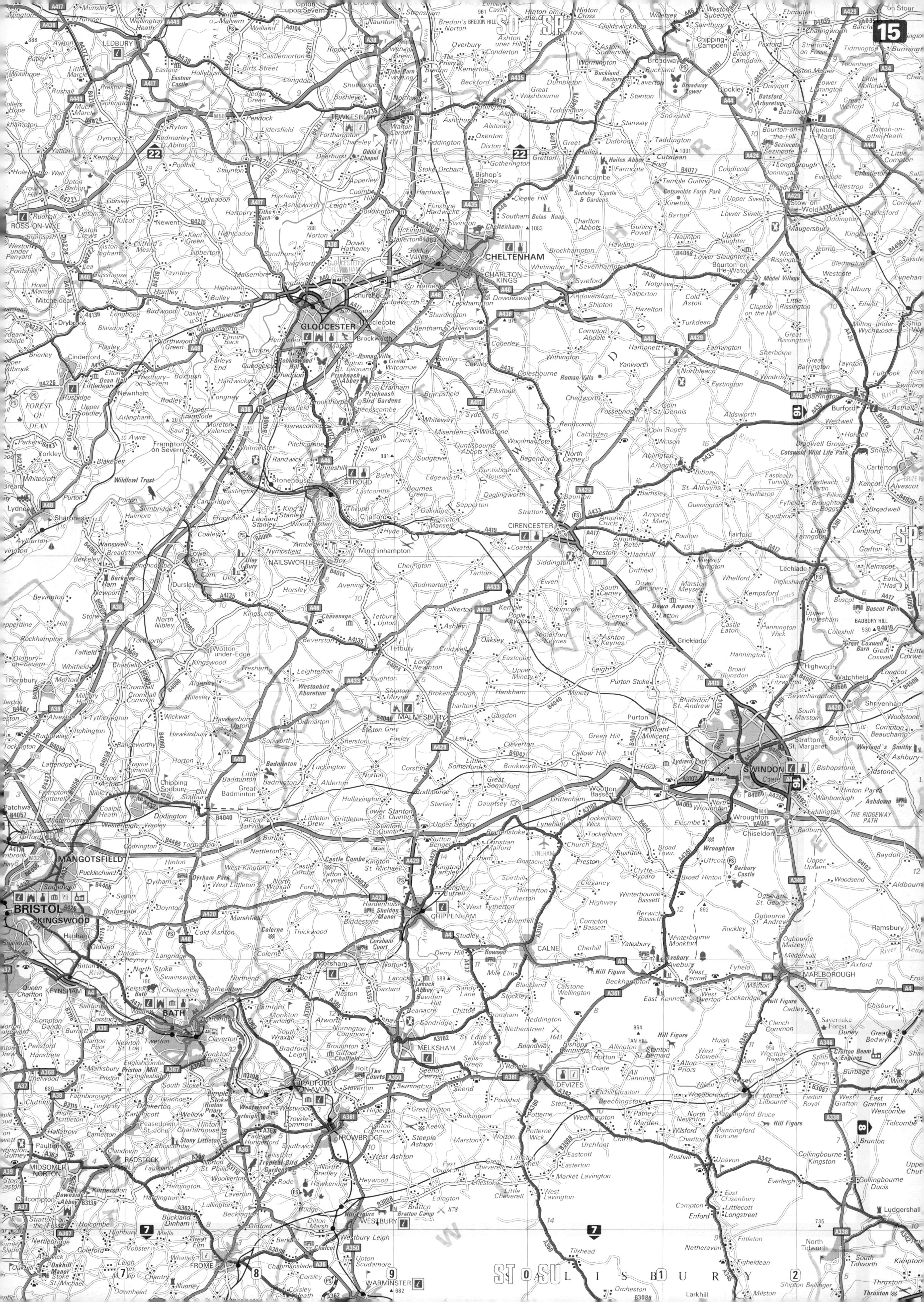

LEDBURY
TEWKESBURY
CHELTENHAM
GLOUCESTER
ROSS-ON-WYE
STROUD
NAILSWORTH
CIRENCESTER
MALMESBURY
SWINDON
CHIPPENHAM
CALNE
MARLBOROUGH
DEVIZES
MELKSHAM
BRADFORD ON AVON
TROWBRIDGE
WESTBURY
WARMINSTER
FROME
BATH
BRISTOL
KINGSWOOD
MANGOTSFIELD
KEYNSHAM
RADSTOCK
MIDSOMER NORTON
Burford
Stow-on-the-Wold
Moreton-in-Marsh
Chipping Campden
Broadway
Winchcombe
Tetbury
Wotton-under-Edge
Dursley
Berkeley
Lechlade
Highworth
Wootton Bassett
Ludgershall
FOREST OF DEAN
SALISBURY
SO
SP
ST
SU

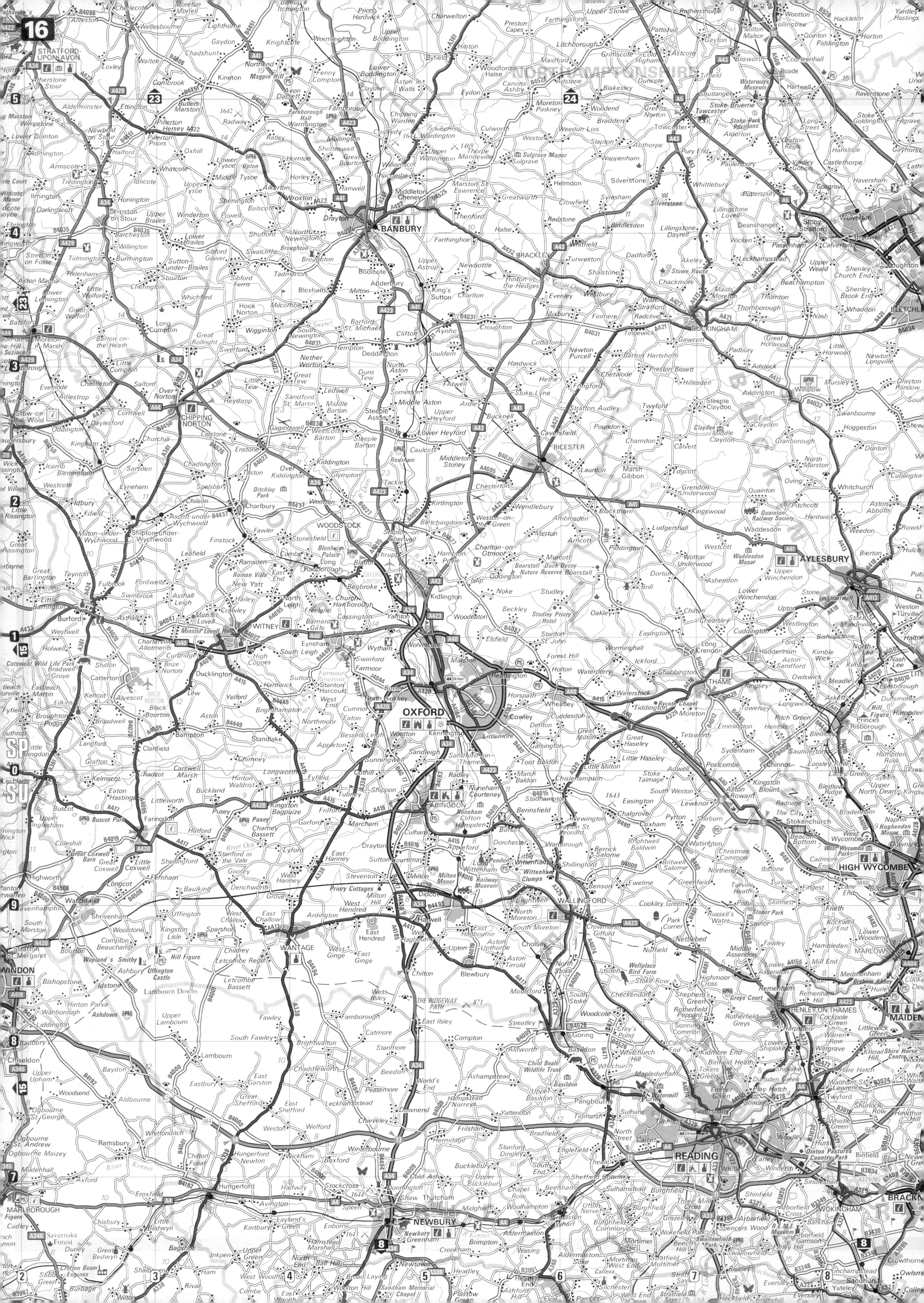
16
STRATFORD-UPON-AVON
NORTHAMPTONSHIRE
BANBURY
BRACKLEY
BUCKINGHAM
CHIPPING NORTON
BICESTER
WOODSTOCK
AYLESBURY
WITNEY
OXFORD
THAME
ABINGDON
WALLINGFORD
WANTAGE
HIGH WYCOMBE
MARLOW
HENLEY-ON-THAMES
READING
NEWBURY
WOKINGHAM
MARLBOROUGH
Hungerford
Towcester
Stony Stratford
Wolverton
Kidlington
Didcot
Faringdon
Burford
Carterton
Bampton
Lechlade
Shrivenham
Lambourn
Goring
Pangbourne
Caversham
Princes Risborough
Winslow
THE RIDGEWAY PATH
Lambourn Downs
Silverstone
Stowe House
Blenheim Palace
OXFORD AIRPORT
Waddesdon Manor
Buscot Park
Uffington Castle
Wellplace Bird Farm
Child Beale Wildlife Trust
Dinton Pastures Country Park
Quainton Railway Society
Waterways Museum
Didcot Railway Museum
Rycote Chapel
Sandham Memorial Chapel
Stoke Park Pavilions
Cotswold Wild Life Park
Sulgrave Manor
Mapledurham
Basildon
Stonor Park
Greys Court
Hill Figure
Priory Cottages
Milton Manor
Rousham
Upton
SP
SU

17
SP
CAMBRIDGE
BEDFORD
SANDY
BIGGLESWADE
ROYSTON
SAFFRON WALDEN
AMPTHILL
LETCHWORTH
BALDOCK
HITCHIN
LEIGHTON BUZZARD
STEVENAGE
LUTON
DUNSTABLE
BISHOP'S STORTFORD
HARPENDEN
HERTFORD
WELWYN GARDEN CITY
HARLOW
TRING
ST. ALBANS
HODDESDON
HEMEL HEMPSTEAD
CHESHAM
CHESHUNT
POTTERS BAR
WATFORD
AMERSHAM
ENFIELD
BUSHEY
BARNET
RICKMANSWORTH
BEACONSFIELD
HARINGEY
WALTHAM FOREST
HARROW
REDBRIDGE
HAVERING
ISLINGTON
HACKNEY
BARKING
BRENT
CAMDEN
HILLINGDON
TOWER HAMLETS
NEWHAM
SLOUGH
EALING
CITY OF WESTMINSTER
CITY OF LONDON
HAMMERSMITH
KENSINGTON AND CHELSEA
SOUTHWARK
LONDON
GREENWICH
WINDSOR
LAMBETH
HOUNSLOW
RICHMOND UPON THAMES
WANDSWORTH
LEWISHAM
BEXLEY
DARTFORD
EGHAM
STAINES
KINGSTON UPON THAMES
MERTON
SUNBURY
CHERTSEY
WALTON-ON-THAMES
ESHER
CROYDON
BROMLEY
SUTTON
SU

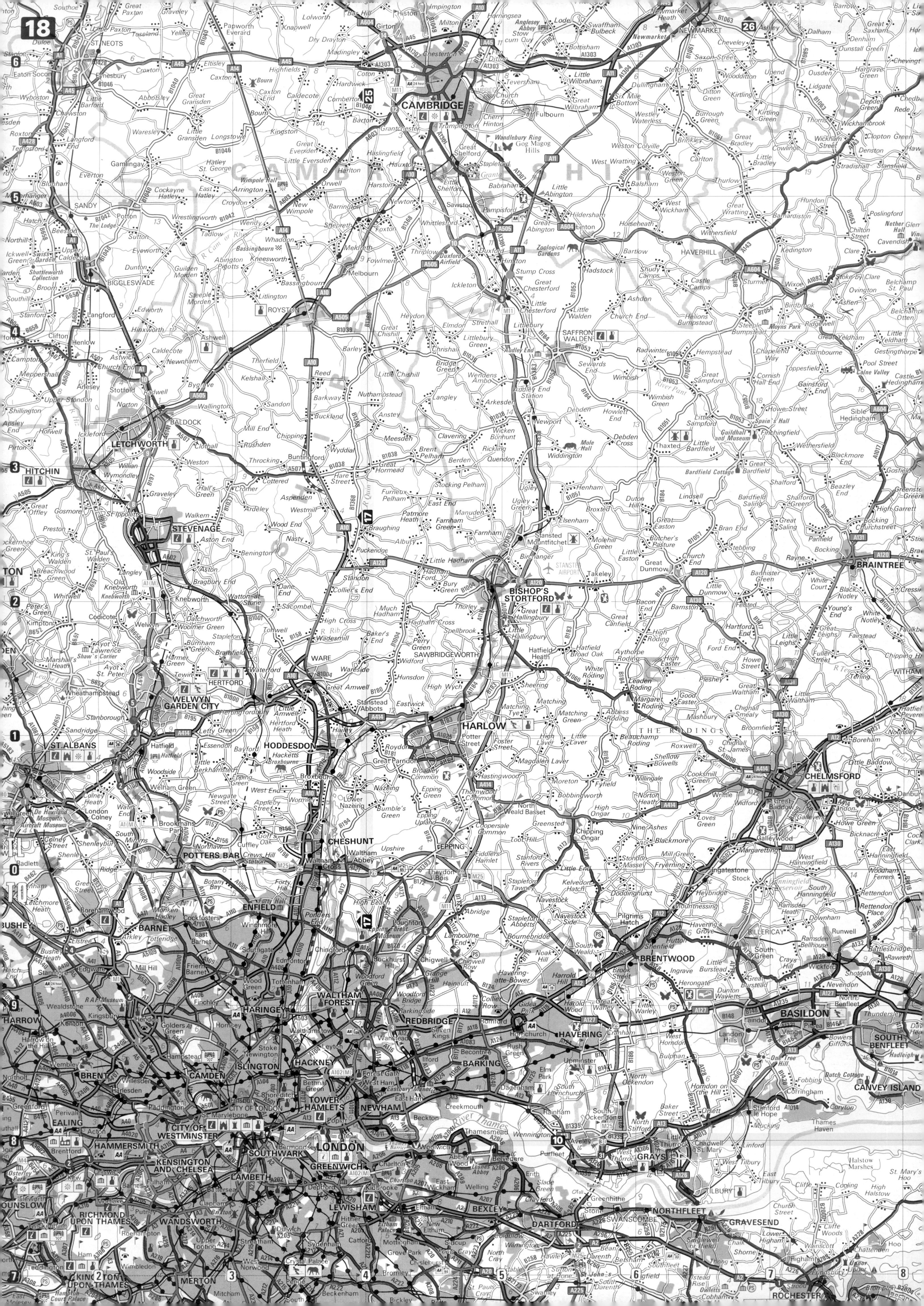
CAMBRIDGE
ST. NEOTS
SANDY
BIGGLESWADE
ROYSTON
BALDOCK
LETCHWORTH
HITCHIN
STEVENAGE
HERTFORD
WELWYN GARDEN CITY
ST. ALBANS
HODDESDON
HARLOW
BISHOP'S STORTFORD
SAFFRON WALDEN
HAVERHILL
BRAINTREE
CHELMSFORD
BRENTWOOD
BILLERICAY
BASILDON
SOUTH BENFLEET
CANVEY ISLAND
CHESHUNT
POTTERS BAR
ENFIELD
BARNET
HARROW
HARINGEY
WALTHAM FOREST
REDBRIDGE
HAVERING
BARKING
BRENT
CAMDEN
ISLINGTON
HACKNEY
TOWER HAMLETS
NEWHAM
EALING
HAMMERSMITH
CITY OF WESTMINSTER
KENSINGTON AND CHELSEA
SOUTHWARK
LONDON
GREENWICH
LAMBETH
LEWISHAM
WANDSWORTH
RICHMOND UPON THAMES
KINGSTON UPON THAMES
MERTON
BEXLEY
DARTFORD
GRAYS
NORTHFLEET
GRAVESEND
ROCHESTER
NEWMARKET
CAMBRIDGESHIRE
THE RODINGS
River Thames
STANSTED AIRPORT

STOWMARKET
SAXMUNDHAM
LEISTON
ALDEBURGH
Aldeburgh Bay
Framlingham
WOODBRIDGE
IPSWICH
Hadleigh
FELIXSTOWE
HARWICH
Harwich Harbour
ZEEBRUGGE
KRISTIANSAND Summer Only
ESBJERG GOTEBORG
HAMBURG HOEK VAN HOLLAND
HIRTSHALS OSLO
SCALE 1:250,000
4 miles to 1 inch
miles
kilometres
COLCHESTER
WIVENHOE
WALTON ON THE NAZE
The Naze
FRINTON-ON-SEA
BRIGHTLINGSEA
MERSEA ISLAND
WEST MERSEA
CLACTON-ON-SEA
Holland-on-Sea
Jaywick
St Osyth Marsh
Colne Point
River Stour
River Orwell
River Blackwater
OSEA IS
NORTHEY IS
BURNHAM-ON-CROUCH
Southminster
FOULNESS ISLAND
POTTON IS
Foulness Point
Great Wakering
North Shoebury
Shoeburyness
SOUTHEND -ON-SEA
Rochford
VLISSINGEN (FLUSHING)
SHEERNESS
Minster
Queenborough
Warden
Warden Point
Leysdown on Sea
ISLE OF SHEPPEY
HERNE BAY
Reculver
Westgate on Sea
MARGATE
NORTH FORELAND
Open to Public
TM
TR

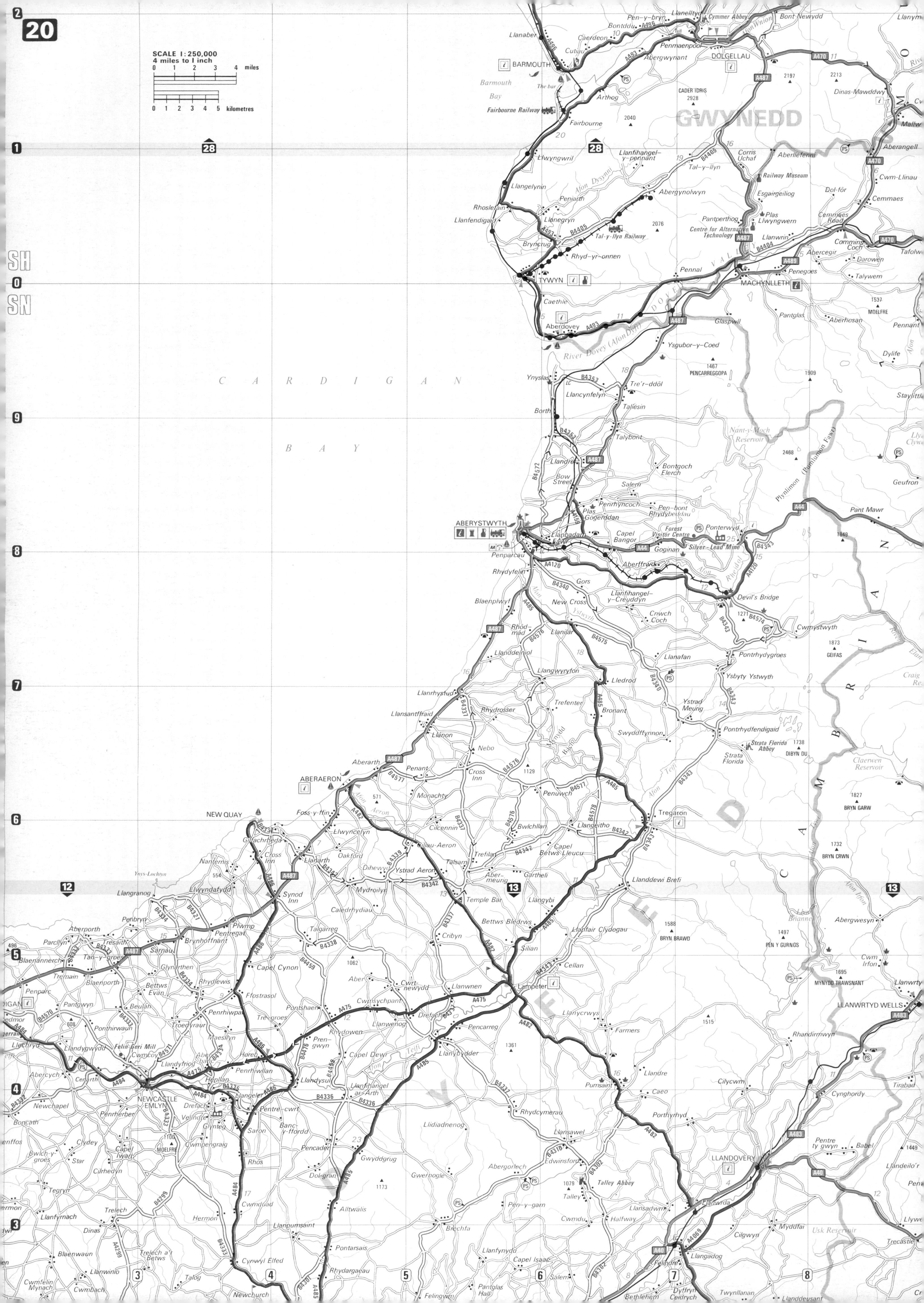
SCALE 1:250,000
4 miles to 1 inch
miles
kilometres
GWYNEDD
CARDIGAN
BAY
DYFED
CAMBRIAN
BARMOUTH
DOLGELLAU
Barmouth Bay
Fairbourne Railway
Fairbourne
Arthog
CADER IDRIS 2928
Llwyngwril
Llangelynin
Rhoslefain
Llanfendigaid
Tal-y-llyn Railway
Abergynolwyn
Tal-y-llyn
Corris Uchaf
Aberllefenni
Railway Museum
Dinas-Mawddwy
Centre for Alternative Technology
TYWYN
MACHYNLLETH
Aberdovey
River Dovey (Afon Dyfi)
Ynyslas
Borth
Talybont
Bow Street
ABERYSTWYTH
Penparcau
Llanbadarn Fawr
Capel Bangor
Ponterwyd
Forest Visitor Centre
Silver-Lead Mine
Devil's Bridge
Nant-y-Moch Reservoir
Plynlimon (Pumlumon Fawr)
Llanrhystud
Aberarth
ABERAERON
NEW QUAY
Llanarth
Synod Inn
Llangranog
Aberporth
Tregaron
Strata Florida Abbey
Pontrhydfendigaid
Llanddewi Brefi
Lampeter
Llanybydder
Llandysul
NEWCASTLE EMLYN
Cenarth
Felin Geri Mill
Talley Abbey
LLANDOVERY
LLANWRTYD WELLS
Claerwen Reservoir
Usk Reservoir

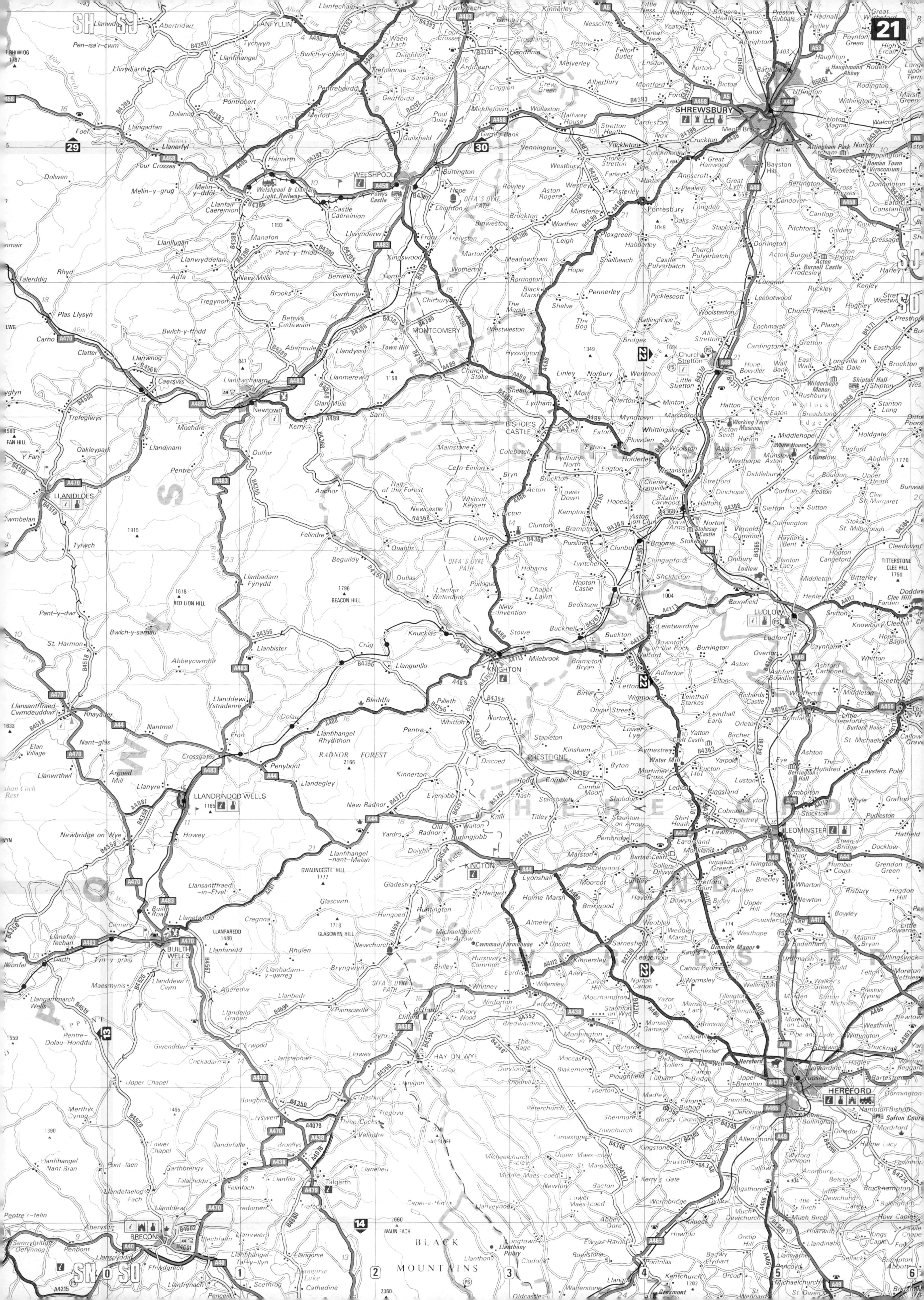
SH SJ
LLANFYLLIN
Llanfechain
Abertridwr
Pen-isa'r-cwm
Llanfihangel
Llwydiarth
Pontrobert
Dolanog
Meifod
Llangadfan
Foel
Llanerfyl
Four Crosses
Dolwen
Melin-y-grug
Melin-y-ddol
Llanfair Caereinion
Welshpool & Llanfair Light Railway
Castle Caereinion
WELSHPOOL
Powys Castle
Guilsfield
Trefnannau
Pool Quay
Buttington
Leighton
OFFA'S DYKE PATH
Llanllugan
Llanwyddelan
Manafon
Pant-y-ffridd
Adfa
New Mills
Berriew
Forden
Kingswood
Talerddig
Rhyd
Tregynon
Brooks
Garthmyl
Plas Llysyn
Carno
Clatter
Bwlch-y-ffridd
Bettws Cedewain
Abermule
Llandyssil
MONTGOMERY
Town Hill
Chirbury
Caersws
Llanwnog
Llanllwchaiarn
Newtown
Kerry
Sarn
Glan-Mule
Trefeglwys
Mochdre
Llandinam
Oakleypark
LLANIDLOES
Dolfor
Pentre
Tylwch
Anchor
Hall of the Forest
Newcastle
Felindre
Beguildy
Dutlas
BEACON HILL
RED LION HILL
Llanbadarn Fynydd
Pant-y-dwr
Bwlch-y-sarnau
St. Harmon
Llanbister
Abbeycwmhir
Knucklas
Llangunllo
KNIGHTON
Bleddfa
Llanddewi Ystradenni
Rhayader
Nantmel
Elan Village
Nant-glas
Crossgates
Penybont
Llanfihangel Rhydithon
RADNOR FOREST
Llandegley
LLANDRINDOD WELLS
Llanyre
Howey
Newbridge on Wye
New Radnor
Old Radnor
KINGTON
PRESTEIGNE
Llanfihangel-nant-Melan
GWAUNCESTE HILL
Gladestry
Glascwm
Llansantffraed-in-Elvel
Builth Road
Cilmery
BUILTH WELLS
Llanelwedd
Llanfaredd
GLASCWYN HILL
Newchurch
Garth
Llandewi'r Cwm
Aberedw
Rhulen
Bryngwyn
Painscastle
Llanbedr
Clifford
HAY-ON-WYE
Cusop
Glasbury
Erwood
Crickadarn
Upper Chapel
Merthyr Cynog
Boughrood
Llyswen
Three Cocks
Talgarth
Bronllys
Llanfilo
Felinfach
Llanddew
BRECON
Llanfaes
Llanspyddid
Llangorse
Llangorse Lake
Cathedine
BLACK MOUNTAINS
WAUN FACH
HAY BLUFF
Llanthony Priory
SHREWSBURY
Atcham
Attingham Park
Bayston Hill
Condover
Pontesbury
Minsterley
Westbury
Yockleton
Church Stretton
Church Stoke
Bishop's Castle
Lydham
Clun
Clunton
Clunbury
Craven Arms
Stokesay Castle
LUDLOW
Leintwardine
Wigmore
Mortimer Cross
Kingsland
LEOMINSTER
Pembridge
Weobley
Dilwyn
HEREFORD
Madley
Kingstone
Dorstone
Peterchurch
Vowchurch
Abbey Dore
Ewyas Harold
Kentchurch
Longtown
SHROPSHIRE
HEREFORD AND WORCESTER
POWYS
SN SO

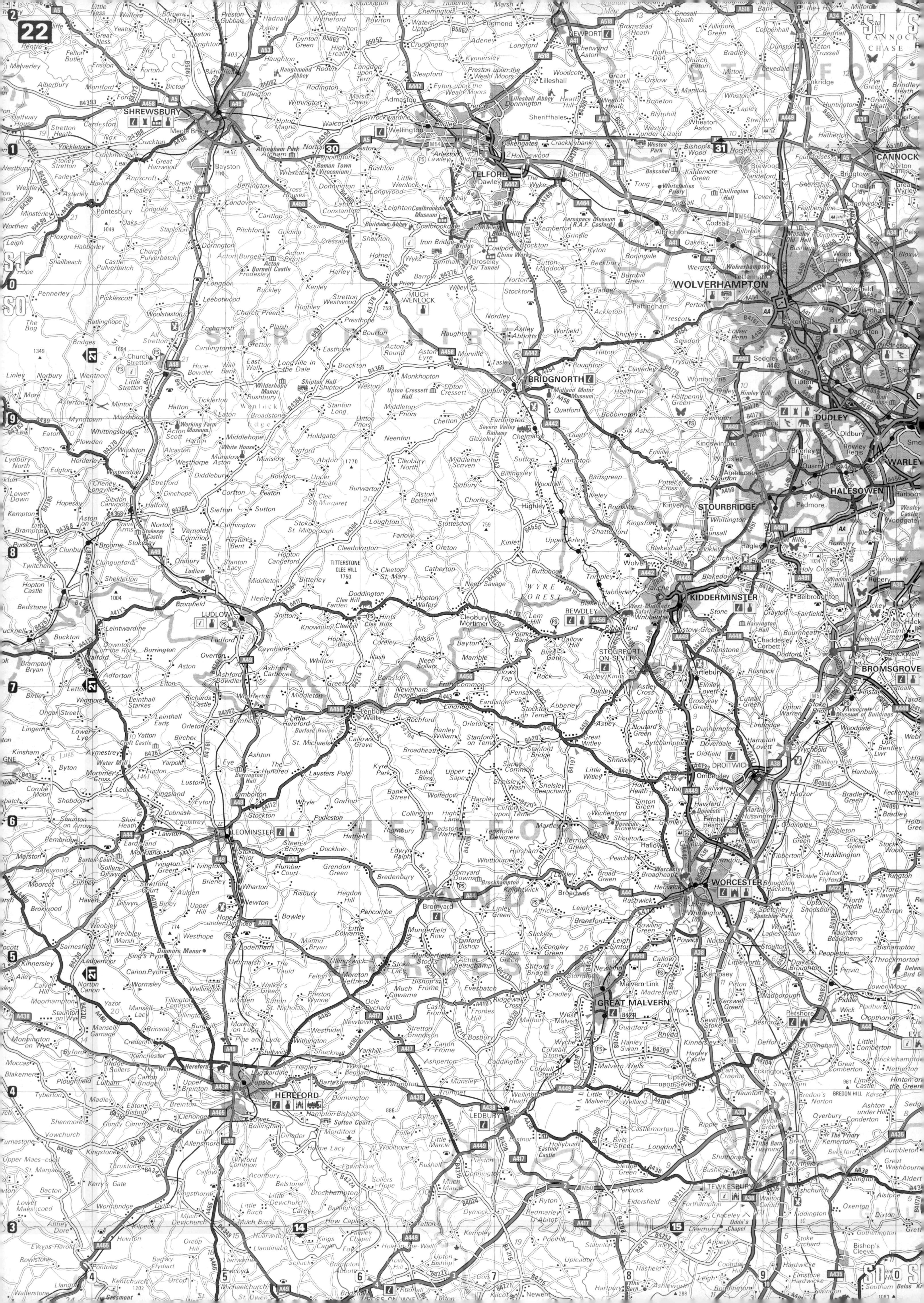
SHREWSBURY
TELFORD
NEWPORT
CANNOCK
WOLVERHAMPTON
MUCH WENLOCK
BRIDGNORTH
DUDLEY
WARLEY
HALESOWEN
STOURBRIDGE
KIDDERMINSTER
BEWDLEY
STOURPORT ON-SEVERN
BROMSGROVE
LUDLOW
DROITWICH
LEOMINSTER
WORCESTER
GREAT MALVERN
HEREFORD
LEDBURY
TEWKESBURY
SHROPSHIRE
HEREFORD AND WORCESTER
STAFFORDSHIRE
WYRE FOREST
CANNOCK CHASE
TITTERSTONE CLEE HILL 1750
SJ
SO

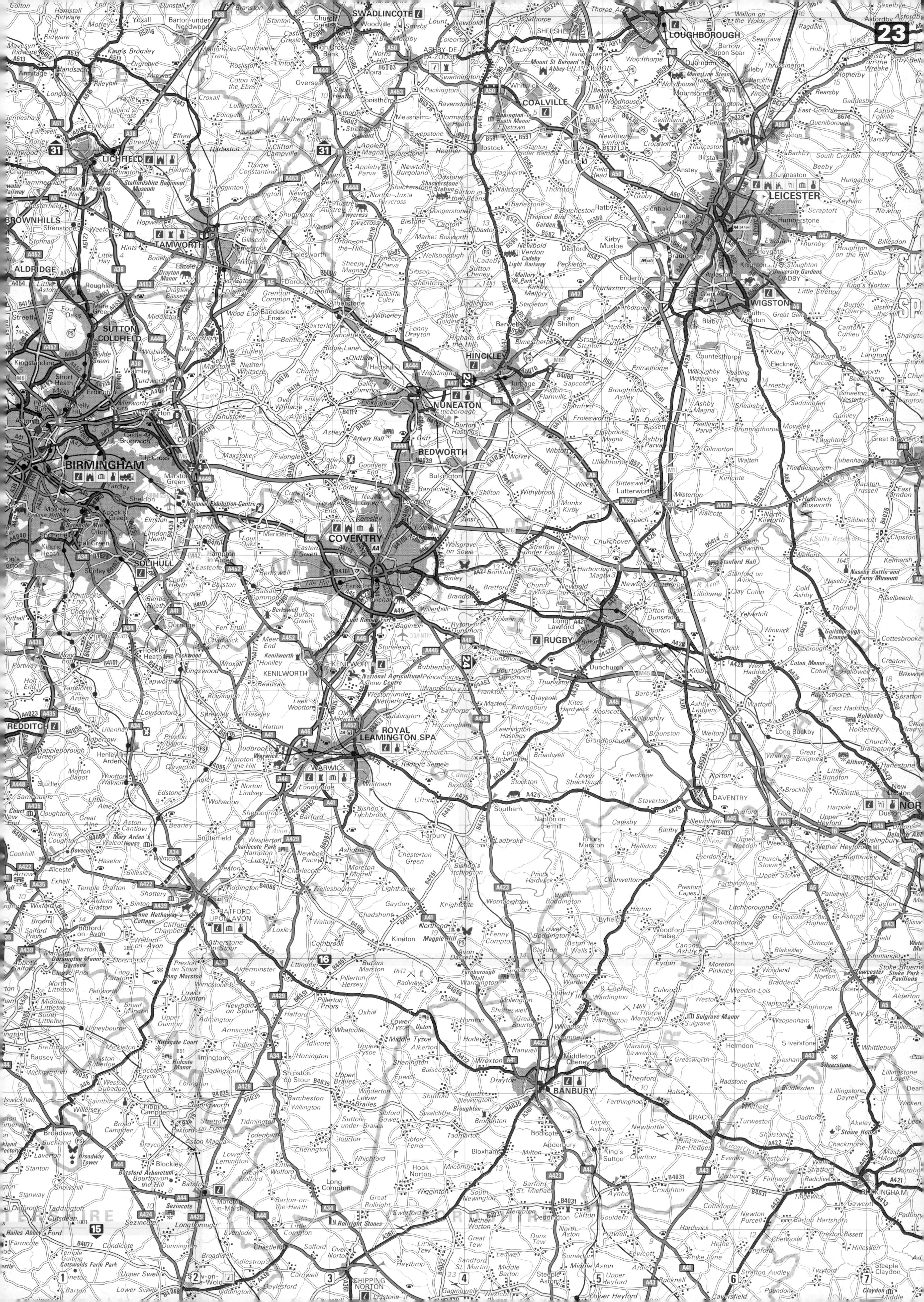

23
SWADLINCOTE
LOUGHBOROUGH
SHEPSHED
ASHBY-DE-LA-ZOUCH
COALVILLE
Mount St Bernard's Abbey
CHARNWOOD FOREST
Main Line Steam Trust
LICHFIELD
Staffordshire Regiment Museum
31
LEICESTER
BROWNHILLS
ALDRIDGE
TAMWORTH
Drayton Manor
Shackerstone Station
Tropical Bird Garden
Battlefield Line
Market Bosworth
Newbold Verdon
Cadeby Light Railway
Mallory Park
Kirby Muxloe
Braunstone
Enderby
Oadby
University Gardens
WIGSTON
SUTTON COLDFIELD
Atherstone
Hinckley
NUNEATON
Arbury Hall
BEDWORTH
BIRMINGHAM
National Exhibition Centre
Coleshill
SOLIHULL
COVENTRY
Kenilworth
24
National Agricultural Show Centre
ROYAL LEAMINGTON SPA
WARWICK
RUGBY
Lutterworth
Stanford Hall
Naseby Battle and Farm Museum
Guilsborough Grange
Coton Manor
Holdenby
Althorp
REDDITCH
DAVENTRY
Southam
Stratford-upon-Avon
Anne Hathaway's Cottage
Mary Arden's House
Charlecote Park
Upton House
16
Farnborough Hall
Kiftsgate Court
Hidcote Manor
BANBURY
Sulgrave Manor
Silverstone
BRACKLEY
Towcester
Stoke Bruerne
Stoke Park Pavilions
Stowe House
BUCKINGHAM
Broadway Tower
Batsford Arboretum
Sezincote
Chipping Campden
Moreton-in-Marsh
Rollright Stones
Cotswolds Farm Park
15
Stow-on-the-Wold
CHIPPING NORTON
1
2
3
4
5
6
7

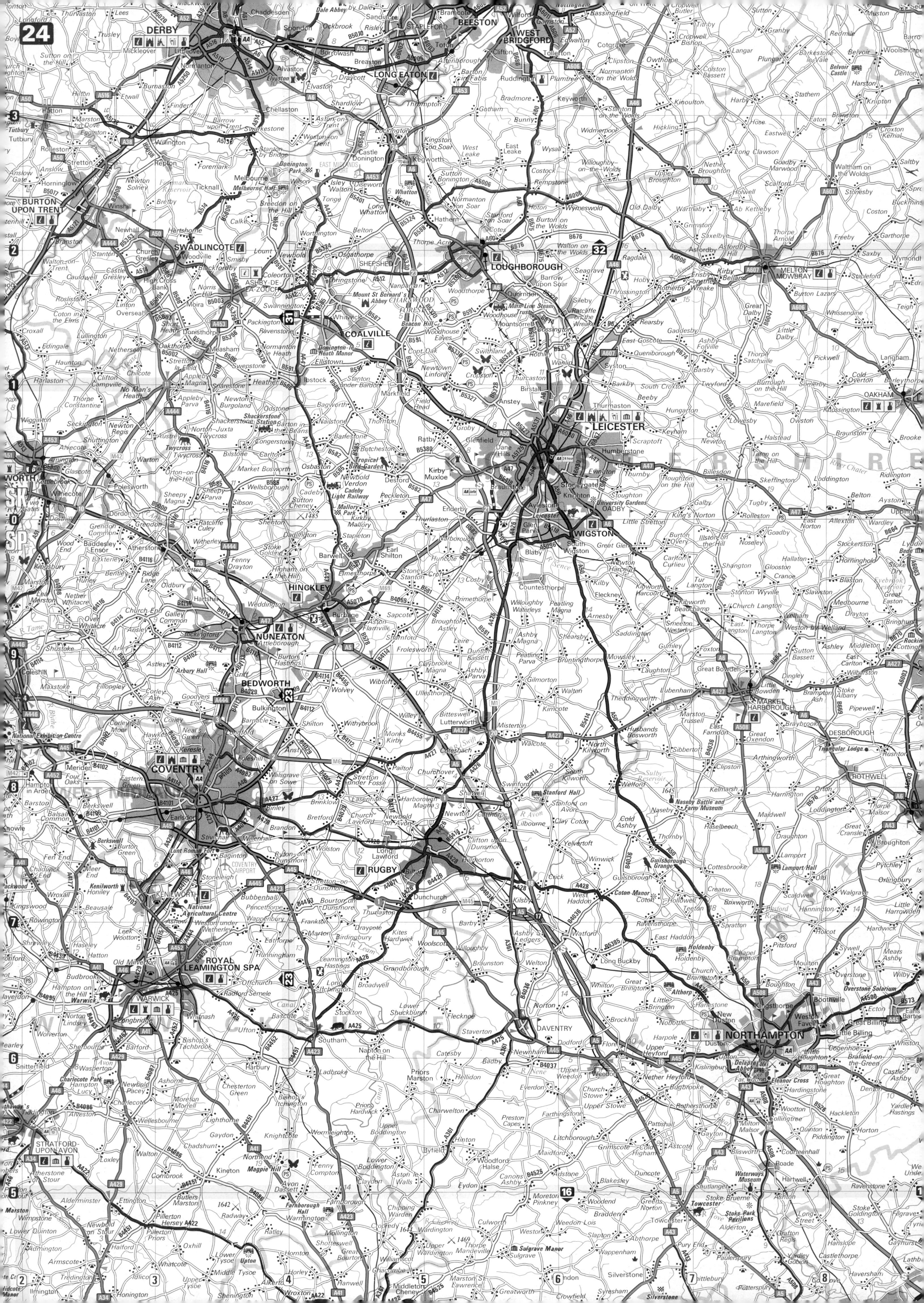
24
DERBY
LONG EATON
BEESTON
WEST BRIDGFORD
BURTON UPON TRENT
SWADLINCOTE
ASHBY-DE-LA-ZOUCH
LOUGHBOROUGH
SHEPSHED
COALVILLE
MELTON MOWBRAY
OAKHAM
LEICESTER
LEICESTERSHIRE
WIGSTON
OADBY
HINCKLEY
NUNEATON
BEDWORTH
COVENTRY
WEST MIDLANDS
National Exhibition Centre
KENILWORTH
RUGBY
ROYAL LEAMINGTON SPA
WARWICK
WARWICKSHIRE
STRATFORD-UPON-AVON
DAVENTRY
MARKET HARBOROUGH
DESBOROUGH
ROTHWELL
NORTHAMPTON
NORTHAMPTONSHIRE
Silverstone
Towcester
East Midlands Airport
Coventry Airport
Donington Park
Belvoir Castle
Stanford Hall
Althorp
Sulgrave Manor
Naseby Battle and Farm Museum
Lamport Hall
Stoke Park Pavilions
Waterways Museum
Mount St Bernard's Abbey
Charnwood Forest
Bosworth Battlefield
Lunt Roman Fort
National Agricultural Centre
Main Line Steam Trust
Twycross
Tropical Bird Garden
Cadeby Light Railway
Shackerstone Station
Donington-le-Heath Manor
Charlecote Park
Holdenby
Coton Manor
Farnborough Hall
Upton
Magpie Hill
Arbury Hall
Triangular Lodge
Overstone Solarium

GRANTHAM
SK
TF
SPALDING
BOURNE
33
STAMFORD
PETERBOROUGH
WHITTLESEY
OLD FLETTON
MARCH
WISBECH
26
BEDFORD LEVELS
OUNDLE
RAMSEY
CHATTERIS
ELY
HUNTINGDON
ST. IVES
GODMANCHESTER
ST. NEOTS
RUSHDEN
HIGHAM FERRERS
RAUNDS
Thrapston
BEDFORDSHIRE
BEDFORD
KEMPSTON
SANDY
17
BIGGLESWADE
CAMBRIDGE
18
SP
TL
1
2
3
4
5
Deeping St. James
Market Deeping
Crowland
Thorney
Yaxley
Sawtry
Kimbolton
Buckden
Eynesbury
Potton
Gamlingay
Royston
Histon
Girton
Cottenham
Willingham
Somersham
Haddenham
Littleport
Holbeach
Long Sutton
Sutton Bridge
Terrington St. Clement
Pinchbeck
Surfleet
Donington
Bicker
Colsterworth
Corby Glen
Ketton
Wansford
Nassington
Elton
Warboys
Stilton
Norman Cross
Alconbury
Brampton
Papworth Everard
Bar Hill
Longstanton
Trumpington
Great Shelford
Sawston
Duxford
Melbourn
Bassingbourn
Wimpole Hall
Northill
Cardington
Clapham
Sharnbrook
Wollaston
Irchester

26
BOSTON
THE WASH
HUNSTANTON
KING'S LYNN
SPALDING
WISBECH
PETERBOROUGH
WHITTLESEY
MARCH
DOWNHAM MARKET
SWAFFHAM
CHATTERIS
RAMSEY
HUNTINGDON
ST IVES
GODMANCHESTER
ELY
NEWMARKET
ST NEOTS
CAMBRIDGESHIRE
BEDFORD LEVELS
Sandringham
Heacham
Holbeach
Long Sutton
Crowland
Littleport
Mildenhall
Brandon
Thetford Warren
Soham
Burwell
Lakenheath
Methwold
Feltwell
Stoke Ferry
Hilgay
Denver
Upwell
Outwell
Manea
Doddington
Somersham
Haddenham
Cottenham
Waterbeach
Fordham
33
25
18
19

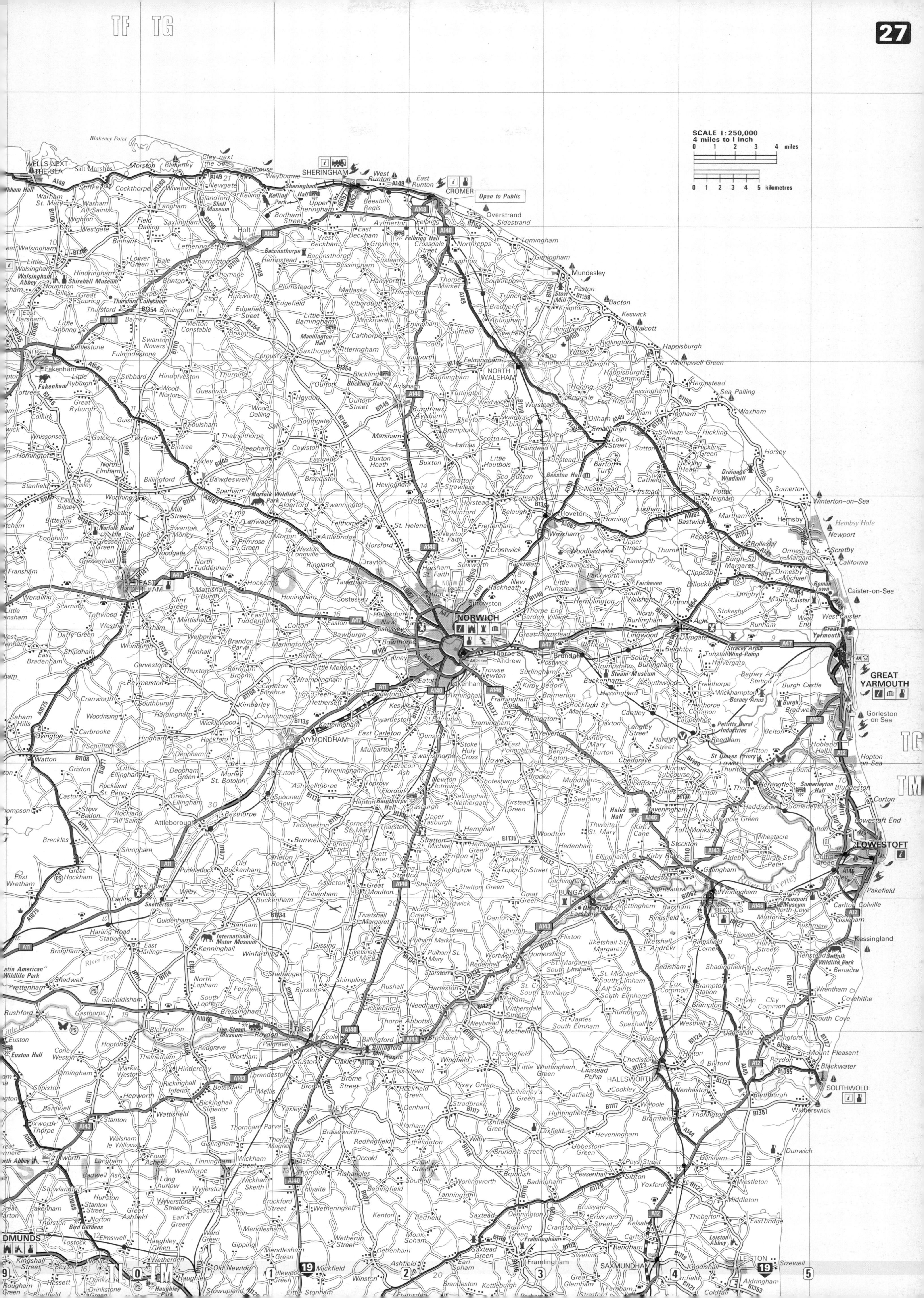
TF
TG
TM
SCALE 1:250,000
4 miles to 1 inch
0 1 2 3 4 miles
0 1 2 3 4 5 kilometres
Blakeney Point
WELLS-NEXT-THE-SEA
Salt Marshes
Morston
Blakeney
Cley next the Sea
Salthouse
Weybourne
SHERINGHAM
West Runton
East Runton
CROMER
Open to Public
Overstrand
Sidestrand
Trimingham
Mundesley
Bacton
Walcott
Happisburgh
Sea Palling
Waxham
Horsey
Winterton-on-Sea
Hemsby
Hemsby Hole
Newport
Scratby
California
Caister-on-Sea
GREAT YARMOUTH
Gorleston on Sea
Hopton on Sea
Corton
Lowestoft End
LOWESTOFT
Pakefield
Kessingland
Covehithe
South Cove
Southwold
SOUTHWOLD
Walberswick
Dunwich
Holt
Aylsham
NORTH WALSHAM
Fakenham
EAST DEREHAM
NORWICH
WYMONDHAM
Attleborough
Watton
DISS
BUNGAY
BECCLES
HALESWORTH
Eye
Framlingham
SAXMUNDHAM
LEISTON
Sizewell
River Waveney
River Thet
Little Ouse
Euston Hall
Blickling Hall
Felbrigg Hall
Mannington Hall
Norfolk Wildlife Park
Norfolk Rural Life
Thursford Collection
Shirehall Museum
Steam Museum
International Motor Museum
Live Steam Museum
Transport Museum
Suffolk Wildlife Park
Somerleyton Hall
Raveningham Hall
Rainthorpe Hall
Drainage Windmill
Stracey Arms Wind Pump
Pettitts Rural Industries
A11
A47
A140
A143
A144
A146
A148
A149
A12
A1066
A1067
A1088
A1120
19

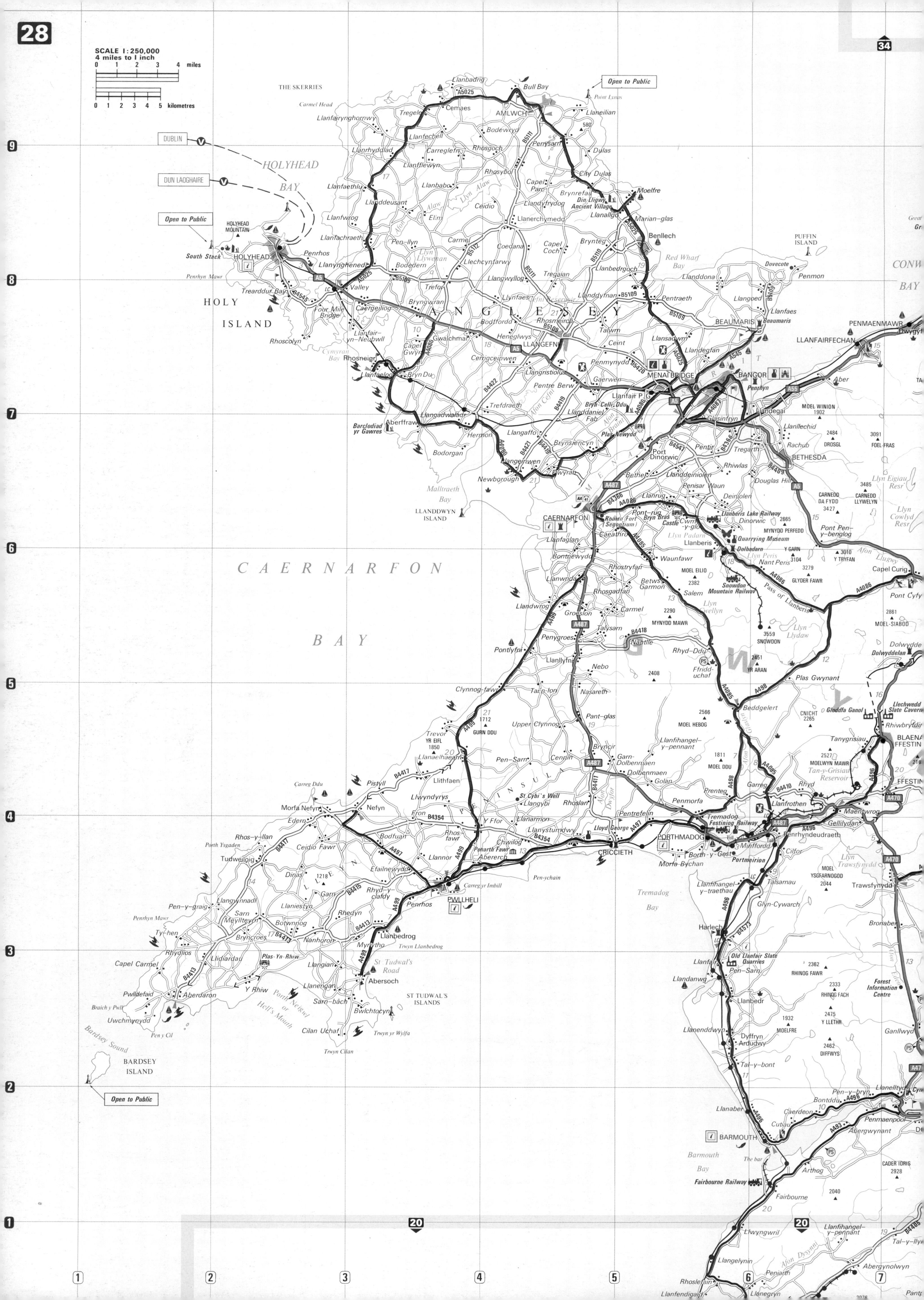
SCALE 1:250,000
4 miles to 1 inch
miles
kilometres
34
DUBLIN
DUN LAOGHAIRE
Open to Public
THE SKERRIES
Carmel Head
HOLYHEAD BAY
HOLYHEAD MOUNTAIN
South Stack
HOLYHEAD
Penrhyn Mawr
HOLY ISLAND
Trearddur Bay
Four Mile Bridge
Rhoscolyn
Valley
Llanfairynghornwy
Cemaes
Llanbadrig
Bull Bay
AMLWCH
Point Lynas
Llaneilian
Tregele
Llanfechell
Bodewryd
Penysarn
Dulas
City Dulas
Llanrhyddlad
Carreglefn
Rhosgoch
Llanfflewyn
Rhosybol
Llanfaethlu
Llanbabo
Llyn Alaw
Capel Parc
Brynrefail
Din Lligwy Ancient Village
Moelfre
Llanddeusant
Ceidio
Llandyfrydog
Llanallgo
Llanfwrog
Elim
Llanerchymedd
Marian-glas
Llanfachraeth
Benllech
Pen-llyn
Carmel
Coedana
Capel Coch
Brynteg
Red Wharf Bay
Penrhos
Llanynghenedl
Llyn Llywenan
Llechcynfarwy
Bodedern
Llanbedrgoch
Tregaian
Llangwyllog
Trefor
Llanddona
Dovecote
PUFFIN ISLAND
Penmon
Caergeiliog
Bryngwran
ANGLESEY
Llynfaes
Cefni Reservoir
Llanddyfnan
Pentraeth
Llangoed
Llanfaes
Llanfair-yn-Neubwll
Bodffordd
Rhosmeirch
Talwrn
Gwalchmai
Heneglwys
LLANGEFNI
Ceint
Llansadwrn
BEAUMARIS
Beaumaris
Capel Gwyn
Cymyran Bay
Rhosneigr
Cerrigceinwen
Penmynydd
Llandegfan
Llangristiolus
Gaerwen
MENAI BRIDGE
BANGOR
Penrhyn
Llanfaelog
Bryn Du
Pentre Berw
Llanfair P.G.
Bryn-Celli-Ddu
Trefdraeth
Llanddaniel Fab
Llandegai
Barclodiad yr Gawres
Aberffraw
Llangadwaladr
Plas Newydd
Glasinfryn
Hermon
Llangaffo
Brynsiencyn
Port Dinorwic
Pentir
Tregarth
Bodorgan
Newborough
Llangeinwen
Dwyran
Rhiwlas
BETHESDA
Malltraeth Bay
Bethel
Llanddeiniolen
Penisar Waun
LLANDDWYN ISLAND
Deiniolen
Llanrug
Pont-rug
Bryn Bras Castle
Cwm-y-glo
Llanberis Lake Railway
Dinorwic
CAERNARFON
Roman Fort (Segontium)
Caeathro
Llyn Padarn
Llanberis
Quarrying Museum
Dolbadarn
Llanfaglan
Bontnewydd
Waunfawr
Llyn Peris
Nant Peris
Rhostryfan
Betws Garmon
MOEL EILIO
Salem
Snowdon Mountain Railway
Pass of Llanberis
Llanwnda
Rhosgadfan
Llyn Cwellyn
Llandwrog
Groeslon
Carmel
MYNYDD MAWR
Talysarn
Penygroes
Nantlle
Rhyd-Ddu
Ffridd-uchaf
SNOWDON
Llyn Llydaw
Pontllyfni
Llanllyfni
Nebo
YR ARAN
Nasareth
Plas Gwynant
Clynnog-fawr
Tai-n-lon
Beddgelert
Pant-glas
MOEL HEBOG
Upper Clynnog
GURN DDU
Trevor
YR EIFL
Llanaelhaearn
Bryncir
Garn-Dolbenmaen
Dolbenmaen
Llanfihangel-y-pennant
MOEL DDU
Pen-Sarn
Cennin
Golan
Llithfaen
Pistyll
Carreg Ddu
Llwyndyrys
St Cybi's Well
Llangybi
Rhoslan
Prenteg
Garreg
Penmorfa
Tremadog
Festiniog Railway
Morfa Nefyn
Nefyn
Edern
Fron
Y Ffor
Llanarmon
Pentrefelin
Llanystumdwy
Lloyd George
PORTHMADOG
Minffordd
Penrhyndeudraeth
Rhos-y-llan
Porth Ysgaden
Ceidio Fawr
Bodfuan
Rhos-fawr
Chwilog
Penarth Fawr
Abererch
CRICCIETH
Borth-y-Gest
Portmeirion
Morfa Bychan
Tudweiliog
Llannor
Efailnewydd
Dinas
Pen-ychain
Carreg yr Imbill
Rhyd-y-clafdy
PWLLHELI
Tremadog Bay
Llanfihangel-y-traethau
Talsarnau
Pen-y-graig
Langwnnadl
Llaniestyn
Garn
Penrhos
Glyn-Cywarch
Penrhyn Mawr
Sarn Meyllteyrn
Rhedyn
Botwnnog
Llanbedrog
Trwyn Llanbedrog
Ty-hen
Bryncroes
Nanhoron
Harlech
Rhydlios
Plas-Yn-Rhiw
Mynytho
St Tudwal's Road
Old Llanfair Slate Quarries
Capel Carmel
Llidiardau
Llangian
Abersoch
Llanfair
Pen-Sarn
RHINOG FAWR
Y Rhiw
Porth Neigwl or Hell's Mouth
Llanengan
Llandanwg
Pwlldefaid
Aberdaron
Sarn-bâch
ST TUDWAL'S ISLANDS
Llanbedr
RHINOG FACH
Forest Information Centre
Braich y Pwll
Uwchmynydd
Bwlchtocyn
Y LLETHR
Cilan Uchaf
Trwyn yr Wylfa
MOELFRE
Llanenddwyn
Dyffryn Ardudwy
Bardsey Sound
Pen y Cil
Trwyn Cilan
DIFFWYS
BARDSEY ISLAND
Tal-y-bont
Llanaber
Bontddu
Cutiau
Caerdeon
BARMOUTH
Barmouth Bay
The bar
Arthog
CADER IDRIS
Fairbourne Railway
Fairbourne
Llwyngwril
Llanfihangel-y-pennant
Tal-y-llyn
Llangelynin
Afon Dysynni
Abergynolwyn
Rhoslefain
Peniarth
Llanegryn
Llanfendigaid
20
CAERNARFON BAY
LLEYN PENINSULA
PENMAENMAWR
LLANFAIRFECHAN
Aber
MOEL WINION
DROSGL
FOEL-FRAS
Llanllechid
Rachub
Llyn Eigiau Resr
CARNEDD DA FYDD
CARNEDD LLYWELYN
Llyn Cowlyd Resr
MYNYDD PERFEDD
Pont Pen-y-benglog
Y GARN
Y TRYFAN
GLYDER FAWR
Capel Curig
Pont Cyfyng
MOEL-SIABOD
Dolwyddelan
Gloddfa Ganol
Llechwedd Slate Caverns
CNICHT
Tanygrisiau
MOELWYN MAWR
Tan-y-Grisiau Reservoir
Rhiwbryfdir
BLAENAU FFESTINIOG
Rhyd
Llanfrothen
Maentwrog
Gellilydan
Cilfor
MOEL YSGFARNOGOD
Llyn Trawsfynydd
Trawsfynydd
Bronaber
Ganllwyd
Pen-y-bryn
Llanelltyd
Penmaenpool
Abergwynant
1
2
3
4
5
6
7
8
9

29
SH 34 SJ
LIVERPOOL BAY
CROSBY
BOOTLE
WALLASEY
LIVERPOOL
HOYLAKE
BIRKENHEAD
WEST KIRBY
BEBINGTON
HESWALL
NESTON
ELLESMERE PORT
CHESTER
LLANDUDNO
COLWYN BAY
RHYL
PRESTATYN
ABERGELE
HOLYWELL
FLINT
CONNAH'S QUAY
MOLD
BUCKLEY
DENBIGH
RUTHIN
LLANRWST
WREXHAM
LLANGOLLEN
BALA
OSWESTRY
LLANFYLLIN
WELSHPOOL
RIVER DEE (AFON DYFRDWY)
WIRRAL
CLOCAENOG FOREST
Brenig Reservoir
Alwen Reservoir
OFFA'S DYKE PATH
Bala Lake Railway
Welshpool & Llanfair Light Railway
Railway Museum
MOEL FAMMAU
ARENIG FAWR
MOEL FFERNA
FOEL WEN
ARAN FAWDDWY
CARNEDD Y FILIAST
Berwyn
30
21
8
9
1
2
3
4
SH 0 SJ

LIVERPOOL
BAY
SCALE 1:250,000
4 miles to 1 inch
miles
kilometres
BELFAST
DOUGLAS
DUBLIN
CROSBY
34
35
29
21
22
LIVERPOOL
BOOTLE
WALLASEY
BIRKENHEAD
BEBINGTON
KIRKBY
ST HELENS
NEWTON-LE-WILLOWS
WARRINGTON
WIDNES
RUNCORN
ELLESMERE PORT
RIVER MERSEY
RIVER DEE (AFON DYFRDWY)
WIRRAL
HOYLAKE
WEST KIRBY
HESWALL
NESTON
FLINT
HOLYWELL
CONNAH'S QUAY
MOLD
BUCKLEY
CHESTER
RUTHIN
WREXHAM
LLANGOLLEN
OSWESTRY
WHITCHURCH
NANTWICH
CREWE
NORTHWICH
WINSFORD
MIDDLEWICH
SANDBACH
MARKET DRAYTON
SHREWSBURY
TELFORD
WELSHPOOL
LLANFYLLIN
ECCLES
URMSTON
OFFA'S DYKE PATH
MOEL FAMMAU
MOEL FFERNA
POWYS
Speke Hall
Chester Zoo
Attingham Park
Hodnet Hall
Cholmondeley Castle
Welshpool & Llanfair Light Railway
Liverpool Botanic Gardens

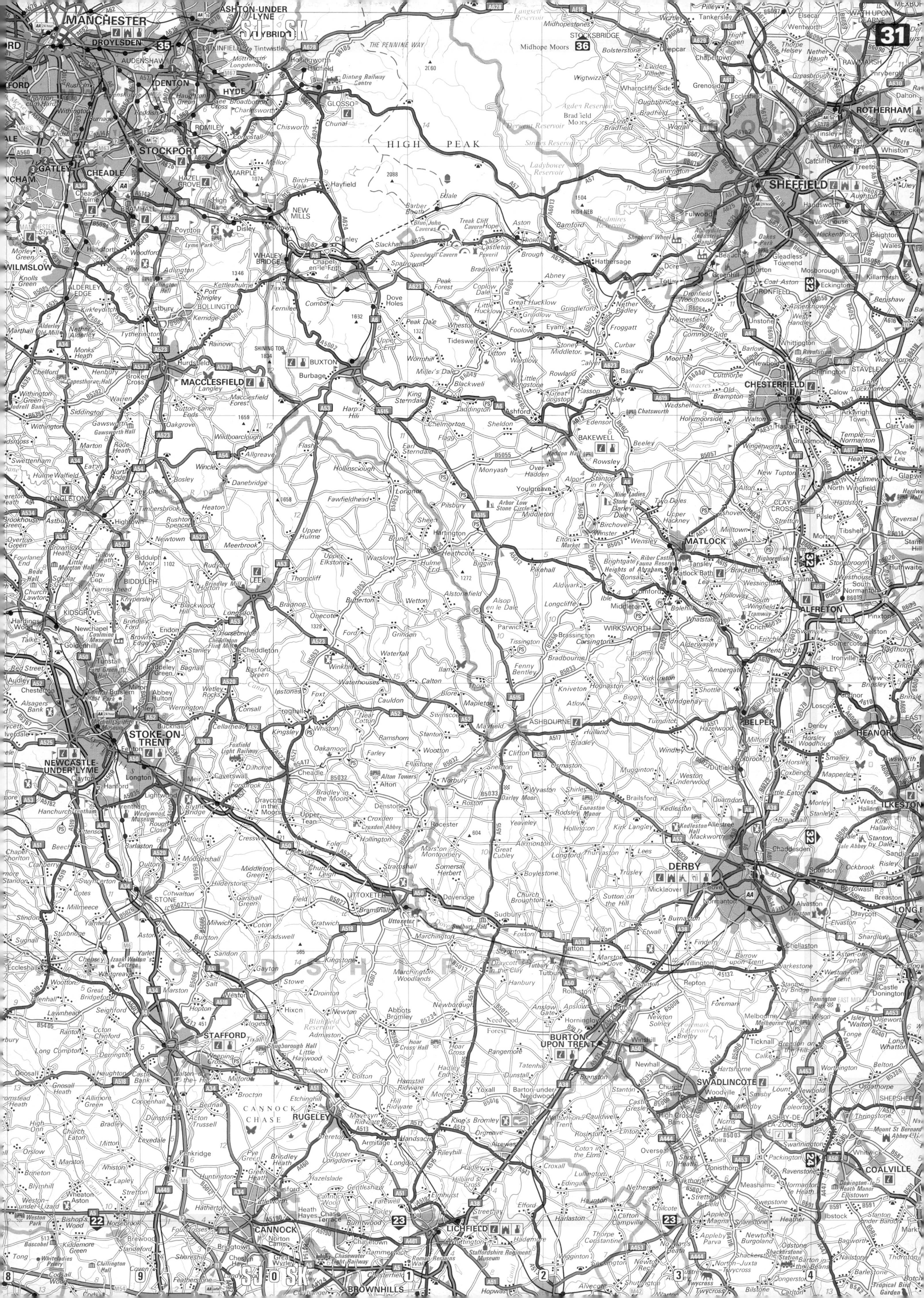
MANCHESTER
ASHTON-UNDER-LYNE
DROYLSDEN
AUDENSHAW
DENTON
HYDE
STOCKPORT
GATLEY
CHEADLE
MARPLE
HAZEL GROVE
BRAMHALL
WILMSLOW
ALDERLEY EDGE
BOLLINGTON
MACCLESFIELD
CONGLETON
KIDSGROVE
BIDDULPH
LEEK
STOKE-ON-TRENT
NEWCASTLE-UNDER-LYME
STONE
STAFFORD
RUGELEY
CANNOCK
LICHFIELD
BROWNHILLS
BURTON UPON TRENT
SWADLINCOTE
ASHBY-DE-LA-ZOUCH
COALVILLE
DERBY
BELPER
HEANOR
ILKESTON
RIPLEY
ALFRETON
MATLOCK
BAKEWELL
CHESTERFIELD
SHEFFIELD
ROTHERHAM
STOCKSBRIDGE
GLOSSOP
BUXTON
ASHBOURNE
UTTOXETER
WIRKSWORTH
HIGH PEAK
THE PENNINE WAY
CANNOCK CHASE
STAFFORDSHIRE

SHEFFIELD
ROTHERHAM
CHESTERFIELD
WORKSOP
RETFORD
GAINSBOROUGH
LINCOLN
MANSFIELD
MANSFIELD WOODHOUSE
SUTTON IN ASHFIELD
KIRKBY IN ASHFIELD
NEWARK-ON-TRENT
NOTTINGHAM
DERBY
ILKESTON
HEANOR
BELPER
ALFRETON
MATLOCK
HUCKNALL
ARNOLD
CARLTON
BEESTON
WEST BRIDGFORD
LONG EATON
STAPLEFORD
GRANTHAM
MELTON MOWBRAY
LOUGHBOROUGH
COALVILLE
SWADLINCOTE
LEICESTER
OAKHAM
BOLSOVER
DRONFIELD
CLAY CROSS
EASTWOOD
RIPLEY
SHERWOOD FOREST

SCALE 1:250,000
4 miles to 1 inch
0 1 2 3 4 miles
0 1 2 3 4 5 kilometres
THE WASH
LINCOLNSHIRE
NORFOLK
MARKET RASEN
LOUTH
MABLETHORPE
Sutton-on-Sea
Sandilands
ALFORD
Chapel St. Leonards
Ingoldmells
SKEGNESS
HORNCASTLE
WOODHALL SPA
Coningsby
Tattershall
Spilsby
Wainfleet All Saints
BOSTON
SLEAFORD
Donington
SPALDING
Holbeach
Long Sutton
BOURNE
Market Deeping
STAMFORD
Crowland
WISBECH
KING'S LYNN
HUNSTANTON
Heacham
Wragby
Binbrook
Caistor
Saltfleet
Anderby Creek
Gibraltar
Frampton
Kirton
Sutterton
Gosberton
Pinchbeck
Billingborough
Folkingham
Terrington St. Clement
Gaywood
Dersingham
Sandringham
37
26
25

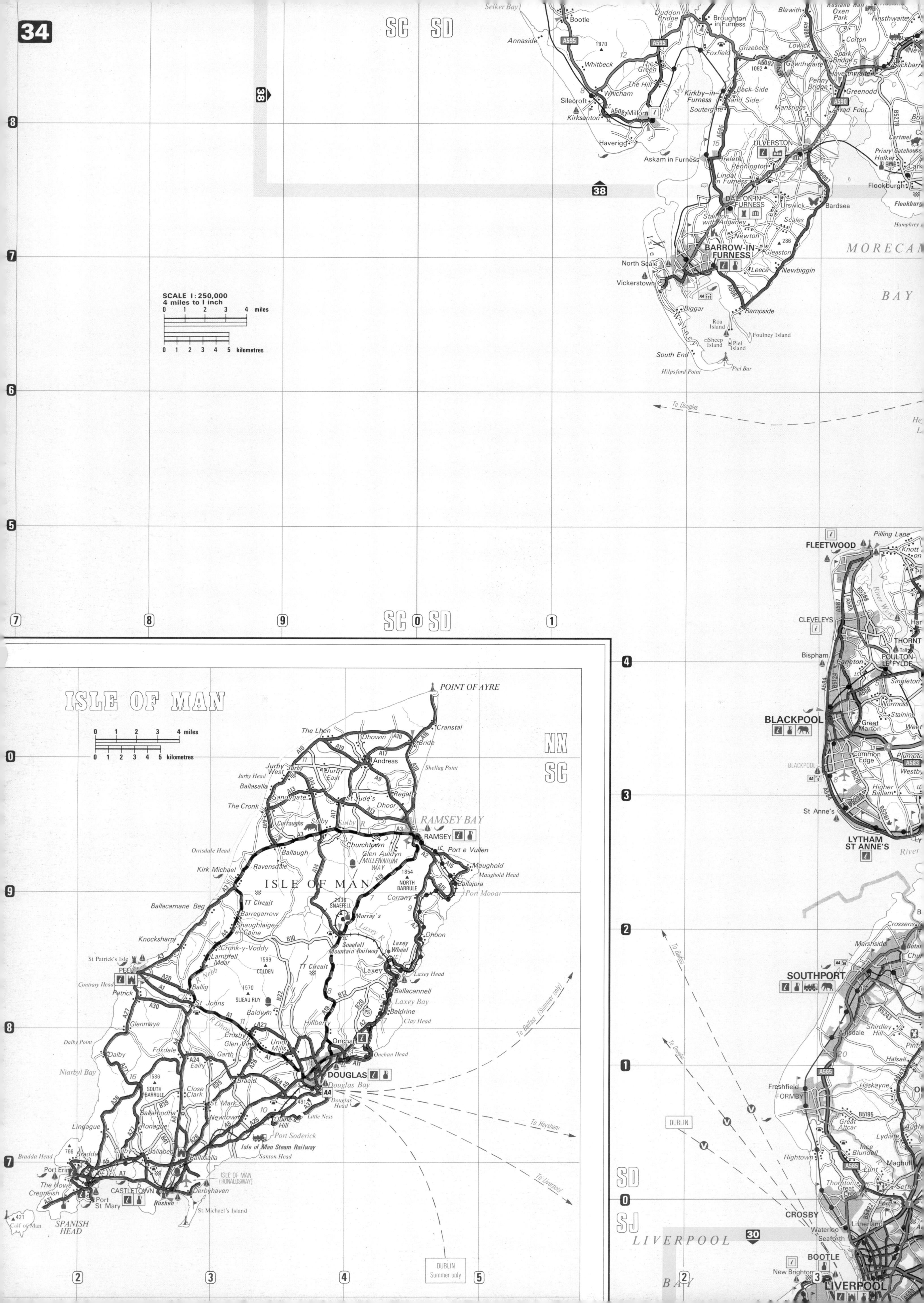
SC SD
Selker Bay
Bootle
Annaside
Duddon Bridge
Broughton in Furness
Blawith
Oxen Park
Finsthwaite
Whitbeck
Foxfield
Lowick
Grizebeck
Colton
Spark Bridge
Gawthwaite
Penny Bridge
Haverthwaite
Backbarrow
The Green
The Hill
Whicham
Silecroft
Kirksanton
Millom
Kirkby-in-Furness
Beck Side
Sand Side
Soutergate
Mansriggs
Greenodd
Arrad Foot
Haverigg
Askam in Furness
ULVERSTON
Cartmel
Priory Gatehouse
Holker
Ireleth
Pennington
Lindal in Furness
Flookburgh
DALTON-IN-FURNESS
Urswick
Bardsea
Stainton with Adgarley
Scales
Newton
BARROW-IN-FURNESS
Gleaston
North Scale
Vickerstown
Leece
Newbiggin
MORECAMBE BAY
Biggar
Rampside
Roa Island
Foulney Island
Sheep Island
Piel Island
South End
Hilpsford Point
Piel Bar
To Douglas
SCALE 1:250,000
4 miles to 1 inch
0 1 2 3 4 miles
0 1 2 3 4 5 kilometres
FLEETWOOD
Pilling Lane
CLEVELEYS
Bispham
THORNTON
POULTON-LE-FYLDE
Carleton
Singleton
Normoss
Staining
BLACKPOOL
Great Marton
Common Edge
Plumpton
Westby
Higher Ballam
St Anne's
LYTHAM ST ANNE'S
ISLE OF MAN
0 1 2 3 4 miles
0 1 2 3 4 5 kilometres
NX SC
POINT OF AYRE
Cranstal
The Lhen
Dhowin
Bride
Andreas
Shellag Point
Jurby West
Jurby
Jurby East
Jurby Head
Ballasalla
Sandygate
St Jude's
Regaby
Dhoor
The Cronk
Curraghs
Sulby
RAMSEY BAY
RAMSEY
Churchtown
Glen Auldyn
MILLENNIUM WAY
Port e Vullen
Ballaugh
Orrisdale Head
Ravensdale
Maughold
Maughold Head
Kirk Michael
1854 NORTH BARRULE
Ballajora
Port Mooar
TT Circuit
2036 SNAEFELL
Corrany
Ballacarnane Beg
Barregarrow
Murray's
Shaughlaige-e-Caine
Dhoon
Knocksharry
Cronk-y-Voddy
Snaefell Mountain Railway
Laxey Wheel
St Patrick's Isle
Lambfell Moar
1599 COLDEN
PEEL
Laxey
Laxey Head
Contrary Head
Ballig
1570 SLIEAU RUY
Ballacannell
Patrick
St Johns
Laxey Bay
Baldrine
Baldwin
Glenmaye
Clay Head
Crosby
Hillberry
Dalby Point
Glen Vine
Union Mills
Onchan
Foxdale
Onchan Head
Dalby
Garth
Eairy
DOUGLAS
Niarbyl Bay
Douglas Bay
1586 SOUTH BARRULE
Braaid
Close Clark
Douglas Head
St Mark's
Ballamodha
Newtown
Little Ness
Lingague
Ronague
Quine's Hill
Port Soderick
Isle of Man Steam Railway
Bradda Head
Bradda
Colby
Ballabeg
Ballasalla
Santon Head
Port Erin
ISLE OF MAN (RONALDSWAY)
The Howe
CASTLETOWN
Derbyhaven
Cregneish
Port St Mary
Rushen
St Michael's Island
Calf of Man
SPANISH HEAD
To Belfast (Summer only)
To Heysham
To Liverpool
DUBLIN Summer only
To Belfast
To Douglas
DUBLIN
SOUTHPORT
Marshside
Crossens
Ainsdale
Shirdley Hill
Halsall
Freshfield
FORMBY
Haskayne
Great Altcar
Lydiate
Ince Blundell
Hightown
Maghull
Thornton
Great Crosby
CROSBY
Litherland
Waterloo
Seaforth
BOOTLE
New Brighton
LIVERPOOL
LIVERPOOL BAY
SD SJ

SD
SE
NORTH
YORKSHIRE
WEST
LANGSTROTHDALE CHASE
THE PENNINE WAY
Forest of Bowland
MORECAMBE
HEYSHAM
LANCASTER
CARNFORTH
GRANGE-OVER-SANDS
Kirkby Lonsdale
Ingleton
High Bentham
Settle
Grassington
SKIPTON
KEIGHLEY
BARNOLDSWICK
CLITHEROE
COLNE
NELSON
BURNLEY
BLACKBURN
ACCRINGTON
PRESTON
LEYLAND
CHORLEY
DARWEN
HALIFAX
TODMORDEN
ROCHDALE
BURY
BOLTON
WIGAN
SKELMERSDALE
ST HELENS
NEWTON-LE-WILLOWS
LEIGH
ECCLES
SALFORD
MANCHESTER
OLDHAM
STALYBRIDGE
ASHTON-UNDER-LYNE
STRETFORD
URMSTON
38
39
36
30
31

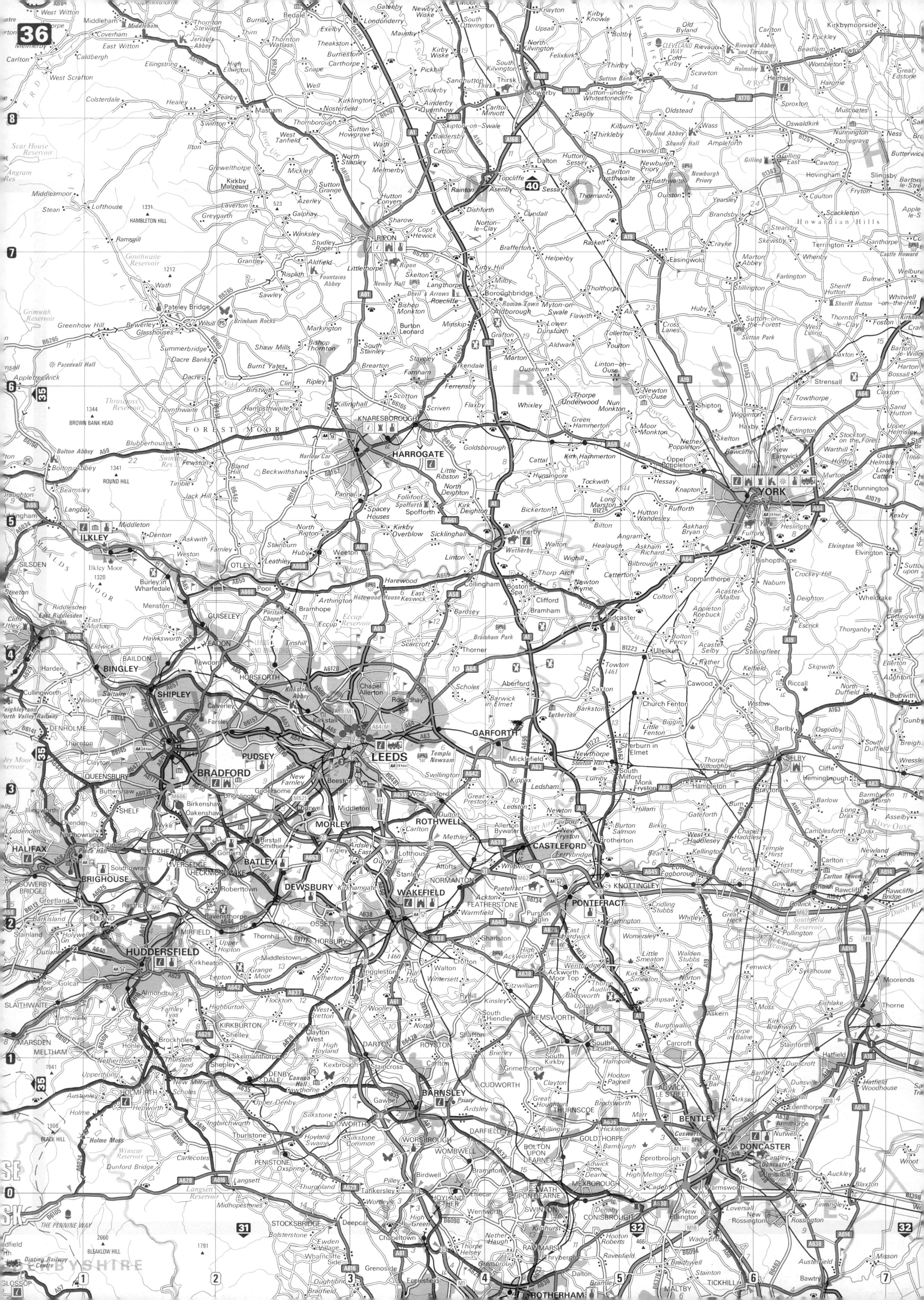
36
RIPON
KNARESBOROUGH
HARROGATE
YORK
ILKLEY
OTLEY
BINGLEY
SHIPLEY
BRADFORD
PUDSEY
LEEDS
GARFORTH
SELBY
HALIFAX
BRIGHOUSE
HUDDERSFIELD
DEWSBURY
BATLEY
MORLEY
WAKEFIELD
CASTLEFORD
PONTEFRACT
KNOTTINGLEY
HEMSWORTH
BARNSLEY
BENTLEY
DONCASTER
MEXBOROUGH
ROTHERHAM
Thirsk
Masham
Pateley Bridge
Boroughbridge
Wetherby
Tadcaster
FOREST MOOR
Howardian Hills
THE PENNINE WAY
35
31
32
40

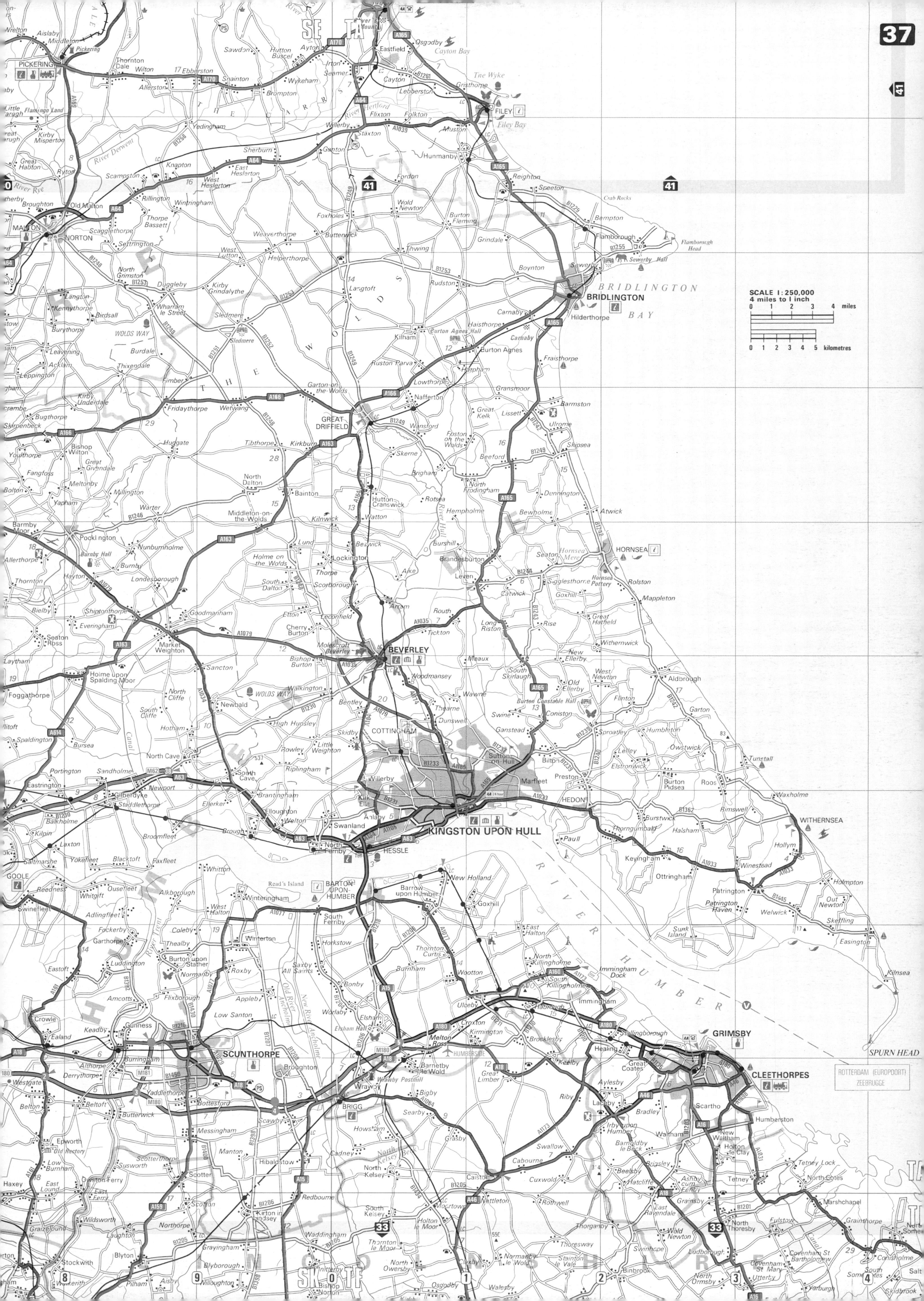
SCALE 1:250,000
4 miles to 1 inch
miles
kilometres
PICKERING
Thornton Dale
Ebberston
Snainton
Brompton
Wykeham
Ayton
Seamer
Eastfield
Osgodby
Cayton Bay
Cayton
Lebberston
The Wyke
Gristhorpe
FILEY
Filey Bay
Flixton
Folkton
Muston
Staxton
Willerby
Ganton
Sherburn
Hunmanby
Yedingham
River Derwent
Knapton
East Heslerton
West Heslerton
Scampston
Rillington
Wintringham
Old Malton
MALTON
NORTON
Scagglethorpe
Settrington
Thorpe Bassett
Weaverthorpe
Foxholes
Butterwick
Wold Newton
Fordon
Burton Fleming
Grindale
Reighton
Speeton
Crab Rocks
Bempton
Flamborough
Flamborough Head
Sewerby Hall
Sewerby
BRIDLINGTON
BRIDLINGTON BAY
Hilderthorpe
Boynton
Rudston
Thwing
Helperthorpe
West Lutton
North Grimston
Duggleby
Kirby Grindalythe
Langton
Kennythorpe
Birdsall
Burythorpe
Wharram le Street
Sledmere
Langtoft
THE WOLDS
WOLDS WAY
Leavening
Acklam
Burdale
Thixendale
Leppington
Fimber
Kirby Underdale
Bugthorpe
Fridaythorpe
Wetwang
Garton-on-the-Wolds
Kilham
Burton Agnes Hall
Burton Agnes
Haisthorpe
Carnaby
Ruston Parva
Lowthorpe
Harpham
Fraisthorpe
Nafferton
Gransmoor
GREAT DRIFFIELD
Wansford
Great Kelk
Lissett
Barmston
Ulrome
Skipsea
Foston on the Wolds
Beeford
Skerne
Brigham
North Frodingham
Dunnington
Atwick
Hutton Cranswick
Rotsea
Hempholme
Bewholme
Watton
Kilnwick
HORNSEA
Hornsea Mere
Seaton
Hornsea Pottery
Rolston
Mappleton
Beswick
Burshill
Brandesburton
Lockington
Lund
Aike
Leven
Catwick
Goxhill
Sigglesthorne
Great Hatfield
Rise
Long Riston
Routh
Arram
Tickton
Scorborough
Leconfield
Etton
Cherry Burton
South Dalton
Holme on the Wolds
Thorpe
Huggate
Tibthorpe
Kirkburn
Bishop Wilton
Great Givendale
Youlthorpe
Fangfoss
Bolton
Meltonby
Yapham
Millington
North Dalton
Bainton
Warter
Middleton-on-the-Wolds
Barmby Moor
Pocklington
Burnby Hall
Nunburnholme
Burnby
Allerthorpe
Thornton
Hayton
Londesborough
Bielby
Shiptonthorpe
Evringham
Goodmanham
Seaton Ross
Market Weighton
Laytham
Holme upon Spalding Moor
Sancton
Molescroft
BEVERLEY
Bishop Burton
Meaux
Withernwick
New Ellerby
West Newton
Aldbrough
South Skirlaugh
Old Ellerby
Flinton
Woodmansey
Wawne
Walkington
North Cliffe
Foggathorpe
South Cliffe
Newbald
Hotham
Bentley
Thearne
Dunswell
Burton Constable Hall
Coniston
Swine
Ganstead
Garton
Humbleton
Sproatley
High Hunsley
Skidby
COTTINGHAM
Little Weighton
Rowley
Bursea
Spaldington
North Cave
Riplingham
Sutton-on-Hull
Bilton
Lelley
Elstronwick
Owstwick
Tunstall
Portington
Sandholme
Eastrington
Gilberdyke
Newport
South Cave
Willerby
Brantingham
Marfleet
Preston
HEDON
Burton Pidsea
Roos
Waxholme
Staddlethorpe
Balkholme
Ellerker
Kirk Ella
Anlaby
Elloughton
Welton
Swanland
KINGSTON UPON HULL
Burstwick
Rimswell
WITHERNSEA
Kilpin
Laxton
Broomfleet
Brough
North Ferriby
HESSLE
Thorngumbald
Paull
Halsham
Hollym
Saltmarshe
Yokefleet
Blacktoft
Faxfleet
Keyingham
Winestead
Ottringham
Whitton
GOOLE
Reedness
Whitgift
Ousefleet
Alkborough
Read's Island
BARTON-UPON-HUMBER
Barrow upon Humber
New Holland
Goxhill
RIVER HUMBER
Patrington
Holmpton
Out Newton
Welwick
Patrington Haven
Skeffling
Swinefleet
Adlingfleet
West Halton
Winteringham
South Ferriby
Fockerby
Garthorpe
Coleby
Thealby
Winterton
Horkstow
East Halton
Sunk Island
Easington
Thornton Curtis
North Killingholme
Immingham Dock
Kilnsea
Eastoft
Luddington
Burton upon Stather
Normanby
Roxby
Saxby All Saints
Burnham
Wootton
South Killingholme
Immingham
Bonby
Amcotts
Flixborough
Appleby
Worlaby
Ulceby
Habrough
Crowle
Keadby
Gunness
Low Santon
Elsham
Elsham Hall
Croxton
Kirmington
Brocklesby
Stallingborough
GRIMSBY
Healing
Eaand
Burringham
SCUNTHORPE
Broughton
Melton Ross
HUMBERSIDE
Barnetby le Wold
Great Limber
Keelby
Great Coates
SPURN HEAD
CLEETHORPES
ROTTERDAM (EUROPOORT) ZEEBRUGGE
Althorpe
Derrythorpe
Westgate
Yaddlethorpe
Bottesford
Wrawby
Wrawby Postmill
Bigby
Aylesby
Riby
Laceby
Bradley
Scartho
Belton
Beltoft
Butterwick
Scawby
BRIGG
Searby
Irby upon Humber
Humberston
Epworth
Old Rectory
Messingham
Howsham
Grasby
Swallow
Barnoldby le Beck
Waltham
New Waltham
Holton le Clay
Low Burnham
Susworth
Scotterthorpe
Manton
Hibaldstow
Cadney
North Kelsey
Kelsey Beck
Cabourne
Beelsby
Brigsley
Tetney Lock
Haxey
East Lound
Owston Ferry
East Ferry
Scotter
Caistor
Cuxwold
Hatcliffe
Ashby cum Fenby
Tetney
North Cotes
Redbourne
Nettleton
Rothwell
East Ravendale
Grainsby
Marshchapel
Wildsworth
Scotton
Kirton in Lindsey
Mocrtown
South Kelsey
Holton le Moor
Thorganby
Wold Newton
North Thoresby
Fulstow
Grainthorpe
Graizelound
Northorpe
Laughton
Waddingham
Thornton le Moor
Thoresway
Swinhope
Ludborough
Covenham St Bartholomew
Covenham St Mary
Stockwith
Blyton
Grayingham
Snitterby
North Owersby
Normanby le Wold
Stainton le Vale
Binbrook
Conisholme
North Ormsby
Utterby
Walkerith
Pilham
Aisby
Blyborough
Willoughton
Bishop Norton
Osgodby
Walesby
Yarburgh
Skidbrook

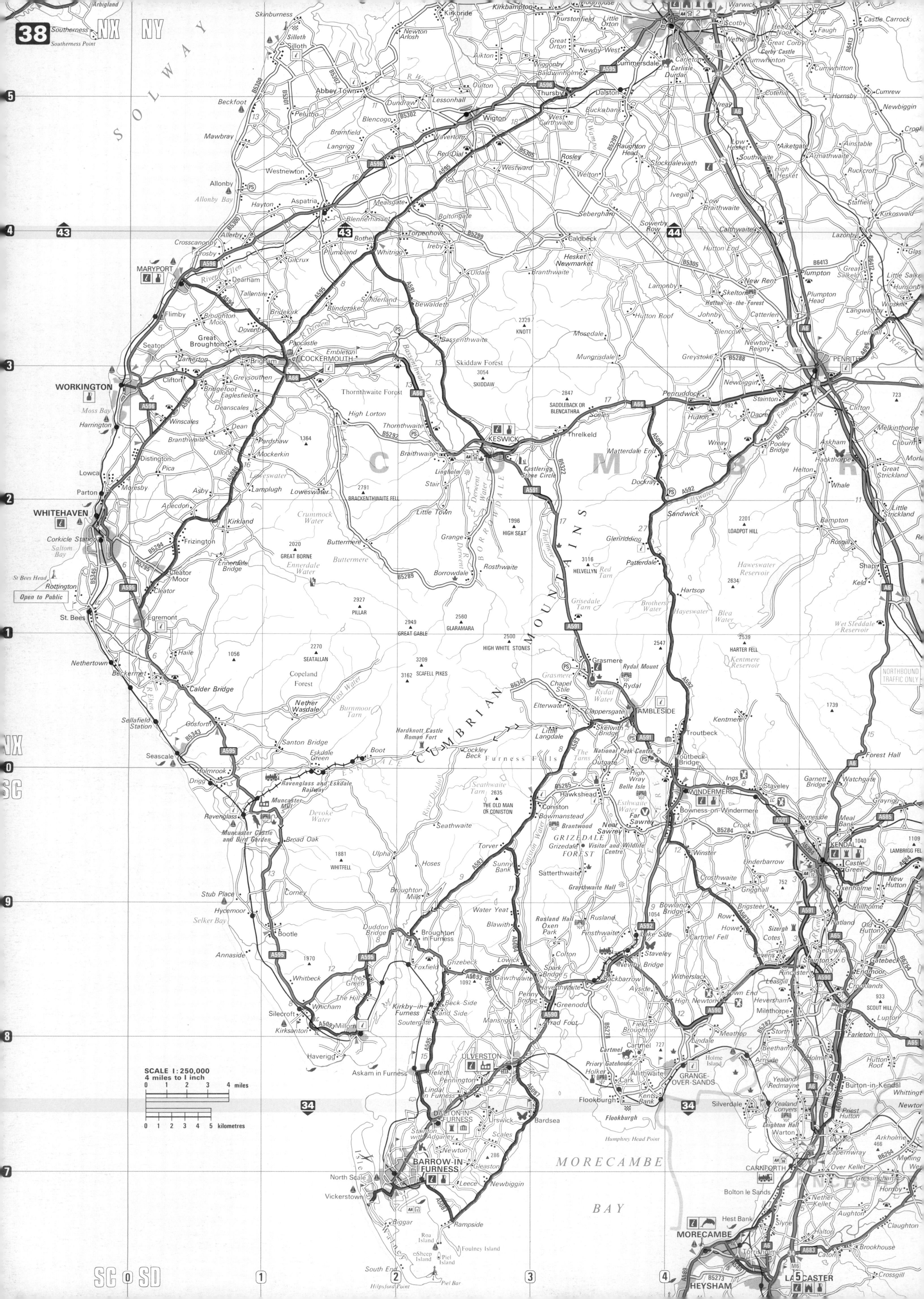
NX
NY
SOLWAY
Southerness
Southerness Point
Arbigland
Skinburness
Silloth
Kirkbride
Kirkbampton
Thurstonfield
Little Orton
Great Orton
Newby West
Carlisle
Scotby
Wetheral
Heads Nook
Great Corby
Corby Castle
Cumwhinton
Cumwhitton
Castle Carrock
How
Faugh
Warwick
Cummersdale
Carleton
Durdar
Newton Arlosh
Aikton
Wiggonby
Baldwinholme
Abbey Town
Oulton
Thursby
Dalston
Beckfoot
Dundraw
Lessonhall
Pelutho
Blencogo
Wigton
West Curthwaite
Buckabank
Wreay
Cotehill
Cumrew
Hornsby
Newbiggin
Mawbray
Bromfield
Langrigg
Waverton
Red Dial
Rosley
Raughton Head
Low Hesket
Southwaite
Aiketgate
Ainstable
Armathwaite
Westnewton
Westward
Welton
Stockdalewath
High Hesket
Ruckcroft
Allonby
Allonby Bay
Hayton
Aspatria
Mealsgate
Blennerhasset
Boltongate
Ivegill
Low Braithwaite
Staffield
Kirkoswald
Seberghan
Sowerby Row
Calthwaite
Lazonby
Allerby
Crosscanonby
Crosby
Torpenhow
Bothel
Plumbland
Whitrigg
Ireby
Caldbeck
Hesket Newmarket
Hutton End
MARYPORT
Gilcrux
River Ellen
Dearham
Tallentire
Uldale
Branthwaite
Plumpton
Great Salkeld
Little Salkeld
Lamonby
New Rent
Skelton
Hutton-in-the-Forest
Plumpton Head
Flimby
Broughton Moor
Bridekirk
Sunderland
Blindcrake
Bewaldeth
Hutton Roof
Johnby
Catterlen
Langwathby
Dovenby
Great Broughton
Seaton
Camerton
Pap castle
COCKERMOUTH
Embleton
Bassenthwaite
Bassenthwaite Lake
Skiddaw Forest
2329
KNOTT
Mosedale
Blencow
Newton Reigny
Edenhall
Mungrisdale
Greystoke
Newbiggin
PENRITH
WORKINGTON
Clifton
Brigham
Greysouthen
Bridgefoot
Eaglesfield
Thornthwaite Forest
3054
SKIDDAW
2847
SADDLEBACK OR BLENCATHRA
Penruddock
Stainton
Dacre
Clifton
Moss Bay
Harrington
Deanscales
Winscales
Dean
High Lorton
Thornthwaite
Scales
Threlkeld
Hutton
Branthwaite
Pardshaw
1364
KESWICK
Matterdale End
Pooley Bridge
Askham
Hackthorpe
Distington
Ullock
Mockerkin
Braithwaite
Castlerigg Stone Circle
Wreay
Lowca
Pica
Loweswater
Lingholm
Helton
Great Strickland
Parton
Moresby
Asby
Lamplugh
Loweswater
Stair
2791
BRACKENTHWAITE FELL
Derwent Water
Dockray
Whale
WHITEHAVEN
Arlecdon
Crummock Water
Little Town
BORROWDALE
Ullswater
Sandwick
Little Strickland
Bampton
Corkickle Station
Saltom Bay
Kirkland
Frizington
Grange
1996
HIGH SEAT
Glenridding
2201
LOADPOT HILL
2020
GREAT BORNE
Buttermere
Rosthwaite
3116
HELVELLYN
Red Tarn
Patterdale
Rosgill
Haweswater Reservoir
Shap
St Bees Head
Rottington
Open to Public
Cleator Moor
Ennerdale Bridge
Ennerdale Water
Cleator
Borrowdale
Hartsop
2634
Keld
2927
PILLAR
Grisedale Tarn
Brothers Water
Hayeswater
Blea Water
St. Bees
Egremont
2949
GREAT GABLE
2560
GLARAMARA
Wet Sleddale Reservoir
Haile
2270
SEATALLAN
1056
2500
HIGH WHITE STONES
2547
2539
HARTER FELL
Nethertown
Beckermet
3209
SCAFELL PIKES
3162
Copeland Forest
Grasmere
Rydal Mount
Rydal
Kentmere Reservoir
NORTHBOUND TRAFFIC ONLY
Calder Bridge
Grasmere
Chapel Stile
Rydal Water
Sellafield Station
Nether Wasdale
Wast Water
Burnmoor Tarn
Elterwater
Clappersgate
AMBLESIDE
Kentmere
1739
Gosforth
Hardknott Castle Roman Fort
CUMBRIAN MOUNTAINS
Little Langdale
Skelwith Bridge
Troutbeck
Santon Bridge
Seascale
Eskdale Green
Boot
Cockley Beck
Furness Fells
The Tarns
National Park Centre
Troutbeck Bridge
Forest Hall
Holmrook
Drigg
Ravenglass and Eskdale Railway
Outgate
High Wray
Belle Isle
Ings
Staveley
Garnett Bridge
Watchgate
Seathwaite Tarn
2635
THE OLD MAN OF CONISTON
Hawkshead
Esthwaite Water
WINDERMERE
Bowness-on-Windermere
Muncaster Mill
Ravenglass
Muncaster Castle and Bird Garden
Devoke Water
River Duddon
Coniston
Bowmanstead
Brantwood
Near Sawrey
Far Sawrey
Crook
Burneside
Meal Bank
Grayrigg
Seathwaite
GRIZEDALE FOREST
Grizedale
Visitor and Wildlife Centre
B5284
KENDAL
1040
LAMBRIGG FELL
1109
Broad Oak
Torver
Winster
Castle Green
1881
WHITFELL
Ulpha
Hoses
Sunny Bank
Satterthwaite
Underbarrow
Oxenholme
New Hutton
Crosthwaite
Grigghall
752
Graythwaite Hall
Millholme
Stub Place
Hycemoor
Corney
Broughton Mills
Water Yeat
Bowland Bridge
Brigsteer
Selker Bay
Rusland Hall
Rusland
Oxen Park
Row
Sizergh
Cotes
Natland
Old Hutton
Blawith
Finsthwaite
Lake Side
Howe
Bootle
Duddon Bridge
Broughton in Furness
1054
Cartmel Fell
Staveley
Annaside
1970
Foxfield
Grizebeck
Colton
Lowick
Newby Bridge
Levens
Sedgwick
Stainton
Gatebeck
Whitbeck
The Green
1092
Gawthwaite
Spark Bridge
Haverthwaite
Backbarrow
Ayside
Witherslack
Rinceater
Leasgill
Endmoor
Crooklands
The Hill
Beck Side
Penny Bridge
Greenodd
High Newton
Town End
Heversham
933
SCOUT HILL
Silecroft
Whicham
Kirkby-in-Furness
Sand Side
Mansriggs
Milnthorpe
Lupton
Kirksanton
Millom
Soutergate
Arrad Foot
Field Broughton
Meathop
Farleton
Storth
Haverigg
ULVERSTON
Cartmel
727
Lindale
Holme Island
Beetham
Arnside
Holme
Cartmel
Priory Gatehouse
Askam in Furness
Ireleth
Pennington
Holker
Cark
Allithwaite
GRANGE-OVER-SANDS
Hutton Roof
Lindal in Furness
Yealand Redmayne
Burton-in-Kendal
Whittington
Flookburgh
Kents Bank
Silverdale
Yealand Conyers
Priest Hutton
Newton
DALTON-IN-FURNESS
Urswick
Bardsea
Flookburgh
Leighton Hall
Warton
Humphrey Head Point
Stainton with Adgarley
Scales
Borwick
Arkholme
Isle of Walney
Newton
286
MORECAMBE
Capernwray
466
Gleaston
CARNFORTH
Over Kellet
Gressingham
North Scale
BARROW-IN-FURNESS
Leece
Newbiggin
Hornby
Vickerstown
Bolton le Sands
Nether Kellet
BAY
Biggar
Rampside
Aughton
Hest Bank
Claughton
Roa Island
Slyne
MORECAMBE
Halton
Sheep Island
Piel Island
Foulney Island
Torrisholme
Caton
Brookhouse
South End
Crossgill
Hilpsford Point
Piel Bar
HEYSHAM
LANCASTER
SC
SD
SCALE 1:250,000
4 miles to 1 inch
miles
kilometres
43
44
34
39

39
44
45
35
40
NY NZ
SD SE
NORTHUMBERLAND
DURHAM
NORTH YORKSHIRE
PENNINES
Allendale Town
Broadwell House
Knarsdale
Slaggyford
Ninebanks
Sinderhope
Ayle
South Tynedale Railway
Alston
Bayles
Gilderdale Forest
Leadgate
Carr Shield
Coalcleugh
Allenheads
Nenthead
Garrigill
Coanwood
Cowshill
Burnhope Reservoir
Ireshopeburn
St. John's Chapel
Daddry Shield
Westgate
Eastgate
Stanhope
Frosterley
Wolsingham
Tow Law
Rookhope
1694 COLLIER LAW
Crawleyside
Blanchland
Edmundbyers
Hunstanworth
1773 BOLT'S LAW
Waskerley
Muggleswick
Castleside
Carterway Heads
CONSETT
Healeyfield
Knitsley
Whittonstall
Hamsterley
Newlands
Ebchester
Kiln Pit Hill
Shotley Bridge
Hobson
Tantobie
Dipton
STANLEY
Beamish
Open-air Museum
Kibblesworth
Birtley
Ouston
Pelton
Fatfield
Leadgate
Iveston
ANNFIELD PLAIN
South Moor
Craghead
Grange Villa
CHESTER-LE-STREET
Waldridge
Edmondsley
Great Lumley
Maiden Law
Burnhope
Lanchester
Sacriston
Kimblesworth
Witton Gilbert
Plawsworth
Framwellgate Moor
Esh
Langley Park
Bearpark
Quebec
Cornsay
Satley
Esh Winning
Ushaw Moor
Waterhouses
DURHAM
East Hedleyhope
Sunniside
BRANDON
Brancepeth
Bowburn
Sunderland Bridge
Croxdale
Thornley
Billy Row
Oakenshaw
CROOK
WILLINGTON
Tudhoe
Fir Tree
Howden-le-Wear
Newfield
Byers Green
SPENNYMOOR
Hunwick
Middlestone Moor
High Grange
Witton-le-Wear
Kirk Merrington
Bedburn
Hamsterley
Witton Park
HAMSTERLEY FOREST
Low Redford
BISHOP AUCKLAND
Coundon
Chilton
High Etherley
St Helen Auckland
West Auckland
Coundon Grange
Rushyford
Morley
Butterknowle
SHILDON
Middridge
Woodland
Copley
Evenwood
NEWTON AYCLIFFE
Cockfield
Wackerfield
Redworth
Raby Castle
Staindrop
Hilton
Bolam
Heighington
Ingleton
Killerby
Kinninvie
Langton
Headlam
Denton
Walworth
Stainton
Cleatlam
Little Newsham
Gainford
High Coniscliffe
Winston
Piercebridge
BARNARD CASTLE
Startforth
Whorlton
Ovington
Manfield
Cleasby
Stapleton
Hurworth-on-Tees
Egglestone Abbey
Boldron
Greta Bridge
Caldwell
Epoleby
Hutton Magna
Forcett
Aldbrough St John
West Layton
East Layton
Brignall
Scargill
Barningham
Newsham
Melsonby
Barton
Dalton-on-Tees
Dalton
Gayles
Ravensworth
Kirby Hill
Whashton
Gilling West
Croft Autodrome
Middleton Tyas
Scotch Corner
Moulton
North Cowton
Skeeby
RICHMOND
Uckerby
Easby Abbey
Brompton-on-Swale
Catterick Bridge
Scorton
Bolton-on-Swale
Whitwell
Catterick
Hudswell
Downholme
Catterick Camp
Scotton
Tunstall
Kirkby Fleetham
Fencote
Marrick
Skelton
Marske
Hurst
Washfold
Langthwaite
Whaw
Reeth
Healaugh
Grinton
Stainton
Barden
East Hauxwell
Hunton
Arrathorne
Hackforth
Constable Burton
Patrick Brompton
Langthorne
Crakehall
Aiskew
Bedale
Leyburn
Harmby
Spennithorne
Finghall
Newton-le-Willows
Bellerby
Preston-under-Scar
Redmire
Castle Bolton
Wensley
Middleham
Coverham
East Witton
Thornton Steward
Jervaulx Abbey
Thornton Watlass
Exelby
Theakston
Burrill
Thirn
High Ellington
Ellingstring
Healey
Fearby
Masham
Swinton
West Tanfield
Nosterfield
Kirklington
Thornborough
Carthorpe
Burneston
Snape
Well
Ilton
Grewelthorpe
Kirkby Malzeard
Mickley
Sutton Grange
Laverton
Azerley
Galphay
523
Greygarth
Winksley
Studley Roger
Grantley
Aldfield
Fountains Abbey
Risplith
Sawley
Pateley Bridge
Wilsill
Brimham Rocks
Bewerley
Glasshouses
Markington
Summerbridge
Dacre Banks
Shaw Mills
Bishop Thornton
Burnt Yates
Greenhow Hill
Grimwith Reservoir
Gouthwaite Reservoir
Ramsgill
Wath
1212
Lofthouse
Middlesmoor
Stean
1331 HAMBLETON HILL
1984 LITTLE WHERNSIDE
Scar House Reservoir
Angram Res
2308 GREAT WHERNSIDE
Parcevall Hall
Burnsall
Hebden
Grassington
National Park Centre
Threshfield
Thorpe
Conistone
Kilnsey
Kettlewell
Hawkswick
Arncliffe
Arncliffe Cote
Starbotton
Buckden
2302 BUCKDEN PIKE
Cray
Walden Head
Halton Gill
Litton
Foxup
Yockenthwaite
LANGSTROTHDALE CHASE
Kidstones
Walden
Horsehouse
Bradley
Woodale
Carlton
West Scrafton
Melmerby
Caldbergh
Agglethorpe
West Witton
West Burton
Newbiggin
Thoralby
Aysgarth
Carperby
Swinithwaite
Woodhall
Askrigg
Newbiggin
Thornton Rust
Countersett
Stalling Busk
Bainbridge
Burtersett
Hawes
National Park Centre
Hardrow
Sedbusk
High Shaw
Cotterdale
Crackpot
Low Row
Gunnerside
Feetham
Ivelet
Muker
Thwaite
Keld
West Stonesdale
Kearton
2349 GREAT SHUNNER FELL
1914 GREAT PINSEAT
2191
1674 CLEASBY HILL
2171
2328
Outhgill
Nateby
Kirkby Stephen
Hartley
Winton
Kaber
Brough Sowerby
Brough
Hillbeck
Great Musgrave
Warcop
North Stainmore
1439
1701 MOODY MEA
Stainmore Forest
Bowes
Deep Dale
Baldersdale Reservoir
Hury
Hunderthwaite
Lartington
Cotherstone
Romaldkirk
Mickleton
Eggleston
Grassholme
Selset Reservoir
Thringarth
Bowbank
Middleton-in-Teesdale
Holwick
Newbiggin
1854
Forest
Langdon Beck
Harwood
Cow Green Res
2284 CHAPELFELL TOP
2249 ROUND HILL
2930 CROSS FELL
River Tees
Milburn Forest
Kirkland
Blencarn
Milburn
Dufton Fell
Newbiggin
Knock
Dufton
THE PENNINE WAY
Kirkby Thore
Long Marton
Crackenthorpe
Brampton
Murton
2446
APPLEBY-IN-WESTMORLAND
Hilton
Lune Forest
Kings Meaburn
Colby
Great Ormside
Sandford
Maulds Meaburn
Drybeck
563
1843
Great Asby
Soulby
Crosby Garrett
Waitby
Orton
Raisbeck
1353
Kelleth
Newbiggin-on-Lune
1284
Tebay
Ravenstonedale
2219 THE CALF
Cautley
2217
Sedbergh
National Park Centre
Garsdale Head
Millthrop
Gawthrop
Dent
Cowgill
Lea Yeat
Stone House
Middleton
1999 CALF TOP
Deepdale
2192
2419 WHERNSIDE
Barbon
Casterton
Kirkby Lonsdale
Chapel le Dale
Cowan Bridge
Ireby
Westhouse
2373 INGLEBOROUGH HILL
High Birkwith
2731
THE PENNINE WAY
New Houses
2273 PEN-Y-GHENT
New Inn
Horton in Ribblesdale
Skirwith
Ingleton
Cantsfield
Burton in Lonsdale
Lower Bentham
High Bentham
Newby
Clapham
National Park Centre
Austwick
Wharfe
Keasden
Lawkland
Eldroth
Stainforth
Malham Tarn
Stackhouse
Langcliffe
1815
Settle
Giggleswick
Lowgill
Thrushgill
Wham
Malham
National Park Centre
Hanlith
Bordley
River Skirfare
River Wharfe
River Derwent
River Wear
River Greta
River Swale
River Ure
River Dee
A686
A689
A68
A692
A693
A691
A167
A177
A688
A689
A6
A66
A67
A66(M)
A1(M)
A1
A685
A683
A684
A6108
A6136
A65
B6295
B6277
B6278
B6276
B6259
B6270
B6255
B6479
B6160
B6265
B6282
B6279
B6274
B6275
B6297
B6296
B6301
B6302
B6310
B6278
B6265
B6268
B6260
B6542
B6413
B6532
B6165
7
8
9
0
1
2
3

40
45
39
36
WASHINGTON
STANLEY
CONSETT
CHESTER-LE-STREET
HOUGHTON LE SPRING
SEAHAM
DURHAM
PETERLEE
HARTLEPOOL
Hartlepool Bay
Tees Bay
REDCAR
MARSKE-BY-THE-SEA
SALTBURN
BISHOP AUCKLAND
SPENNYMOOR
NEWTON AYCLIFFE
SHILDON
CROOK
WILLINGTON
TOW LAW
STOCKTON ON-TEES
MIDDLESBROUGH
GUISBOROUGH
SKELTON
DARLINGTON
BARNARD CASTLE
RICHMOND
NORTHALLERTON
Thirsk
Sowerby
Bedale
Masham
RIPON
Boroughbridge
Pateley Bridge
Leyburn
Middleham
Helmsley
Easingwold
Sedgefield
Billingham
Yarm
Stokesley
Great Ayton
Hendon
Ryhope
Horden
Blackhall Colliery
Seaton Carew
Greatham
Thornaby on Tees
Eaglescliffe
Egglescliffe
Hurworth-on-Tees
Croft Autodrome
Catterick Camp
Catterick
Scotton
Leeming Bar
Osmotherley
Mount Grace Priory
Rievaulx Abbey
Byland Abbey
Newburgh Priory
Fountains Abbey
Jervaulx Abbey
Easby Abbey
Egglestone Abbey
Raby Castle
Castle Bolton
Captain Cook Monument
CLEVELAND WAY
HAMSTERLEY FOREST
Gouthwaite Reservoir
Grimwith Reservoir
Scar House Reservoir
Angram Res
River Wear
River Tees
River Swale
River Greta
River Ure
River Leven
R Rye
Beacon Point
Horden Point
DURHAM
NORTH
YORKSHIRE
CLEVELAND
HAMBLETON HILL
LITTLE WHERNSIDE
COLLIER LAW
Howardian Hills

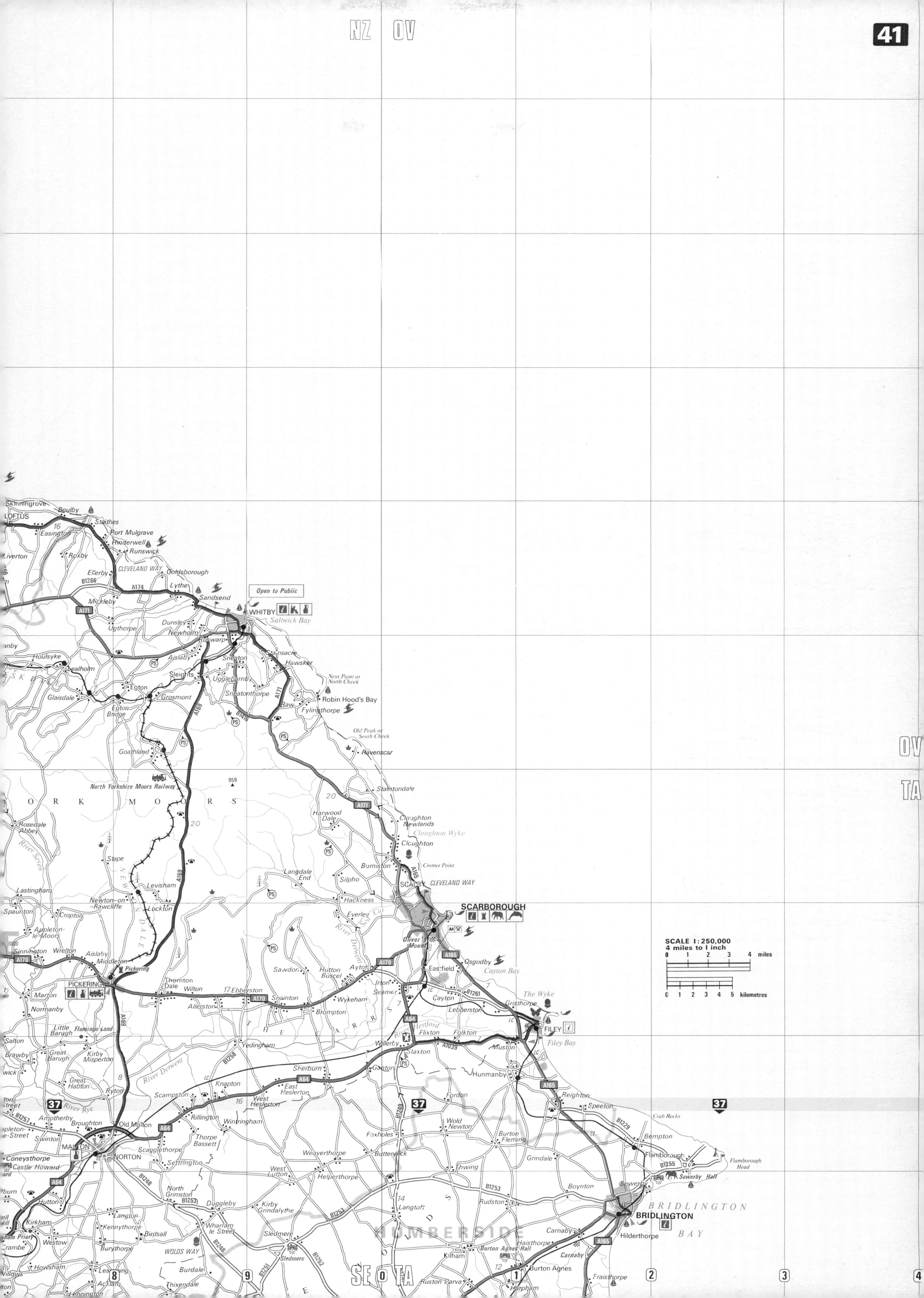
NZ
OV
TA
SE
TA
Skinningrove
LOFTUS
Boulby
Staithes
Easington
Port Mulgrave
Hinderwell
Runswick
Liverton
Roxby
Ellerby
CLEVELAND WAY
Goldsborough
B1266
A174
Lythe
Sandsend
Open to Public
WHITBY
Saltwick Bay
Mickleby
A171
Ugthorpe
Dunsley
Newholm
Ruswarp
Aislaby
Sneaton
Stainsacre
Hawsker
Houlsyke
Lealholm
Sleights
Ugglebarnby
Ness Point or North Cheek
Robin Hood's Bay
Egton
Glaisdale
Grosmont
Sneatonthorpe
Raw
Fylingthorpe
Egton Bridge
A169
B1416
Old Peak or South Cheek
Ravenscar
Goathland
959
North Yorkshire Moors Railway
Staintondale
Y O R K M O O R S
20
A171
Harwood Dale
Cloughton Newlands
Rosedale Abbey
Cloughton Wyke
Cloughton
River Seven
Stape
Burniston
Cromer Point
Langdale End
Silpho
A165
SCALBY
CLEVELAND WAY
Lastingham
Levisham
Hackness
SCARBOROUGH
Newton-on-Rawcliffe
Lockton
Everley
Sea Cut
Spaunton
Cropton
River Derwent
NEWTON DALE
Appleton-le-Moors
Oliver's Mount
Sinnington
Wrelton
Aislaby
Middleton
A165
Osgodby
A170
Pickering
Sawdon
Hutton Buscel
Ayton
Cayton Bay
A170
Eastfield
PICKERING
Thornton Dale
Wilton
17 Ebberston
Irton
Seamer
The Wyke
Marton
A170
Snainton
Wykeham
Cayton
B1261
Gristhorpe
Allerston
Normanby
Brompton
Lebberston
A169
T H E C A R R S
A64
FILEY
Little Barugh
Flamingo Land
River Hertford
Flixton
Folkton
Filey Bay
Salton
Yedingham
Willerby
A1039
Muston
Brawby
Great Barugh
Kirby Misperton
Staxton
B1258
River Derwent
Sherburn
Ganton
Hunmanby
Great Habton
A64
Ryton
Knapton
East Heslerton
Scampston
West Heslerton
A165
Fordon
Reighton
37
River Rye
16
37
Speeton
37
Crab Rocks
Amotherby
Rillington
Wintringham
B1249
Wold Newton
B1257
Broughton
Old Malton
A64
B1229
Swinton
Thorpe Bassett
Foxholes
Burton Fleming
Bempton
MALTON
Scagglethorpe
Flamborough
Coneysthorpe
NORTON
Weaverthorpe
Butterwick
Grindale
Flamborough Head
Castle Howard
Settrington
B1255
Sewerby Hall
A64
B1248
West Lutton
Helperthorpe
Thwing
North Grimston
Boynton
Sewerby
B1253
B1253
Hutton
Duggleby
Kirby Grindalythe
Rudston
B R I D L I N G T O N
Kirkham
Langton
Kennythorpe
B1253
Langtoft
BRIDLINGTON
Wharram le Street
H U M B E R S I D E
Hilderthorpe
Westow
Birdsall
Sledmere
Carnaby
B A Y
Burythorpe
A165
WOLDS WAY
B1248
Haisthorpe
Sledmere
B1252
Kilham
Burton Agnes Hall
Carnaby
Howsham
Leavening
Burdale
B1251
Burton Agnes
Acklam
Fraisthorpe
Thixendale
Ruston Parva
Harpham
8
9
1
2
3
4
SCALE 1:250,000
4 miles to 1 inch
0 1 2 3 4 miles
0 1 2 3 4 5 kilometres

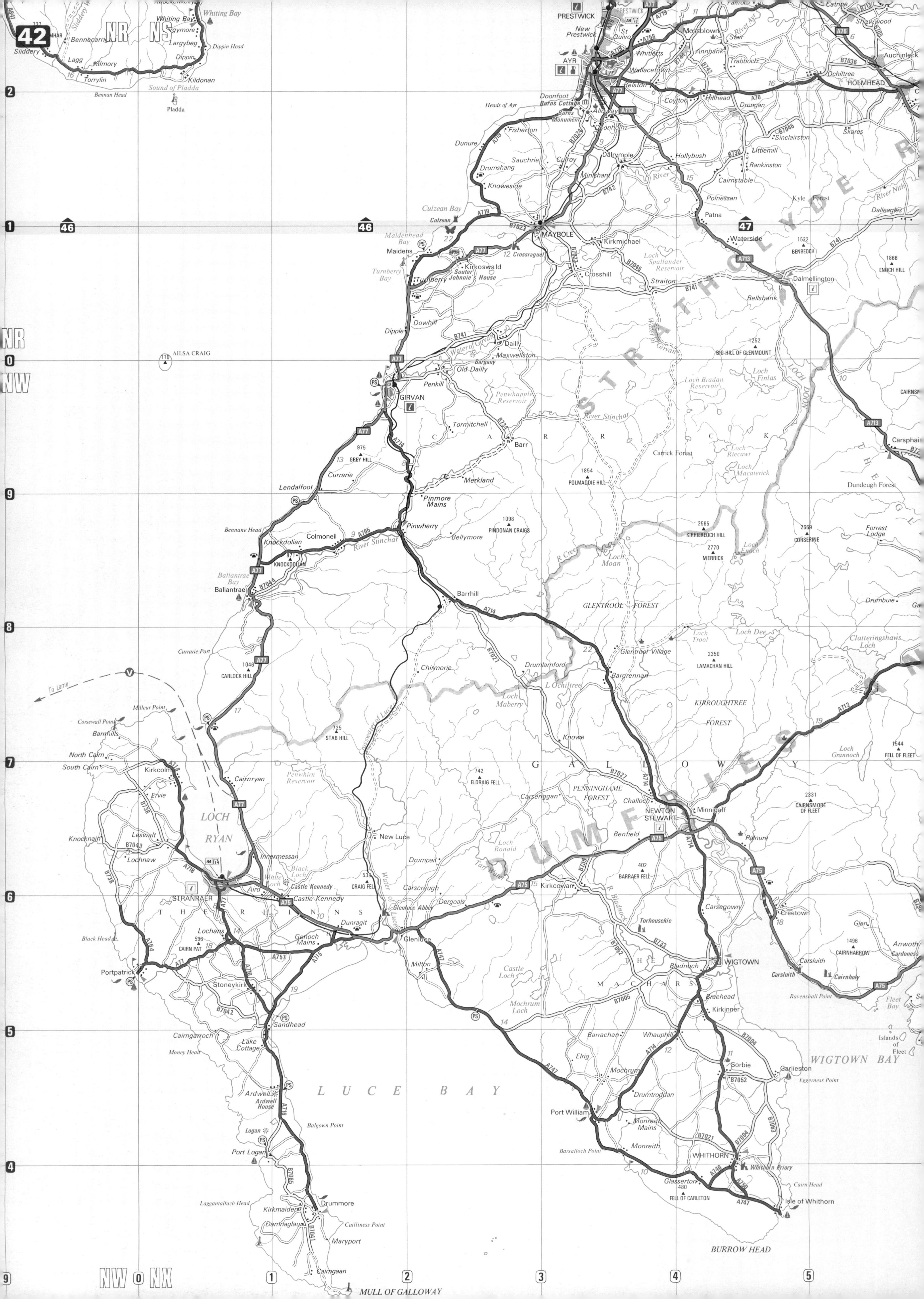

42
NR
NS
46
47
NR
0
NW
NW
0
NX
9
1
2
3
4
5
PRESTWICK
New Prestwick
St Quivox
Mossblown
Annbank
Stair
Trabboch
Shawwood
Catrine
Auchinleck
Ochiltree
HOLMHEAD
AYR
Whitletts
Wallacetown
Belston
Coylton
Hillhead
Drongan
Sinclairston
Skares
Doonfoot
Burns Cottage
Burns Monument
Alloway
Doonholm
Heads of Ayr
Fisherton
Dunure
Sauchrie
Culroy
Dalrymple
Hollybush
Littlemill
Rankinston
Drumshang
Minishant
Cairnstable
Knoweside
River Doon
Polnessan
Kyle Forest
River Nith
Dalleagles
Patna
Waterside
Culzean Bay
Culzean
Maidenhead Bay
Maidens
MAYBOLE
Kirkmichael
Crossraguel
Kirkoswald
Souter Johnnie's House
Turnberry Bay
Turnberry
Crosshill
Loch Spallander Reservoir
Straiton
1522 BENBEOCH
1866 ENOCH HILL
Dalmellington
Bellsbank
Dowhill
Dipple
Dailly
Water of Girvan
Maxwellston
Bargany
Old Dailly
1252 BIG HILL OF GLENMOUNT
110 AILSA CRAIG
GIRVAN
Penkill
Penwhapple Reservoir
Loch Bradan Reservoir
Loch Finlas
LOCH DOON
River Stinchar
CAIRNSM
Tormitchell
Barr
C A R R I C K
Catrick Forest
Loch Riecawr
Loch Macaterick
Carsphai
975 GREY HILL
Currarie
Merkland
1854 POLMADDIE HILL
Dundeugh Forest
Lendalfoot
Pinmore Mains
Bennane Head
Pinwherry
Colmonell
Knockdolian
Bellymore
1098 PINDONAN CRAIGS
2565 KIRRIEREOCH HILL
2668 CORSERINE
Forrest Lodge
871 KNOCKDOLIAN
R. Cree
Loch Moan
2770 MERRICK
Loch Enoch
Ballantrae Bay
Ballantrae
Barrhill
GLENTROOL FOREST
Drumbuie
Loch Trool
Loch Dee
Clatteringshaws Loch
Currarie Port
Glentrool Village
2350 LAMACHAN HILL
1046 CARLOCK HILL
Chirmorie
Drumlamford
Bargrennan
To Larne
L. Ochiltree
Milleur Point
Loch Maberry
KIRROUGHTREE FOREST
Corsewall Point
Barnhills
725 STAB HILL
Cross Water of Luce
Knowe
Loch Grannoch
1544 FELL OF FLEET
North Cairn
South Cairn
Kirkcolm
G A L L O W A Y
Ervie
Cairnryan
Penwhirn Reservoir
742 ELDRAIG FELL
PENNINGHAME FOREST
Carseriggan
2331 CAIRNSMORE OF FLEET
LOCH RYAN
NEWTON STEWART
Minnigaff
Challoch
Knocknain
Leswalt
Lochnaw
New Luce
Benfield
Palnure
Innermessan
Drumpail
Loch Ronald
Tarf Water
402 BARRAER FELL
Black Loch
White Loch
Castle Kennedy
538 CRAIG FELL
Water of Luce
Kirkcowan
R. Bladnoch
STRANRAER
Aird
Carscreugh
Dergoals
Carsegown
Creetown
T H E R H I N N S
Glenluce Abbey
Torhousekie
Glen
Lochans
Dunragit
Black Head
596 CAIRN PAT
Genoch Mains
Glenluce
1496 CAIRNHARROW
Anwoth
Cardoness
Portpatrick
Milton
Castle Loch
THE MACHARS
WIGTOWN
Bladnoch
Carsluith
Cairnholy
Stoneykirk
Mochrum Loch
Braehead
Kirkinner
Ravenshall Point
Fleet Bay
Sandhead
Cairngarroch
Lake Cottage
Barrachan
Whauphill
Islands of Fleet
Money Head
Elrig
Sorbie
WIGTOWN BAY
Garlieston
Eggerness Point
L U C E B A Y
Mochrum
Drumtroddan
Ardwell
Ardwell House
Port William
Balgown Point
Monreith Mains
Logan
Monreith
Port Logan
Barsalloch Point
WHITHORN
Whithorn Priory
Glasserton
480 FELL OF CARLETON
Cairn Head
Isle of Whithorn
Laggantalluch Head
Drummore
Kirkmaiden
Damnaglaur
Cailliness Point
Maryport
BURROW HEAD
Cairngaan
MULL OF GALLOWAY
Kildonan
Dippin Head
Dippin
Largybeg
Whiting Bay
Sliddery
Bennecarrigan
Lagg
Kilmory
Torrylin
Bennan Head
Sound of Pladda
Pladda
STRATHCLYDE
DUMFRIES

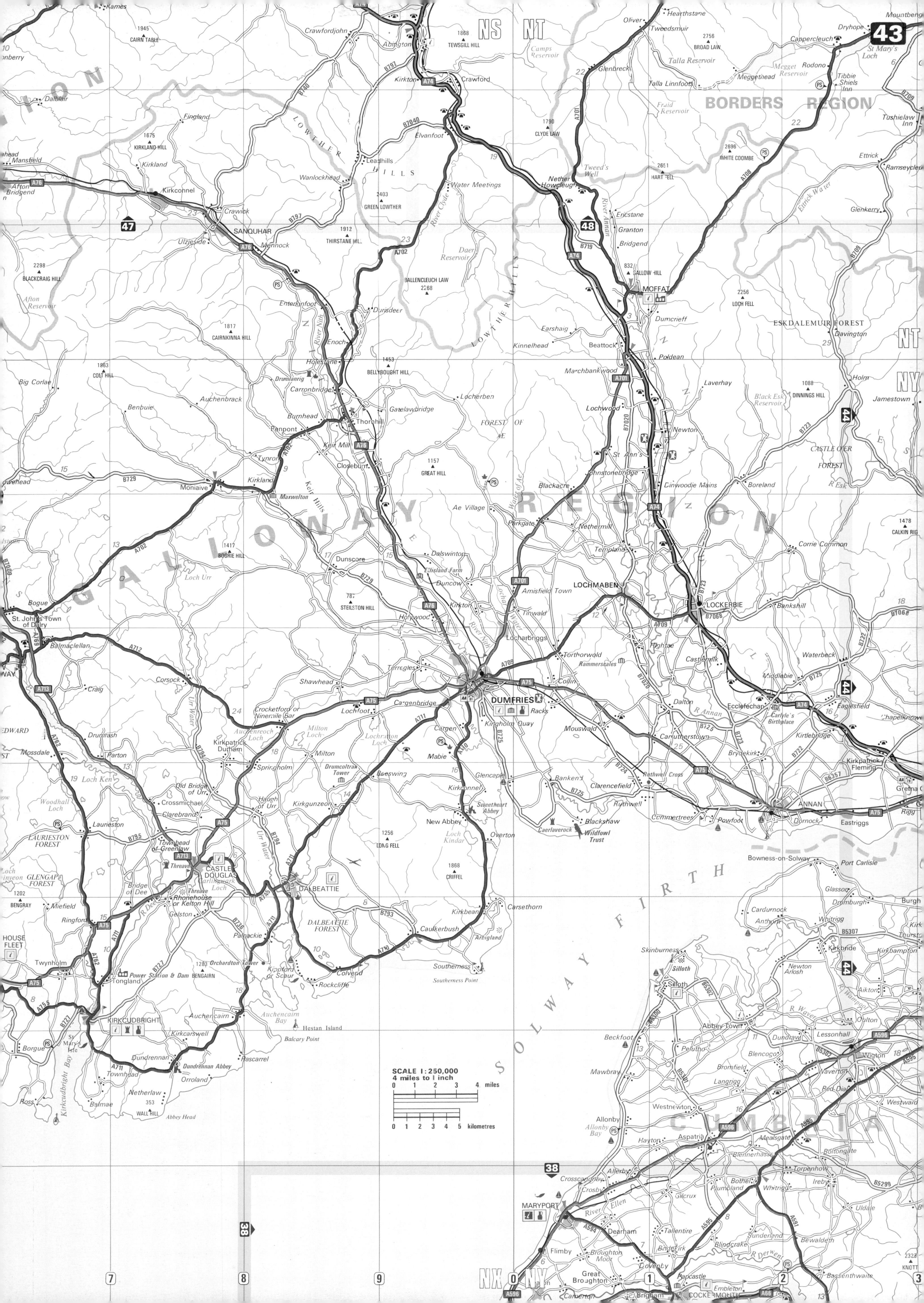

43
47
48
44
38
NS
NT
NX
NY
BORDERS REGION
DUMFRIES AND GALLOWAY REGION
CUMBRIA
SOLWAY FIRTH
LOWTHER HILLS
Kames
1945 CAIRN TABLE
Crawfordjohn
Abington
1868 TEWSGILL HILL
Camps Reservoir
Kirkton
Crawford
Elvanfoot
Leadhills
Wanlockhead
2403 GREEN LOWTHER
Water Meetings
River Clyde
Dalblair
Fingland
1675 KIRKLAND HILL
Kirkland
Mansfield
Afton Bridgend
Kirkconnel
Crawick
SANQUHAR
Ulzieside
Mennock
1912 THIRSTANE HILL
2298 BLACKCRAIG HILL
Afton Reservoir
Enterkinfoot
Durisdeer
Daer Reservoir
2268 BALLENCLEUCH LAW
1817 CAIRNKINNA HILL
Enoch
Holestane
River Nith
1453 BELLYBOUGHT HILL
1863 COLT HILL
Big Corlae
Drumlanrig
Carronbridge
Auchenbrack
Benbuie
Burnhead
Penpont
Thornhill
Gatelawbridge
Locherben
FOREST OF AE
Keir Mill
Closeburn
Tynron
1157 GREAT HILL
Moniaive
Kirkland
Maxwelton
Keir Hills
Ae Village
Water of Ae
Hearthstane
Oliver
Tweedsmuir
2756 BROAD LAW
Talla Reservoir
Glenbreck
Talla Linnfoots
Megget Reservoir
Meggethead
Fruid Reservoir
1790 CLYDE LAW
Tweed's Well
Nether Howcleugh
River Annan
Ericstane
Granton
Bridgend
832 GALLOW HILL
MOFFAT
Dumcrieff
Earshaig
Kinnelhead
Beattock
Poldean
Marchbankwood
Lochwood
Newton
St Ann's
Johnstonebridge
Blackacre
Dinwoodie Mains
Parkgate
Nethermill
Templand
LOCHMABEN
Amisfield Town
Tinwald
Locharbriggs
Torthorwold
Rammerscales
Collin
Mountbenger
Dryhope
Cappercleuch
St Mary's Loch
Rodono
Tibbie Shiels Inn
Tushielaw Inn
2696 WHITE COOMBE
2651 HART FELL
Ettrick
Ramseycleugh
Ettrick Water
Glenkerry
2256 LOCH FELL
ESKDALEMUIR FOREST
Davington
Laverhay
Black Esk Reservoir
1088 DINNINGS HILL
Holm
Jamestown
CASTLE O'ER FOREST
Boreland
R Esk
1478 CALKIN RIG
Corrie Common
LOCKERBIE
Bankshill
Waterbeck
Castlemilk
Hightae
Middlebie
Ecclefechan
Carlyle's Birthplace
Eaglesfield
Chapelknowe
Kirtlebridge
Kirkpatrick Fleming
Gretna
Dalton
R Annan
Carrutherstown
Brydekirk
ANNAN
Dornock
Eastriggs
Powfoot
Cummertrees
Ruthwell
Ruthwell Cross
Clarencefield
Mouswald
Bankend
Blackshaw
Caerlaverock
Wildfowl Trust
Dunscore
Dalswinton
Ellisland Farm
Duncow
Kirkton
Holywood
787 STEILSTON HILL
1417 BOGRIE HILL
Loch Urr
Bogue
St. John's Town of Dalry
Balmaclellan
Corsock
Craig
Shawhead
Terregles
Crocketford or Ninemile Bar
Lochfoot
Cargenbridge
DUMFRIES
Racks
Kingholm Quay
Cargen
Mabie
Auchenreoch Loch
Milton Loch
Lochrutton Loch
Milton
Drumcoltran Tower
Beeswing
Kirkpatrick Durham
Springholm
Urr Water
Glencaple
Kirkconnel
Sweetheart Abbey
New Abbey
Loch Kindar
Overton
1256 LONG FELL
1868 CRIFFEL
Drumrash
Mossdale
Parton
Loch Ken
Old Bridge of Urr
Crossmichael
Clarebrand
Haugh of Urr
Kirkgunzeon
Woodhall Loch
Laurieston
LAURIESTON FOREST
GLENGAP FOREST
Townhead of Greenlaw
Threave
CASTLE DOUGLAS
Carlingwark Loch
DALBEATTIE
1202 BENGRAY
Miefield
Bridge of Dee
Rhonehouse or Kelton Hill
Gelston
Ringford
Palnackie
DALBEATTIE FOREST
Carsethorn
Kirkbean
Caulkerbush
Arbigland
HOUSE FLEET
Twynholm
Power Station & Dam
Tongland
1283 BENGAIRN
Orchardton Tower
Kippford or Scaur
Colvend
Rockcliffe
Southerness
Southerness Point
KIRKCUDBRIGHT
Auchencairn
Auchencairn Bay
Hestan Island
Balcary Point
Kirkcarswell
Borgue
Kirkcudbright Bay
Dundrennan
Dundrennan Abbey
Townhead
Rascarrel
Orroland
Netherlaw
Balmae
Ross
353 WALL HILL
Abbey Head
SCALE 1:250,000
4 miles to 1 inch
0 1 2 3 4 miles
0 1 2 3 4 5 kilometres
Bowness-on-Solway
Port Carlisle
Glasson
Drumburgh
Burgh
Cardurnock
Anthorn
Whitrigg
Kirkbride
Kirkbampton
Newton Arlosh
Skinburness
Silloth
Abbey Town
R Waver
Aikton
Oulton
Lessonhall
Beckfoot
Dundraw
Pelutho
Blencogo
Wigton
Waverton
Bromfield
Langrigg
Red Dial
Mawbray
Westward
Westnewton
Allonby
Allonby Bay
Hayton
Aspatria
Mealsgate
Blennerhasset
Boltongate
Allerby
Crosscanonby
Crosby
Torpenhow
Bothel
Plumbland
Ireby
Whitrigg
Uldale
MARYPORT
River Ellen
Gilcrux
Dearham
Tallentire
Sunderland
Bewaldeth
Flimby
Broughton Moor
Bridekirk
Blindcrake
R Derwent
Great Broughton
Dovenby
Papcastle
Embleton
Bassenthwaite
2323 KNOTT
Camerton
Brigham
COCKERMOUTH
A76
A74
A702
A701
A708
A709
A710
A711
A712
A713
A75
A762
A755
A769
A596
A595
A591
A594
A66
B797
B740
B7040
B729
B719
B7020
B7068
B723
B722
B725
B724
B125
B6357
B794
B795
B736
B727
B793
B5302
B5300
B5301
B5307
B5299
7
8
9
0
1
2
3

BLACK LAW
Broadmeadows
Yarrow
Selkirk
Bowhill
Philiphaugh
Bowden
Maxton
Rutherford
Roxburgh
Heiton
Shotton
Longnewton Forest
Longnewton
Midlem
Lilliesleaf
Riddell
Ancrum
Nisbet
Eckford
BOWMONT FOREST
Crookhouse
Town Yetholm
Kirk Yetholm
Linton
Morebattle
THE PENNINE WAY
Mountbenger
Yarrow Feus
Sundhope
Ettrick Bridge
Dryhope
Cappercleuch
St Mary's Loch
Ettrick Forest
Kirkhope
Clerklands
Belses
Greenhouse
BORDERS
Crailing
Cessford
Rodono
Tibbie Shiels Inn
Gilmanscleuch
1209 CAVER'S HILL
Wall
Ashkirk
Chesters
Bonjedward
Crailinghall
1985 THE SCHIL
Lanton
JEDBURGH
Hassendean
Minto
Newton
Hownam Mains
Mowhaugh
Sourhope
Horsleyhill
Hundalee
Hownam
Tushielaw Inn
Crosslee
1056 SMASHA HILL
Appletreehall
Denholm
Bedrule
Oxnam
Chatto
Burnfoot
Swinside Hall
Redfordgreen
Alemoor Loch
Borthwickshiels
Bairnkine
Mossburnford
2032 WINDY GYLE
Ettrick
Ramseycleuch
Buccleuch
Wilton Dean
HAWICK
Hallrule
Halla
Borthwickbrae
Roberton
Kirkton
Mervinslaw
Etterick Water
Burnfoot
Bonchester Bridge
Abbotrule
Deanburnhaugh
Branxholme
Hobkirk
Glenkerry
Newmill
Chesters
48
49
Craik
Broadhaugh
REGION
Carter Bar
Dodburn
1729 RAVENS KNOWE
River Teviot
Teviothead
WAUCHOPE FOREST
THE CHEVIOT HILLS
ESKDALEMUIR FOREST
Davington
1564 EWESLESS KNOWE
Catcleugh Reservoir
REDESDALE FOREST
1996 CAULDCLEUCH HEAD
Sills
1809 OH ME EDGE
Mosspaul Hotel
1965 TUDHOPE HILL
Holm
1088 DINNINGS HILL
Black Esk Reservoir
Jamestown
Rochester
Horsley
Hermitage
Saughtree
Newlands
Bankhead
Larriston
Elishaw
CASTLE O'ER FOREST
Kielder
Steele Road
1303 EARL'S SEAT
R Esk
Kirkstile
Bentpath
ESKDALE
Castleton
Kielder Water
NORTHUMBERLAND
Gatehouse
1478 CALKIN RIG
1464 BLACK EDGE
Newcastleton
1684 GLENDHU HILL
Falstone
Greenhaugh
West Woodburn
Corrie Common
LANGHOLM
KIELDER FOREST
Bellingham
Hesleyside
821 EARSHAW HILL
Bankshill
Liddel Water
LIDDESDALE
KERSHOPE FOREST
Cauldside
1615 BLACK KNOWE
THE PENNINE WAY
Nook
Waterbeck
The Flatt
Birtley
Blackpool Gate
Crossings
Evertown
Rowanburn
Canonbie
WARK FOREST
Whygate
Stonehaugh
Wark
Roughsike
Bewcastle
Milltown
Eaglesfield
Haggbeck
Butterburn
Chapelknowe
Simonburn
Kirtlebridge
Easton
Netherby
Roman Wall (Mithraic Temple)
Stapleton
Spadeadam
Greenlee Lough
Hadrian's Wall
Roman Fort
Kirkpatrick Fleming
Roman Wall & Housesteads Museum
Whiteside
Kirkcambeck
Boltonfelland
Longtown
Gretna Green
Fourstones
West Hill
Gilsland Spa
Gilsland
Newbrough
ANNAN
Gretna
Kirklinton
Hadrian's Wall
Vindolanda Roman Fort
Rigg
Hethersgill
Greenhead
Bardon Mill
Dornock
Eastriggs
Smithfield
Haltwhistle
Melkridge
Henshaw
Haydon Bridge
Westlinton
Banks
Lanercost Priory
Scalebyhill
Todhills
Walton
Newtown
Plenmeller
Willimontswick
Port Carlisle
Scaleby
Low Row
R Eden
Rockcliffe
Blackford
Irthington
Brampton
Glasson
Burgh by Sands
Harker
CARLISLE (CROSBY)
Milton
Rowfoot
Drumburgh
Low Crosby
Beaumont
Cargo
Kingstown
Houghton
Hallbankgate
Tindale
Midgeholme
Whitrigg
Kirkandrews upon Eden
Grinsdale
Linstock
Newby East
Farlam
Lambley
Stonehouse
Whitfield
Bearsbridge
Catton
CARLISLE
Warwick Bridge
Hayton
Talkin
Halton Lea Gate
Forest Head
Kirkbride
Kirkbampton
Moorhouse
Warwick
How
Castle Carrock
Allendale Town
Newton Arlosh
Thurstonfield
Little Orton
Scotby
Heads Nook
Faugh
Great Orton
Wetheral
Great Corby
Knarsdale
Aikton
Newby West
Corby Castle
Ninebanks
Cummersdale
Cumwhinton
Wiggonby
Baldwinholme
Carleton
Carlisle
Durdar
Cumwhitton
Slaggyford
Sinderhope
R Wampool
Oulton
Thursby
Dalston
Cotehill
CUMBRIA
Cumrew
Lessonhall
Wigton
Buckabank
Wreay
Hornsby
Newbiggin
Ayle
Waverton
West Curthwaite
Croglin
South Tynedale Railway
Alston
Carr Shield
Red Dial
Raughton Head
Low Hesket
Aiketgate
Ainstable
Scale Houses
Bayles
Coalcleugh
Allenheads
Westward
Rosley
Stockdalewath
Southwaite
Armathwaite
Ruckcroft
Renwick
Gilderdale Forest
Welton
High Hesket
Nenthead
Ivegill
Staffield
Leadgate
Low Braithwaite
Kirkoswald
Garrigill
Coanwood
Boltongate
Sebergham
Cowshill
Sowerby Row
Calthwaite
38
39
Torpenhow
Caldbeck
Lazonby
Gamblesby
Burnhope Reservoir
Ireby
Hutton End
Glassonby
Ireshopeburn
Hesket Newmarket
Plumpton
Great Salkeld
Melmerby
St John's Chapel
Uldale
Branthwaite
New Rent
Little Salkeld
2249 ROUND HILL
Lamonby
Hunsonby
Skelton
Plumpton Head
Winskill
Bewaldeth
Hutton-in-the-Forest
Ousby
2930
River
THE PENNINES

SCALE 1:250,000
4 miles to 1 inch
0 1 2 3 4 miles
0 1 2 3 4 5 kilometres
NT NU
NU
NZ
NY NZ
Kirknewton
Akeld
Humbleton
Wooler
Greendykes
Chatton
Adderstone
Warenford
Lucker
Newham Hall
Newham
Swinhoe
Beadnell
Benthall
Beadnell Bay
West Fleetham
Newstead
Chathill
Ellingham
Preston
High Newton by-the-Sea
Earle
Haugh Head
Chillingham
Chillingham Wild Cattle
Lilburn Tower
Middleton Hall
Newtown
Rosebrough
Brockdam
Brunton
Embleton
Dunstanburgh
1485
COLD LAW
Middleton
Hepburn
876
CATERAN HILL
Christon Bank
East Lilburn
Old Bewick
West Ditchburn
North Charlton
Langleeford
Ilderton
Roddam
Roseden
Wooperton
Harehope
Eglingham
South Charlton
Rock
Dunstan
Craster
New Bewick
Rennington
Howick
Howick Hall
Beanley
Brandon
Ingram
Branton
Powburn
Littlehoughton
Greensidehill
Titlington
Longhoughton
Glanton Pike
Glanton
River Aln
ALNWICK
Denwick
Boulmer
Great Ryle
Bolton
Broome Park
Abberwick
Hawkhill
Prendwick
Whittingham
Lesbury
River Aln
Little Ryle
Thrunton
Bilton
Alnham
Lemmington Hall
Alnmouth
Alnmouth Bay
Scrainwood
Callaly Castle
Callaly
Edlingham
Yetlington
High Buston
Biddlestone
Shilbottle
Netherton
1047
LONG CRAG
Birling
Alwinton
Burradon
Lorbottle
Eastfield Hall
Warkworth
Hermitage
Coquet Island
High Trewhitt
Newton-on-the-Moor
Cartington
Gloster Hill
AMBLE
River Coquet
Sharperton
Swarland Estate
Guyzance
Hauxley
Holystone
Warton
Snitter
Cragside
Forest
Flotterton
Rothbury
Acklington
Togston
Radcliffe
Swarland
Thropton
Longframlington
Caistron
Hepple
Whitton
Newtown
Great Tosson
Felton
Broomhill
1444
TOSSON HILL
Pauperhaugh
Brinkburn
River Coquet
East Thirston
Red Row
Chevington Drift
Low Hesleyhurst
Eshott
Druridge Bay
West Chevington
Rothbury
Forestburn Gate
Wingates
Causey Park
Widdrington
HARWOOD FOREST
Fontburn Reservoir
Longhorsley
Widdrington Station
Cresswell
Elsdon
Ewesley
Fenrother
Tritlington
Ellington
Raylees
Ulgham
Lynemouth
Netherwitton
Stanton
Hebron
Longhirst
Woodhorn
Beacon Point
Longwitton
Pigdon
ASHINGTON
Pegswood
Hirst
NEWBIGGIN-BY-THE-SEA
Scots' Gap
Hartburn
Throphill
Mitford
MORPETH
Bothal
Guide Post
North Seaton
Knowesgate
Cambo
Middleton
Stakeford
Kirkwhelpington
Wallington
Meldon
Choppington
Scotland Gate
Cambois
River Wansbeck
Hepscott
Tranwell
East Sleekburn
Kirkharle
BEDLINGTON
BLYTH
Whalton
Capheaton
Bebside
Great Bavington
Saltwick
East Hartford
Newsham
River Blyth
Thockrington
Stannington
Kirkheaton
Belsay
Ogle
Nelson Village
Cramlington
New Hartley
Hallington Reservoir
Hallington
River Blyth
Seaton Sluice
New Horton Grange
Hartley
Great Whitington
Milbourne
Higham Dykes
Open to Public
Colwell
Ryal
Ingoe
Berwick Hill
East Cramlington
Seaton
SEATON DELAVAL
Seaton Burn
Fenwick
Heugh
Ponteland
Dinnington
Seghill
WHITLEY BAY
BERGEN STAVANGER Summer only
Wide Open
Chollerton
Bingfield
Dalton
Prestwick
Hazlerigg
Newcastle
Burradon
Earsdon
GOTEBORG Summer only
Chollerford
Matfen
Stamfordham
Backworth
Shiremoor
Cullercoats
Dartas Hall
High Callerton
NEWCASTLE (WOOLSINGTON)
Great Whittington
Black Callerton
Harlow Hill
LONGBENTON
New York
ESBJERG Summer only
Hadrian's Wall
GOSFORTH
TYNEMOUTH
North Shields
Hadrian's Wall
NEWCASTLE UPON TYNE
WALLSEND
Willington
SOUTH SHIELDS
Acomb
Sandhoe
Horsley
Throckley
JARROW
Heddon-on-the-Wall
Heaton
Walker
Harton
Marsden Bay
RYTON
Newton
Corbridge
Wylam
NEWBURN
HEBBURN
Open to Public
Roman Station
Ovingham
Prudhoe
Crawcrook
Byker
Monkton
Cleadon
Whitburn
HAM
Dilston
Ovington
BLAYDON
Dunston
Pelaw
Boldon Colliery
Riding Mill
Broomhaugh
Mickley Square
PRUDHOE
Greenside
FELLING
Stocksfield
Painshawfield
Barlow
WHICKHAM
GATESHEAD
BOLDON
Fulwell
Dye House
Hedley on-the-Hill
High Spen
Gibside Chapel
Highfield
Sunniside
Southwick
Roker
Wrekenton
Castletown
Slaley
Healey
Chopwell
ROWLANDS GILL
Lamesley
SUNDERLAND
Burnopfield
Wildfowl Trust
South Hylton
Chapel
Whittonstall
Hamsterley
Kibblesworth
Birtley
WASHINGTON
Minsteracres
Newlands
Hobson
Herdon
Open-air Museum
Kiln Pit Hill
Ebchester
Tantobie
Tanfield
Beamish
Ouston
Penshaw
adwell House
Shotley Bridge
Dipton
STANLEY
Pelton
Fatfield
Herrington
Ryhope
River Wear
New Silksworth
Carterway Heads
South Moor
Grange Villa
Shiney Row
Blanchland
CONSETT
Leadgate
Craghead
CHESTER-LE-STREET
Bournmoor
HOUGHTON LE SPRING
Edmundbyers
Iveston
ANNFIELD PLAIN
Waldridge
Seaton
SEAHAM
Muggleswick
Castleside
Maiden Law
Edmondsley
Great Lumley
Colliery Row
Hunstanworth
Knitsley
Burnhope
Finchale Priory
HETTON-LE-HOLE
Dalton-le-Dale
Healeyfield
Lanchester
Sacriston
East Rainton
Murton
Cold Hesledon
1773
BOLT'S LAW
Plawsworth
Kimblesworth
West Rainton
Easington Lane
Waskerley
Witton Gilbert
Framwellgate Moor
Pittington
South Hetton
Beacon Point
Butsfield
Langley Park
Carrville
Rookhope
Cornsay
Quebec
Bearpark
Littletown
Haswell
Easington
Horden Point
1694
COLLIER LAW
DURHAM
Satley
Esh
Esh Winning
Ushaw Moor
Sherburn
Shotton Colliery
Horden
Crawleyside
Waterhouses
DURHAM
Shadforth
Ludworth
PETERLEE
East Hedleyhope
Thornley
Wheatley Hill
Shotton
Blackhall Colliery
Eastgate
Stanhope
TOW LAW
BRANDON
Sunniside
Bowburn
Wingate
Hesleden
Frosterley
Wolsingham
Brancepeth
Sunderland Bridge
Quarrington Hill
Castle Eden
Thornley
Billy Row
Oakenshaw
Croxdale
Hett
Coxhoe
Station Town
CROOK
WILLINGTON
Tudhoe
Kelloe
Trimdon Grange
Trimdon Colliery
Hutton Henry
Sheraton
Byers
A1
A697
A68
A69
A695
A696
A189
A192
A193
A194
A195
A19
A1018
A1068
A690
A691
A692
A693
A694
A167
A177
A181
A182
A183
A184
A186
A191
A1231
A179
A689
B6341
B6342
B6343
B6344
B6345
B6346
B6347
B6348
B6349
B6318
B6321
B6323
B6324
B6278
B6296
B6297
B6301
B6302
B6306
B6307
B6309
B6310
B6315
B6309
B1340
B1339
B1281
B1283
B1284
B1285
B1331
49
39
40
1
2
3
4
5
6

SOUND OF JURA
LOCH SWEEN
LOCH CAOLISPORT
LOCH FYNE
KYLES OF BUTE
SOUND OF GIGHA
WEST LOCH TARBERT
KILBRANNAN SOUND
SOUND OF BUTE
ISLAND OF ARRAN
FIRTH OF CLYDE
STRAIT OF
REG
KINTYRE
BUTE
GIGHA ISLAND
HOLY ISLAND
INCHMARNOCK
GREAT CUMBRAE ISLAND
LITTLE CUMBRAE ISLAND
Sanda Island
MULL OF KINTYRE
LOCHGILPHEAD
Tarbert
CAMPBELTOWN
ROTHESAY
DUNOON
MILLPORT
Brodick
Lamlash
Whiting Bay
Crinan
Ardrishaig
Tighnabruaich
Carradale
Machrihanish
Southend
Port Askaig–Kennacraig
Port Ellen–Kennacraig
Brodick–Ardrossan
(Summer only)
NR NS
NR 0 NS
SCALE 1:250,000
4 miles to 1 inch
0 1 2 3 4 miles
0 1 2 3 4 5 kilometres
51
54
42

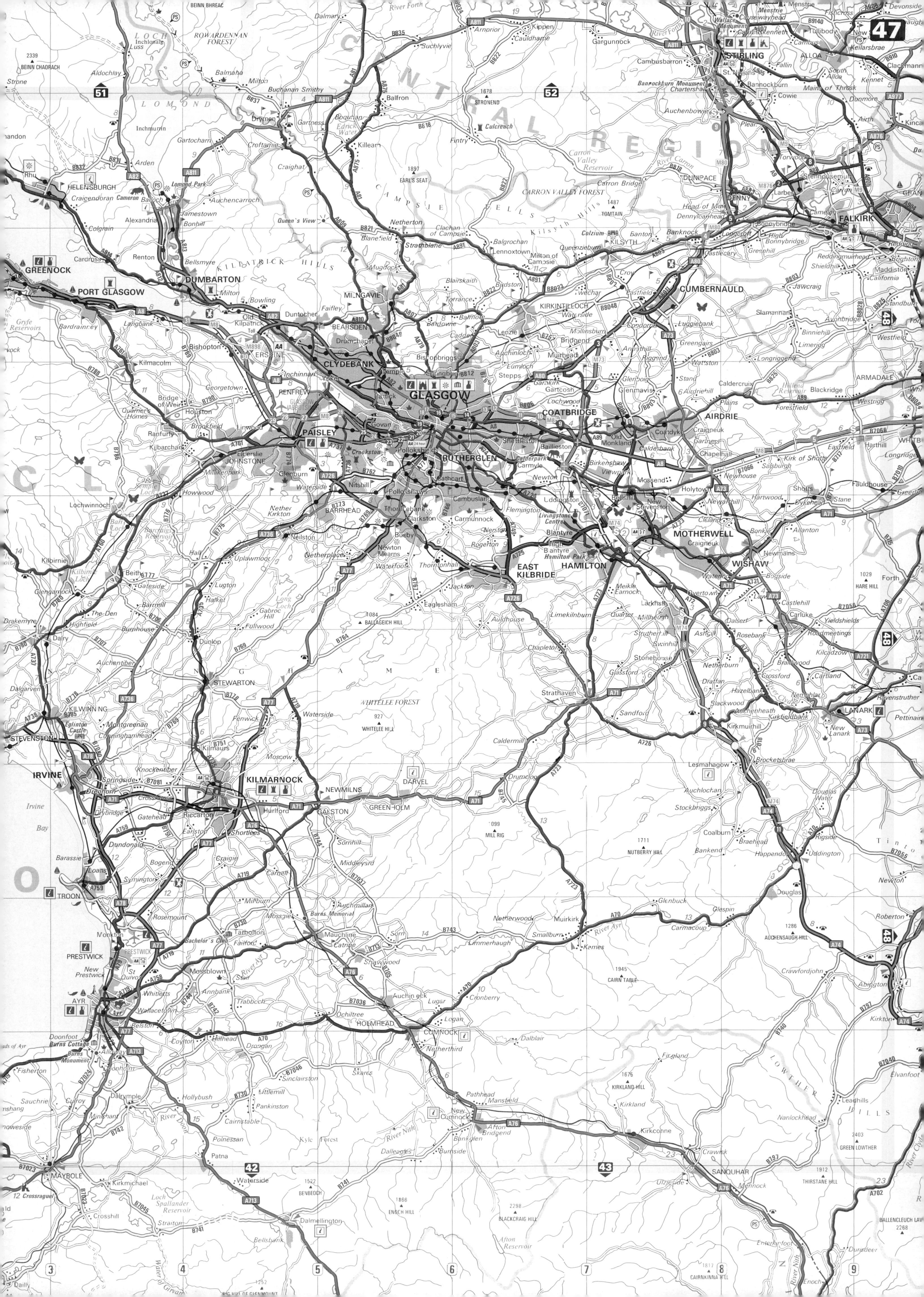
STIRLING
ALLOA
FALKIRK
CUMBERNAULD
HELENSBURGH
GREENOCK
PORT GLASGOW
DUMBARTON
CLYDEBANK
GLASGOW
PAISLEY
RUTHERGLEN
COATBRIDGE
AIRDRIE
MOTHERWELL
HAMILTON
EAST KILBRIDE
WISHAW
KILMARNOCK
IRVINE
TROON
PRESTWICK
AYR
LANARK
CUMNOCK
MAYBOLE
SANQUHAR
CENTRAL REGION
CAMPSIE FELLS
KILPATRICK HILLS
Kilsyth Hills
WHITELEE FOREST
LOWTHER HILLS
Irvine Bay
51
52
48
42
43
3
4
5
6
7
8
9

48
NS NT
Devonside
Blairingone
Cleish Hills
Blairadam Forest
Lochore
Auchterderran
River Ore
Wemyss
Hill End
Loch Glow
Crosshill
Cluny
Gallatown
West Wemyss
Kelty
Glencraig
Cardenden
Balgonar
Saline
Knock Hill
Lochgelly
Chapel
Dysart
Clackmannan
Fife
Lassodie
Cowdenbeath
Kirkcaldy
Kennet
Cowstrandburn
Bowershall
Kingseat
Auchtertool
Linktown
Carnock
Gowkhall
Townhill
Crossgates
Dunfermline
Firth of Forth
Blairhall
Oakley
Wellwood
Fordell
Donibristle
Kinghorn
Airth
Kincardine
Culross Abbey
Mulesmark
Cairneyhill
Valleyfield
Crossford
Aberdour
Burntisland
Pettycur
Dunimarle
Culross
Low Torry
Torryburn
Hillend
St. Colme
Charlestown
Limekilns
Rosyth
Dalgety Bay
North Berwick
Inverkeithing
Inchkeith
Dirleton
Grangemouth
Bo'ness
Grangepans
Carriden
Muirhouses
North Queensferry
Gullane Bay
Gullane
Kingston
Falkirk
Blackness
Kinneil
Champany
Hopetoun
Queensferry
Dalmeny House
Cramond Island
Aberlady Bay
Aberlady
Dirleton
Myreton Motor Museum
Gosford Bay
Luffness
Spittal
Ballencrieff
Museum of Flight
Redding
Brightons
Maddiston
California
Linlithgow
Linlithgow Palace
Philpstoun
Newton
Dalmeny
Granton
Cramond
Lauriston Castle
Leith
Edinburgh
Cockenzie and Port Seton
Longniddry
Athelstaneford
Union Canal
Whitecross
Bridgend
Winchburgh
Dalmeny Rows
Cramond Bridge
Prestonpans
Huntington
Haddington
Loan
Cockleroy
Standburn
Torphichen
Torphichen Preceptory
Ecclesmachan
Newbridge
Kirkliston
Ingliston
Edinburgh (Turnhouse)
Arthur's Seat
Duddingston
Portobello
Musselburgh
Inveresk
Pinkie House
Tranent
Macmerry
Gladsmuir
Westfield
Uphall
Dechmont
Broxburn
Burnside
Gogar
Corstorphine
Morningside
Craigmillar
Wallyford
Elphinstone
New Winton
Samuelston
Lennoxlove
Cairnpapple Hill
Bathgate
Uphall Station
Ratho
Suntrap
Craiglockhart
Liberton
Craigmillar
Danderhall
Whitecraig
New Town
Bolton
Armadale
Livingston
Pumpherston
Bonnington
Long Hermiston
Juniper Green
Colinton
Gilmerton
Millerhill
Ormiston
Pencaitland
Whiteside
East Calder
Wilkieston
Currie
Fairmilehead
Kaimes
Dalkeith
Dalkeith Park
Cousland
East Saltoun
Gifford
Westrigg
Seafield
Livingston Village
Oakbank
Kirknewton
Newmills
Balerno
Malleny
Straiton
Lasswade
Eskbank
Peaston Bank
Peaston
West Saltoun
Whitburn
East Whitburn
Blackburn
Bellsquarry
Malleny Mills
Threipmuir Reservoir
Loanhead
Bonnyrigg
Mayfield
Longyester
Harthill
Stoneyburn
Polbeth
Woodhouselee
Bilston
Roslin
Rosslyn
Polton
Newtongrange
Pathhead
Longridge
West Calder
Addiewell
Black Hill
Milton Bridge
Rosewell
Newlandrig
Humbie
Fauldhouse
Greenburn
Breich
Harperrig Reservoir
Silverburn
Auchendinny
Carrington
Arniston Engine
Gorebridge
Crichton
Fala Dam
Fala
Blegbie
Pentland Hills
Penicuik
North Middleton
Tynehead
Soutra Mains
Crib Law
Cobbinshaw Loch
River North Esk
Howgate
Temple
Middleton
Carlops
Leadburn
Gilston
Tarbrax
Falahill
Forth
Rootpark
Auchengray
Whim
Gladhouse Reservoir
Moorfoot Hills
Heriot
Carfraemill
Oxton
Hare Hill
West Linton
Mendick Hill
Braehead
Waterheads
River South Esk
West Mains
Halmyre Mains
Wether Law
Fountainhall
Thirlestane Castle
Thirlestane
Lauder
Strathclyde
Dunsyre
Romannobridge
Mountain Cross
Eddleston
Torquhan
Carstairs
Carnwath
Dolphinton
Newbigging
Walston
Carstairs Junction
Blyth Bridge
Castlecraig
Killochyett
Stow
Ravenstruther
Lanark
Pettinain
Libberton
Elsrickle
Dunslair Heights
Windlestraw Law
Nether Blainslie
Broughton Heights
Hallyne
Peebles
Glentress
Bowland
Quothquan
Biggar
Skirling
Neidpath
Kings Muir
Lee Pen
Langshaw
Thankerton
Stobo
Broughton Place
Broughton
Kirkton Manor
Kailzie
Cardrona
Walkerburn
Blackhaugh
Buckholm
Galashiels
Symington
Tinto
Tinto Hills
River Tweed
Dawyck House
Bellspool
Cardrona Forest
Scottish Textiles Museum
Innerleithen
Traquair
Elibank and Traquair Forest
Clovenfords
Meigle Hill
Bridgend
Gattonside
Newstead
Coulter
River Clyde
Wiston
Drumelzier
Glen House
Kirkhouse
Caddonfoot
Abbotsford
Boleside
Melrose Abbey
Melrose
Newton
Lamington
Pykestone Hill
Broadmeadows
Lindean
Dryburgh Abbey
Bowden
St Boswells
Roberton
Region
Culter Fell
Stanhope
Yarrow
Selkirk
Bowhill
Philiphaugh
Midlem
Longnewton
Black Law
Yarrow Feus
Mountbenger
Sundhope
Lilliesleaf
Riddell
Abington
Tewsgill Hill
Hearthstane
Oliver
Tweedsmuir
Broad Law
Dryhope
Cappercleuch
St Mary's Loch
Ettrick Forest
Ettrick Bridge
Kirkhope
Clerklands
Greenhouse
Camps Reservoir
Talla Reservoir
Megget Reservoir
Gilmanscleuch
Caver's Hill
Wall
Ashkirk
Kirkton
Crawford
Glenbreck
Talla Linnfoots
Meggethead
Rodono
Tibbie Shiels Inn
Hassendean
Minto
Fruid Reservoir
Tushielaw Inn
Crosslee
Horsleyhill
Denholm
Elvanfoot
Clyde Law
Appletreehall
Smasha Hill
Burnfoot
Redfordgreen
Alemoor Loch
Borthwickshiels
White Coombe
Ettrick
Ramseycleuch
Buccleuch
Borthwickbrae
Wilton Dean
Hawick
Kirkton
Leadhills
Water Meetings
Hart Fell
Tweed's Well
Nether Howcleugh
River Annan
Ettrick Water
Roberton
Bonchester Bridge
Green Lowther
Deanburnhaugh
Burnfoot
Branxholme
Glenkerry
Hobkirk
Ericstane
Newmill
Granton
River Clyde
Bridgend
Craik
Broadhaugh
Daer Reservoir
River Teviot
Dodburn
Ballencleuch Law
Gallow Hill
Moffat
Loch Fell
Teviothead
Waucho
Durisdeer
Dumcrieff
Eskdalemuir Forest
Ewesless Knowe
Davington
Farshaig
Kinnelhead
Beattock
Cauldcleuch Head
Lowther Hills
Borders Region
Lammermuir Hills
Teviotdale
NS 0 NT
43
44
47
52
53

NT NU
53
SCALE 1:250,000
4 miles to 1 inch
0 1 2 3 4 miles
0 1 2 3 4 5 kilometres
DUNBAR
West Barns
Broxburn
Barns Ness
Pitcox
Spott
Stenton
Skateraw
Thorntonloch
Innerwick
1046
COCKLAW HILL
Oldhamstocks
Reed Point
Cockburnspath
Ecclaw
ST ABB'S HEAD
Northfield
St Abbs
Grantshouse
Coldingham
Houndwood
EYEMOUTH
Cairncross
Whiteadder Reservoir
859
CRANSHAWS HILL
Cranshaws
Abbey St. Bathans
Ellemford
Auchencrow
Reston
Ayton
Burnmouth
Marygold
Lintlaw
Preston
Watch Water Reservoir
Longformacus
Chirnside
Chirnsidebridge
Edrom
Foulden
Lamberton
Clappers
1333
1307
DIRRINGTON GREAT LAW
DUNS
Allanton
Hutton
Paxton
BERWICK-UPON-TWEED
Tweedmouth
Spittal
Blackadder
Gavinton
Westruther
Polwarth
Whitsome
Fishwick
Loanend
East Ord
Fogo
Horncliffe
Scremerston
Houndslow
Thorntonpark
Murton
Ladykirk
Norham
Swinton
Thornton
Greenlaw
Swintonmill
Shoreswood
Shoresdean
West Allerdean
Cheswick
CAUSEWAY FLOODED AT HIGH TIDE
Goswick
HOLY ISLAND
Grindon
Ancroft
Simprim
Leitholm
Felkington
Haggerston
Gordon
Berrington
Beal
Holy Island
Lindisfarne Priory
Castle Point
Hume
Howlaws
Duddo
Eccles
Castle Heaton
Bowsden
Burrows Hole
Fans
Lennel
COLDSTREAM
Cornhill on-Tweed
Dundock Wood
730
SWEETHOPE HILL
Mellerstain
Birgham
Stichill
Etal
Heatherslaw Mill
Lowick
Kyloe
Fenwick
Buckton
Crookham
The Lady Waterford Hall
Ford
Elwick
Ross
Staple Sound
FARNE ISLANDS
Nenthorn
Ednam
Carham
Wark
Learmouth
Branxton
Smailholm
Kelso
Hendersyde Park
Hadden
Pressen
Kimmerston
Holburn
Detchant
Middleton
Easington
Budle Bay
Budle
Inner Sound
Bamburgh
Flodden
Floors Castle
Sprouston
Downham
Nesbit
Belford
Waren Mill
KELSO
Lempitlaw
Milfield
Fenton Town
Doddington
Spindlestone
Burton
Open to Public
Maxwellheugh
Mindrum
Pawston
Seahouses
Carr End
Mangrill
Trows
River Tweed
Roxburgh
Blakelaw
Kilham
Lanton
Coupland
Newtown
Horton
Bradford
Bellshill
North Sunderland
Rutherford
Heiton
Shotton
Kirknewton
Akeld
Warenton
Adderstone
Lucker
Newham Hall
Swinhoe
Beadnell
Benthall
BOWMONT FOREST
Town Yetholm
Kirk Yetholm
Hethpool
Humbleton
Wooler
Greendykes
Newham
Warenford
Chatton
Newstead
West Fleetham
Beadnell Bay
Crookhouse
THE PENNINE WAY
Earle
Haugh Head
Chillingham
Rosebrough
Chathill
Ellingham
High Newton by-the-Sea
Nisbet
Eckford
Linton
Middleton Hall
Lilburn Tower
Chillingham Wild Cattle
Preston
Morebattle
Newtown
Hepburn
Brockdam
Crailing
485
COLD LAW
Middleton
876
CATERAN HILL
Brunton
Embleton
Bonjedward
Cessford
1985
THE SCHIL
East Lilburn
Christon Bank
Dunstanburgh
Lanton
JEDBURGH
Crailinghall
Langleeford
Old Bewick
West Ditchburn
North Charlton
Hownam Mains
Mowhaugh
2674
THE CHEVIOT
Ilderton
Roddam
Rosedean
Harehope
Eglingham
South Charlton
Rock
Dunstan
Hundalee
Hownam
Sourhope
Wooperton
New Bewick
Craster
Oxnam
Chatto
Brandon
Beanley
Rennington
Howick
Howick Hall
Swinside Hall
Ingram
Powburn
Littlehoughton
Bairnkine
Mossburnford
2032
WINDY GYLE
Greensidehill
Branton
Titlington
Longhoughton
Falla
Glanton Pike
Glanton
Bolton
River Aln
ALNWICK
Denwick
Boulmer
Mervinslaw
NORTHUMBERLAND
Great Ryle
Broome Park
Abberwick
Hawkhill
Prendwick
River Aln
Whittingham
Lesbury
Little Ryle
Thrunton
Lemmington Hall
Bilton
Chesters
Alnham
Callaly Castle
Callaly
Edlingham
Alnmouth
Alnmouth Bay
Scrainwood
Yetlington
High Buston
Biddlestone
Shilbottle
Stillmoor
Netherton
Carter Bar
Lorbottle
1047
LONG CRAG
Birling
1729
RAVENS KNOWE
Alwinton
Burradon
Eastfield Hall
Warkworth
Hermitage
Linshiels
High Trewhitt
Newton-on-the-Moor
River Coquet
Herbottle
Sharperton
Cartington
AMBLE
Catcleugh Reservoir
Warton
Swarland Estate
Guyzance
Gloster Hill
Hauxley
Holystone
Snitter
Acklington
Rothbury
Cragside
Forest
Togston
Radcliffe
REDESDALE FOREST
Sills
Happle
Thropton
Whitton
Longframlington
Swarland
Felton
Broomhill
THE CHEVIOT HILLS
LAMMERMUIR HILLS
MERSE
44
45
7
8
9
1
2
3
A1
A1107
A6112
B6438
B6437
B6355
B6365
A6105
B6456
B6460
B6461
A697
A6112
B6470
A698
B6525
B6354
B6353
B6350
A6089
B6397
B6404
B6396
B6352
B6351
B6348
B6436
B6401
A699
A68
B6349
B1342
B1341
B1340
B6347
B6346
B1339
B6341
A1068
A6088

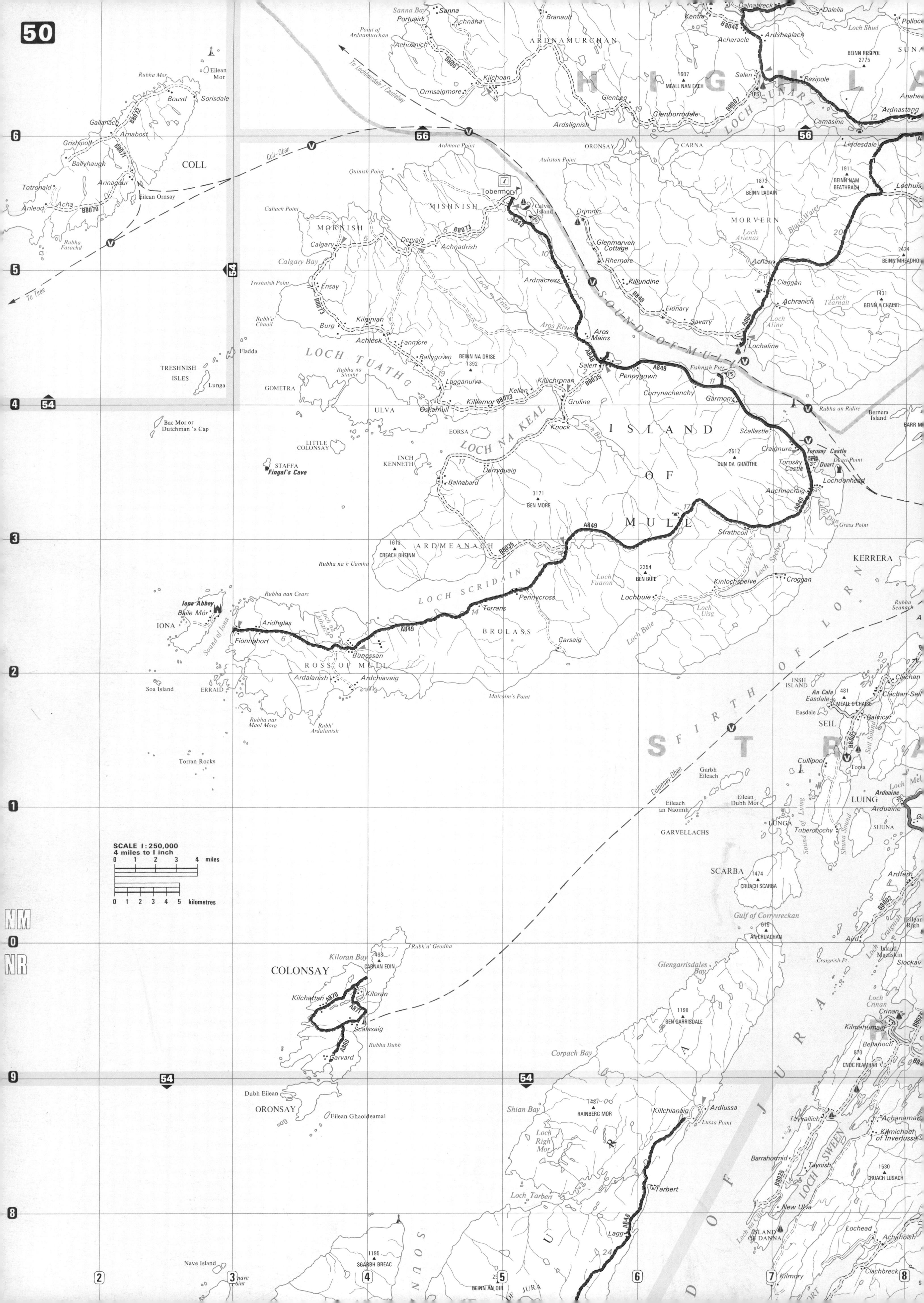
HIGHLAND
STRATHCLYDE
ARDNAMURCHAN
Sanna Bay
Sanna
Portuairk
Achnaha
Point of Ardnamurchan
Achosnich
Kilchoan
Ormsaigmore
Branault
Kentra
Acharacle
Ardshealach
Dalnabreck
Dalelia
Loch Shiel
Salen
Resipole
MEALL NAN EACH
Glenbeg
Glenborrodale
Ardslignish
LOCH SUNART
Camasine
Ardnastang
BEINN RESIPOL
Liddesdale
ORONSAY
CARNA
Auliston Point
To Lochboisdale / Castlebay
Coll-Oban
To Tiree
COLL
Eilean Mor
Rubha Mor
Bousd
Sorisdale
Gallanach
Arnabost
Grishipoll
Ballyhaugh
Arinagour
Totronald
Acha
Arileod
Eilean Ornsay
Rubha Fasachd
TRESHNISH ISLES
Fladda
Lunga
Bac Mor or Dutchman's Cap
GOMETRA
ULVA
LITTLE COLONSAY
STAFFA
Fingal's Cave
INCH KENNETH
EORSA
Ardmore Point
Quinish Point
Tobermory
Calve Island
MISHNISH
MORNISH
Caliach Point
Calgary
Calgary Bay
Dervaig
Achnadrish
Treshnish Point
Ensay
Rubh'a' Chaoil
Burg
Kilninian
Achleck
Fanmore
Ballygown
BEINN NA DRISE
LOCH TUATH
Rubha na Stroine
Lagganulva
Oskamull
Killiemor
Kellan
Killichronan
Gruline
Loch Frisa
Aros River
Ardnacross
Aros Mains
Salen
Pennygown
Fishnish Pier
Corrynachenchy
Garmony
Drimnin
Glenmorven Cottage
Rhemore
Killundine
Fiunary
Savary
Lochaline
SOUND OF MULL
MORVERN
BEINN LADAIN
BEINN NAM BEATHRACH
Loch Arienas
Black Water
Acharn
Claggan
Achranich
Loch Aline
Loch Teàrnait
BEINN A' CHAISIL
BEINN MHEADHOIN
Rubha an Ridire
Bernera Island
ISLAND OF MULL
LOCH NA KEAL
Knock
Loch Ba
Scallastle
Craignure
Torosay Castle
Duart
Duart Point
Lochdonhead
DUN DA GHAOTHE
Dervyguaig
Balnahard
BEN MORE
Auchnacraig
Grass Point
Strathcoil
ARDMEANACH
CREACH BHEINN
Rubha na h Uamha
LOCH SCRIDAIN
Loch Fuaron
BEN BUIE
Kinlochspelve
Loch Spelve
Croggan
Lochbuie
Loch Uisg
Loch Buie
Pennycross
Torrans
BROLASS
Carsaig
Malcolm's Point
KERRERA
Rubha Seanach
FIRTH OF LORN
Rubha nan Cearc
Iona Abbey
Baile Mór
IONA
Sound of Iona
Aridhglas
Fionnphort
Bunessan
ROSS OF MULL
Ardalanish
Ardchiavaig
Soa Island
ERRAID
Rubha nar Maol Mora
Rubh' Ardalanish
Torran Rocks
Colonsay-Oban
Garbh Eileach
Eileach an Naoimh
Eilean Dubh Mor
GARVELLACHS
INSH ISLAND
An Cala
Easdale
MEALL A' CHAISE
Clachan
Clachan-Seil
Balvicar
SEIL
Seil Sound
Cullipool
Torsa
LUING
Ardluaine
Arduaine
LUNGA
Sound of Luing
Toberonochy
Shuna Sound
SHUNA
SCARBA
CRUACH SCARBA
Gulf of Corryvreckan
AN CRUACHAN
Ardfern
Eilean Righ
Craignish Pt
Aird
Island Macaskin
Loch Craignish
Slockavullin
Loch Crinan
Crinan
Kilmahumaig
Bellanoch
CNOC REAMHAR
Glengarrisdale Bay
BEN GARRISDALE
Corpach Bay
SOUND OF JURA
JURA
COLONSAY
Kiloran Bay
CARNAN EOIN
Rubh' a' Geodha
Kiloran
Kilchattan
Scalasaig
Rubha Dubh
Garvard
Dubh Eilean
ORONSAY
Eilean Ghaoideamal
Shian Bay
RAINBERG MOR
Loch Righ Mor
Killchianaig
Ardlussa
Lussa Point
Tarbert
Loch Tarbert
Lagg
SGARBH BREAC
BEINN AN OIR
PAPS OF JURA
Nave Island
Tayvallich
Achanamara
Kilmichael of Inverlussa
Barrahormid
Taynish
LOCH SWEEN
CRUACH LUSACH
New Ulva
ISLAND OF DANNA
Loch na Cille
Lochead
Achahoish
Kilmory
Clachbreck
SCALE 1: 250,000
4 miles to 1 inch
0 1 2 3 4 miles
0 1 2 3 4 5 kilometres
NM
NR

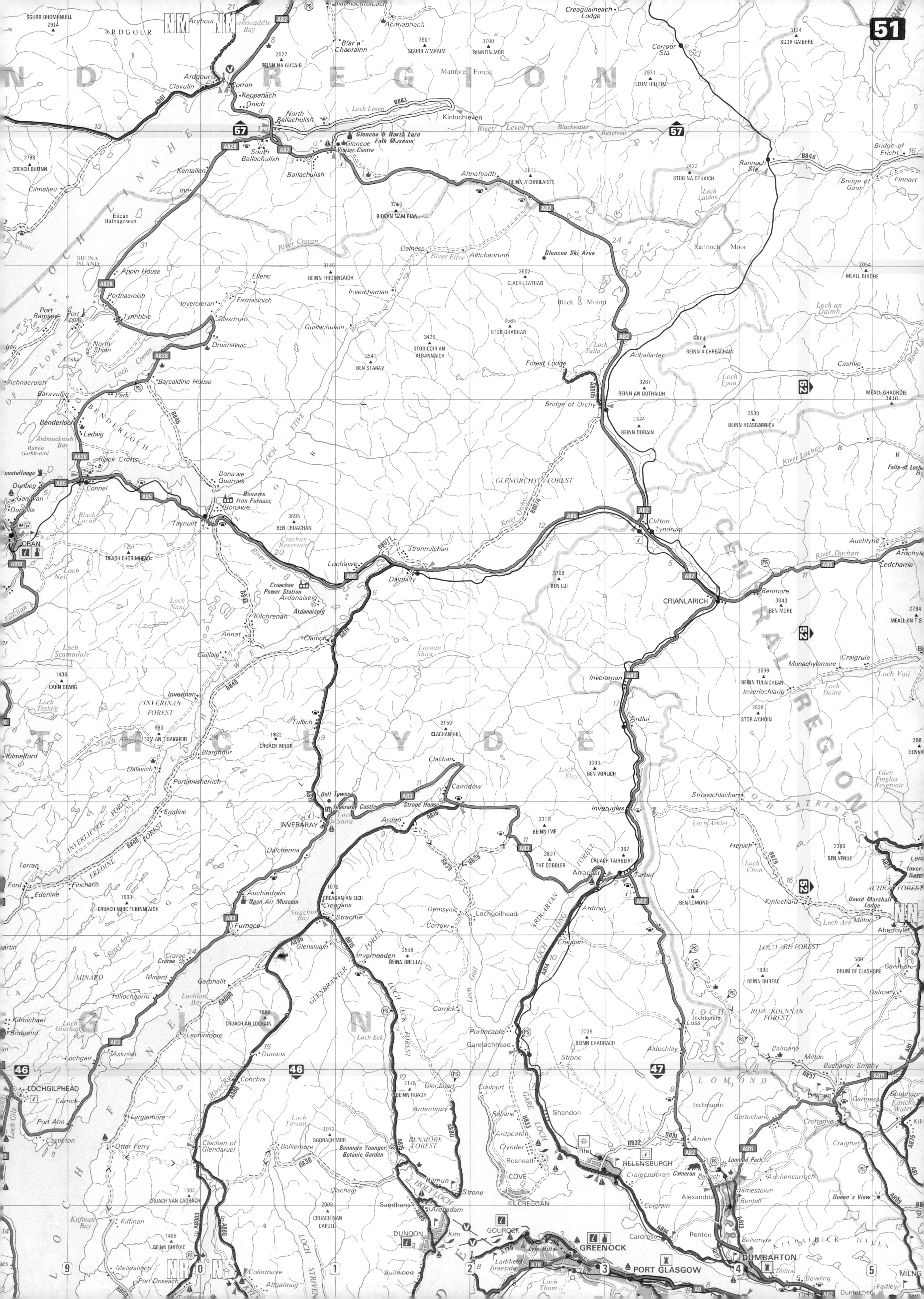

NM NN
ARDGOUR
SGURR DHOMHNUILL 2914
Ardgour
Clovulin
Corran
Keppanach
Onich
North Ballachulish
Loch Leven
Kinlochleven
River Leven
Blackwater Reservoir
Mamore Forest
SGURR A'MHAIM
BINNEIN MOR
BEINN NA GUCAIG
Corrour Sta
LEUM UILLEIM
SGOR GAIBHRE
Creaguaineach Lodge
Glencoe & North Lorn Folk Museum
Glencoe Visitor Centre
South Ballachulish
Ballachulish
Kentallen
CREACH BHEINN
Cilmalieu
Eilean Balnagowan
LOCH LINNHE
SHUNA ISLAND
Appin House
Portnacroish
Port Ramsey
Port Appin
Tynribbie
North Shian
Eriska
Loch Creran
Achnacroish
Baravullin
Park
Benderloch
BENDERLOCH
Ledaig
Black Crofts
Connel
Dunbeg
Ganavan
Dunollie
OBAN
Altnafeadh
BEINN A'CHRULAISTE
BIDEAN NAM BIAN
Dalness
River Etive
Alltchaorunn
Glencoe Ski Area
River Creran
BEINN FHIONNLAIDH
CLACH LEATHAD
Black Mount
Ellerio
Fasnacloich
Invercreran
Glasdrum
Druimavuic
Inverchaman
Gualachulain
STOB GHABHAR
STOB COIR'AN ALBANNAICH
BEN STARAV
Loch Tulla
Forest Lodge
Achallader
BEINN A'CHREACHAIN
Bridge of Orchy
BEINN AN DOTHAIDH
BEINN DORAIN
Rannoch Sta
Rannoch Moor
Loch Laidon
STOB NA CRUAICH
Bridge of Ericht
Bridge of Gaur
Finnart
MEALL BUIDHE
Loch an Daimh
Cashlie
Loch Lyon
MEALL GHAORDIE
BEINN HEASGARNICH
River Lochay
Falls of Lochay
Barcaldine House
LOCH ETIVE
Bonawe Quarries
Bonawe Iron Furnace
Bonawe
Taynuilt
BEN CRUACHAN
Cruachan Reservoir
DEADH CHORIMHEAD
Stronmilchan
Lochawe
Dalmally
River Awe
Loch Nell
Cruachan Power Station
Ardanaiseig
Kilchrenan
Loch Nant
Annat
Cladich
Coillaig
GLENORCHY FOREST
River Orchy
Clifton
Tyndrum
River Lochy
BEN LUI
CRIANLARICH
Benmore
BEN MORE
River Dochart
Auchlyne
Ardchyle
Ledcharrie
CENTRAL REGION
Lochan Shira
Loch Scamadale
CARN DEARG
INVERINAN FOREST
Inverinan
Loch Avich
TOM AN T SAIGHEIR
CRUACH MHOR
Tullich
Kilmelford
Dalavich
Blarghour
Portinnisherrich
CLACHAN HILL
Clachan
Cairndow
Loch Sloy
BEN VORLICH
Ardlui
Inverarnan
Monachylemore
Craigruie
BEINN TULAICHEAN
Inverlochlarig
Loch Voil
Loch Doine
STOB A'CHOIN
Glen Finglas Reservoir
Stronachlachar
LOCH KATRINE
Loch Arklet
INVERARAY
Bell Tower
Inveraray Castle
Strone House
Loch Shira
Ardno
BEINN IME
THE COBBLER
CRUACH TAIRBEIRT
Arrochar
Tarbet
Inveruglas
Frenich
Loch Chon
BEN VENUE
Kinlochard
David Marshall Lodge
Aberfoyle
Milton
Loch Ard
BEN LOMOND
Eredine
INVERLIEVER FOREST
EREDINE FOREST
Torran
Ford
Fincharn
Ederline
Dalchenna
Auchindrain Open Air Museum
CRUACH MHIC FHIONNLAIDH
CREAGAN AN EICH
Creggans
Strachur
Strachur Bay
Furnace
Ardmay
Drimsynie
Lochgoilhead
Corrow
LOCH LONG
ARDGARTAN FOREST
Craggan
Glensluain
Invernoaden
BEINN BHELLA
LOCH ARD FOREST
DRUM OF CLASHORE
BEINN BHREAC
Crarae
Minard
MINARD
Garbhallt
Tullochgorm
Lochlan Bay
Carrick
Loch Goil
Loch Eck
GLENBRANTER
Kilmichael
Loch Glashan
Bridgend
CRUACH AN LOCHAIN
Lephinmore
Portincaple
Garelochhead
BEINN CHAORACH
Aldochlay
Luss
Inchlonaig
LOCH LOMOND
ROWARDENNAN FOREST
Balmaha
Milton
Buchanan Smithy
Drymen
Gartness
Lochgair
Asknish
Dunans
LOCHGILPHEAD
Conchra
River Ruel
Glen Finart
BEINN RUADH
Ardentinny
Coulport
Rahane
Strone
Shandon
Inchmurrin
Gartocharn
Croftamie
Port Ann
Castleton
Largiemore
Otter Ferry
Clachan of Glendaruel
Loch Tarsan
SGORACH MOR
Balliemore
Benmore Younger Botanic Garden
BENMORE FOREST
Ardpeaton
Clynder
Rosneath
COVE
GARE LOCH
Rhu
HELENSBURGH
Craigendoran
Cameron
Arden
Lomond Park
Balloch
Jamestown
Bonhill
Alexandria
Auchencarroch
Queen's View
Kilmun
HOLY LOCH
Sandbank
Ardnadam
KILCREGGAN
Clachaig
CRUACH NAN CAORACH
Kilfinan
Kilfinan Bay
CRUACH NAN CAPULL
DUNOON
Kirn
GOUROCK
GREENOCK
PORT GLASGOW
Larkfield
Braeside
Loch Thom
Colgrain
Cardross
Renton
DUMBARTON
KILPATRICK HILLS
Bellsmyre
Milton
Bowling
Duntocher
Faifley
BEINN BHREAC
Melldalloch
Port Driseach
Colintraive
Altgaltraig
LOCH STRIVEN
Bullwood
LOCH FYNE
NR NS
A82 A828 A85 A816 A819 A83 A815 A886 A880 A814 A818 A811 A813 A8 A78 A770 A8003
B863 B846 B845 B8074 B8077 B840 B828 B839 B8000 B836 B833 B832 B831 B837 B829

NN
NO
NS
NT
Calvine
Struan
Dalchalloch
B847
Blair Atholl
Aldclune
BEN VRACKIE 2760
Straloch
2759 BEINN MHOLACH
BEINN A'CHUALLAICH 2927
Killiecrankie
Visitor Centre
Tummel Forest Centre
B8019
A924
2092 CREAG DHUBA
Craiganour Lodge
Kinloch Rannoch
B846
Dunalastair
River Tummel
Tummel Bridge
Tressait
Queen's View
Loch Tummel
Faskally Wayside Centre
Moulin
PITLOCHRY
Kirkmichael
Bridge of Ericht
Killichonan
LOCH RANNOCH
Rannoch Sta
Bridge of Gaur
Finnart
Dall
Carie
Inverhadden
Dunalastair Water
Foss
Camghouran
SCHIEHALLION 3554
2559 FARRAGON HILL
Loch Derculich
Dalcapon
Ballechin
Logierait
Tulliemet
Ballinluig
Glengoulandie Deer Park
Edradynate
Grandtully
Balnaguard
Moor
CARN GORM 3377
3419 CAIRN MAIRG
3054 MEALL BUIDHE
57
58
Camserney
Weem
Keltneyburn
Dull
B846
River Tay
ABERFELDY
Balmacneil
Kindallachan
Kincraigie
Guay
Dowally
Camusvrachan
Invervar
Fortingall
Innerwick
Loch an Daimh
Bridge of Balgie
Croftgarbh
A827
1747 GRANDTULLY HILL
Loch Skiach
Dalguise
A826
Loch Kennard
Butterstone
A923
Fearnan
Kenmore
Remony
Acharn
MEALL GARBH 3661
River Lyon
Cashlie
Loch Lyon
Dunkeld
Little Dunkeld
Birnam
51
MEALL GHAORDIE 3410
3984 BEN LAWERS
Lawers
LOCH TAY
Ballinlick
Trochrie
A822
A984
3530 BEINN HEASGARNICH
Mountain Visitor Centre
Carie
Ardtalnaig
Garrow
Milton
Loch Freuchie
Amulree
River Braan
Waterloo
Obney
Bankfoot
River Lochay
Falls of Lochay
Boreland
Finlarig
Killin
Milton Morenish
Morenish
Ardeonaig
Corrymuckloch
2045 MEALL NAN CAORAICH
Glenshee
Achmore
A827
2883 CREAG UCHDAG
River Almond
2188 MEALL REAMHAR
3048 BEN CHONZIE
Harrietfield
Chapelhill
B8063
Moneydie
Auchlyne
Ardchyle
Ledcharrie
River Dochart
A85
Loch Lednock
Loch Turret Reservoir
GLEN ALMOND
Buchanty
Invergeldie
SRON MHOR 2203
Busby
Benmore
3843 BEN MORE
2794 MEALL AN T-SEALLAIDH
Lochearnhead
Dalveich
LOCH EARN
St. Fillans
Ardtrostan
Edinample
Ardvorlich
River Earn
Comrie
Tullybannocher
Ross
Dalginross
Fall of Turret
Hosh
Lawers
Quoig
Monzie
Gilmerton
Fowlis Wester
Keillour
Methven
Braegrum
Tibbermore
CRIEFF
Lochlane
Madderty
Findo Gask
St. David's
Balquhidder
Auchtoo
Kingshouse
Monachylemore
Craigruie
Loch Voil
STRATHYRE
A84
3231 BEN VORLICH
Forest of Glenartney
The Balloch
B8062
3099 BEINN TULAICHEAN
Inverlochlarig
Loch Doine
Culloch
Drummond
Muthill
Innerpeffray Library
Kirkton
River Earn
2839 STOB A'CHOIN
Strathyre
Dalchruin
Ochtermuthill
Strathallan Aircraft Museum
Kinkell Bridge
Aberuthven
Dunning
B827
2685 BENVANE
Ardchullarie More
2072 CREAG BEINN NAN EUN
A823
AUCHTERARDER
Glen Finglas Reservoir
Loch Lubnaig
Garrick
1346 CRAIG ROSSIE
Murtown
LOCH KATRINE
2882 BEN LEDI
Anie
Kilmahog Woollen Mill
Braco
Allan Water
Gleneagles
Path of Condie
Brig o'Turk
Coilantogle
Bochastle
CALLANDER
Greenloaning
Blackford
Middle Rig
Frenich
2386 BEN VENUE
A821
Lendrick
L. Venachar
Invertrossachs Nature Reserve
Kinbuck
OCHIL
B934
Loch Chon
B829
ACHRAY FOREST
Menteith Hills
TORRIE FOREST
Ashfield
Glendevon
Dalqueich
Kinlochard
David Marshall Lodge
Port of Menteith
Burn of Cambus
Motor Museum
DOUNE
River Teith
Deanston
B8032
River Devon
Burnfoot
Castlehill Reservoir
Carnbo
Loch Ard
Milton
Aberfoyle
Inchmahome Priory
Ruskie
A873
B826
B824
DUNBLANE
2364 BEN CLEUCH
Yetts o'Muckhart
Pool o'Muckhart
Drum
A977
LOCH ARD FOREST
Lake of Menteith
Thornhill
Doune
Blair Drummond
Keir
Sunnylaw
BRIDGE OF ALLAN
Castle Campbell and Dollar Glen
Rumbling Bridge
560 DRUM OF CLASHORE
Dykehead
B8031
B8075
Blairlogie
ALVA
TILLICOULTRY
DOLLAR
Powmill
1898 BEINN BHREAC
Gartmore
River Forth
B8034
Menstrie
Fishcross
Devonside
Blairingone
Dalmary
Wallace Monument
Causewayhead
A907
Tullibody
Coalsnaughton
Hill End
ROWARDENNAN FOREST
B835
A811
Arnprior
Kippen
Cauldhame
Gargunnock
Cambuskenneth
Cambus
New Sauchie
Forest Mill
Buchlyvie
STIRLING
Kellarsbrae
Balgonar
1194 KNOCK HILL
Cambusbarron
Fallin
ALLOA
Clackmannan
Saline
Balmaha
Milton
Buchanan Smithy
St. Ninians
Bannockburn Monument
Chartershall
Bannockburn
South Alloa
Mains of Throsk
Kennet
A907
Cowstrandburn
48
1678 STRONEND
47
Cowie
Dunmore
A977
Blairhall
Carnock
Balfron
B837
Drymen
Gartness
Boquhan
Edrick Water
B818
Culcreuch
Auchenbowie
Plean
Airth
Kincardine
Culross Abbey
Oakley
Gartocharn
Croftamie
Killearn
Fintry
Carron Valley Reservoir
River Carron
Torwood
A876
A985
Valleyfield
Cairneyhill
Craighat
1897 EARL'S SEAT
Dunipace
Stenhousemuir
Carron
Larbert
Dunimarle
Low Torry
Torryburn
CULROSS
Lomond Park
Auchencarroch
CAMPSIE
Carron Bridge
CARRON VALLEY FOREST
DENNY
GRANGEMOUTH
Charlestown
Jamestown
Bonhill
Queen's View
1487 TOMTAIN
FELLS
Kilsyth Hills
Head of Muir
Dennyloanhead
Camelon
FALKIRK
BO'NESS
Grangepans
Carriden
Muirhouses
Netherton
Clachan of Campsie
Bonnybridge
High Bonnybridge
Banknock
Blanefield
Strathblane
Balgrochan
Lennoxtown
Colzium
Banton
KILSYTH
Longcroft
Greenhill
Kinneil
Champany
A813
KILPATRICK HILLS
Mugdock
Milton of Campsie
Queenzieburn
A803
Castlecary
Reddingmuirhead
Redding
Brightons
Bellsmyre
DUMBARTON
Milton
Bowling
MILNGAVIE
Blairskaith
Birdston
Torrance
Twechar
Croy
Shieldhill
Maddiston
California
Whitecross
Union Canal
LINLITHGOW
Linlithgow Palace
Philipstoun
Bridgend
Old Kilpatrick
ERSKINE
Duntocher
Faifley
BEARSDEN
Balmore
Bardowie
KIRKINTILLOCH
Waterside
Eastfield
CUMBERNAULD
Jawcraig
Slamannan
Avonbridge
Standburn
Loan
Cockleroy
Winchburgh
Ecclesmachan
Bishopton
Drumchapel
Lenzie
Bridgend
Condorrat
Luggiebank
Greengairs
Binniehill
Limerigg
Westfield
Torphichen
Uphall
Dechmont
Cairnpapple Hill
Muirhead
Annathill
Auchinloch

SCALE 1:250,000
4 miles to 1 inch
0 1 2 3 4 miles
0 1 2 3 4 5 kilometres
DUNDEE
EDINBURGH
MONTROSE
ARBROATH
BRECHIN
FORFAR
KIRRIEMUIR
ALYTH
BLAIRGOWRIE
RATTRAY
COUPAR ANGUS
CARNOUSTIE
MONIFIETH
Broughty Ferry
TAYPORT
NEWPORT ON-TAY
Wormit
Leuchars
Guardbridge
ST. ANDREWS
CUPAR
LADYBANK
AUCHTERMUCHTY
NEWBURGH
FALKLAND
GLENROTHES
MARKINCH
LESLIE
LEVEN
METHIL
BUCKHAVEN
KIRKCALDY
KINGHORN
BURNTISLAND
Aberdour
DUNFERMLINE
INVERKEITHING
North Queensferry
COWDENBEATH
LOCHGELLY
KINROSS
CRAIL
KILRENNY
ANSTRUTHER
PITTENWEEM
ST. MONANS
ELIE
EARLSFERRY
NORTH BERWICK
DUNBAR
EAST LINTON
HADDINGTON
TRANENT
MUSSELBURGH
PRESTONPANS
COCKENZIE AND PORT SETON
Portobello
Leith
Granton
Dalmeny
Kirkliston
FIRTH OF TAY
FIRTH OF FORTH
ST ANDREWS BAY
LUNAN BAY
BUDDON NESS
FIFE NESS
LARGO BAY
TENTSMUIR FOREST
Gullane Bay
Aberlady Bay
Gosford Bay
Isle of May
Inchkeith
Glamis Castle
Lochty Private Railway
Kellie Castle
Falkland Palace
Museum of Flight
Tantallon
Mills Observatory
DUNDEE (RIVERSIDE PARK)
PERTH (SCONE)
HILL OF FINAVON
KING'S SEAT
NO
NT
48
49
58
59

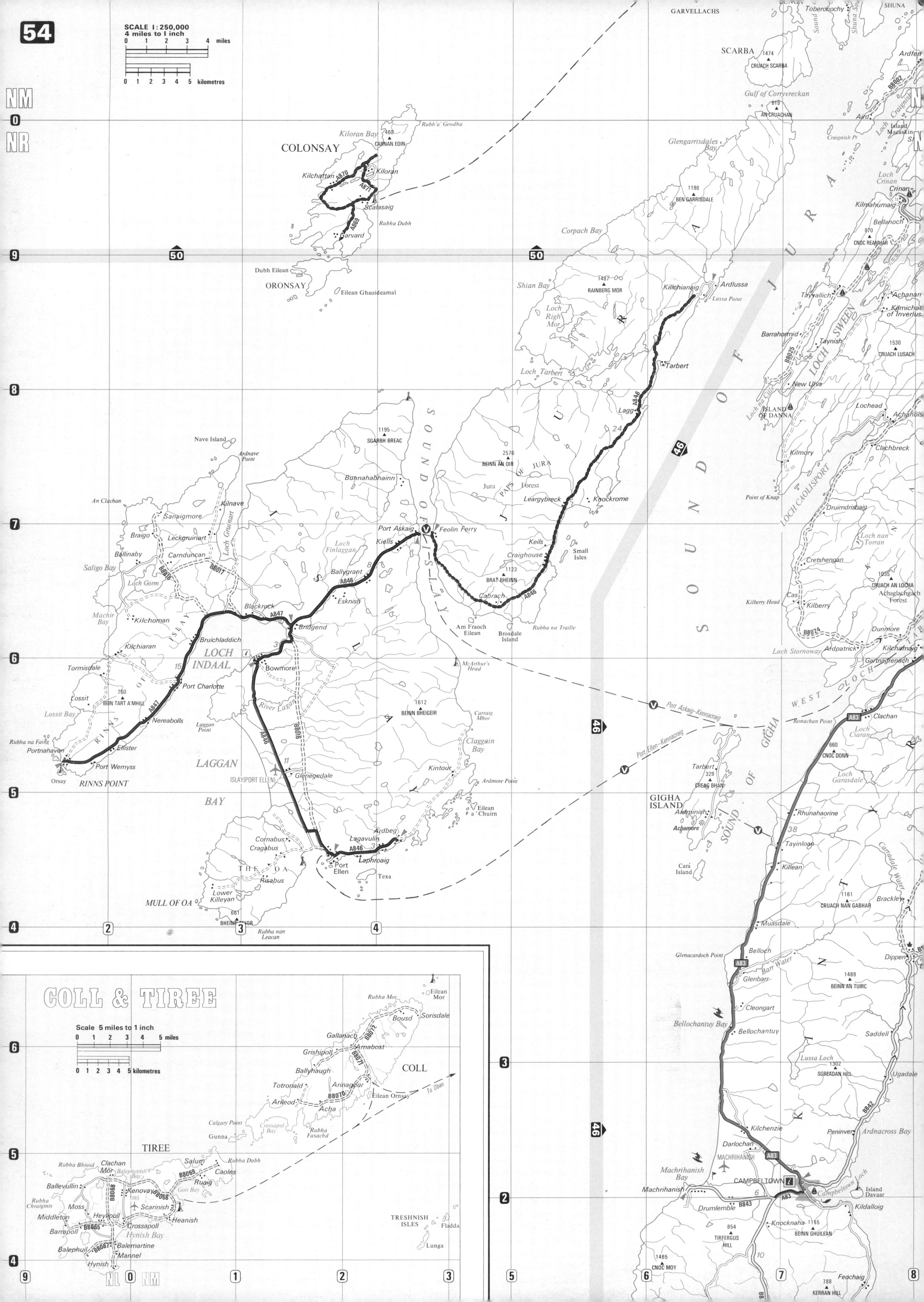
SCALE 1 : 250,000
4 miles to 1 inch
0 1 2 3 4 miles
0 1 2 3 4 5 kilometres
NM
NR
COLONSAY
Kiloran Bay
468 CARNAN EOIN
Rubh'a' Geodha
Kilchattan
Kiloran
Scalasaig
Rubha Dubh
Garvard
A870
A871
A869
Dubh Eilean
ORONSAY
Eilean Ghaoideamal
50
GARVELLACHS
SCARBA
1474 CRUACH SCARBA
Gulf of Corryvreckan
819 AN CRUACHAN
Glengarrisdales Bay
1198 BEN GARRISDALE
Corpach Bay
Shian Bay
1487 RAINBERG MOR
Loch Righ Mor
Killchianaig
Ardlussa
Lussa Point
Loch Tarbert
Tarbert
Lagg
A846
24
2576 BEINN AN OIR
PAPS OF JURA
Jura Forest
Leargybreck
Knockrome
Keils
Craighouse
Small Isles
1123 BRAT BHEINN
Cabrach
Am Fraoch Eilean
Brosdale Island
Rubha na Traille
JURA
SOUND OF JURA
SOUND OF ISLAY
46
Toberonochy
SHUNA
Shuna Sound
Ardfern
B8002
Aird
Craignish Pt
Loch Craignish
Island Macaskin
Loch Crinan
Crinan
Kilmahumaig
Bellanoch
870 CNOC REAMHAR
Tayvallich
Achanamara
Kilmichael of Inverlussa
Barrahormid
Taynish
LOCH SWEEN
1530 CRUACH LUSACH
B8025
New Ulva
Loch na Cille
ISLAND OF DANNA
Lochead
Achahoish
Kilmory
Clachbreck
LOCH CAOLISPORT
Point of Knap
Druimdrishaig
Loch nan Torran
Cretshengan
1035 CRUACH AN LOCHA
Achaglachgach Forest
Kilberry Head
Cas
Kilberry
B8024
Dunmore
Loch Stornoway
Ardpatrick
Kilchamaig
Gartnagrenach
WEST LOCH TARBERT
Ronachan Point
A83
Clachan
Loch Ciaran
660 CNOC DONN
Loch Garasdale
Rhunahaorine
38
Tayinloan
Killean
Carradale Water
1161 CRUACH NAN GABHAR
Brackley
Muasdale
Glenacardoch Point
Belloch
Barr Water
Glenbarr
1489 BEINN AN TUIRC
Dippen
Cleongart
Bellochantuy Bay
Bellochantuy
Saddell
Lussa Loch
1302 SGREADAN HILL
Ugadale
B842
Kilchenzie
Peninver
Ardnacross Bay
Darlochan
MACHRIHANISH
Machrihanish Bay
Machrihanish
CAMPBELTOWN
Campbeltown Loch
Island Davaar
6
Drumlemble
B843
Kildalloig
Knocknaha
1155 BEINN GHUILEAN
854 TIRFERGUS HILL
10
1465 CNOC MOY
Feochaig
788 KERRAN HILL
KINTYRE
Port Askaig–Kennacraig
Port Ellen–Kennacraig
Tarbert
329 CREAG BHAN
GIGHA ISLAND
Ardminish
Achamore
SOUND OF GIGHA
Cara Island
1195 SGARBH BREAC
Nave Island
Ardnave Point
An Clachan
Bunnahabhainn
Kilnave
Sanaigmore
Braigo
Leckgruinart
Loch Gruinart
Ballinaby
Carnduncan
Saligo Bay
B8018
B8017
Loch Gorm
Loch Finlaggan
Port Askaig
Feolin Ferry
Kiells
Ballygrant
A846
8
Esknish
Machir Bay
Kilchoman
Blackrock
A847
Bridgend
Bruichladdich
Kilchiaran
LOCH INDAAL
3
Bowmore
McArthur's Head
Tormisdale
15
Port Charlotte
Lossit
760 BEIN TART A'MHILL
Lossit Bay
River Laggan
1612 BEINN BHEIGEIR
Nereabolls
Laggan Point
B8016
Carraig Mhor
Rubha na Faing
RINNS OF ISLAY
Ellister
Portnahaven
Port Wemyss
LAGGAN
Claggain Bay
Orsay
RINNS POINT
11
ISLAY (PORT ELLEN)
Glenegedale
Kintour
Ardmore Point
BAY
Eilean a'Chuirn
Cornabus
Cragabus
Ardbeg
Lagavulin
A846
Port Ellen
Laphroaig
Texa
THE OA
Risabus
Lower Killeyan
MULL OF OA
661 BEINN MHOR
Rubha nan Leacan
ISLAY
COLL & TIREE
Scale 5 miles to 1 inch
0 1 2 3 4 5 miles
0 1 2 3 4 5 kilometres
Rubha Mor
Eilean Mor
Sorisdale
Bousd
Gallanach
B8072
Arnabost
Grishipoll
B8071
COLL
Ballyhaugh
Totronald
Arinagour
B8070
Eilean Ornsay
To Oban
Arileod
Acha
Calgary Point
Crossapol Bay
Rubha Fasachd
Gunna
TIREE
Rubha Bhiosd
Clachan Mor
Balephetrish Bay
Salum
Rubha Dubh
B8069
Caoles
Ruaig
Balevullin
B8068
Kenovay
Gott Bay
Rubha Chraiginis
Moss
Scarinish
Middleton
Heylipoll
Heanish
Barrapoll
B8065
Crossapoll
Hynish Bay
Balephuil
B8067
Balemartine
Mannel
Hynish
TRESHNISH ISLES
Fladda
Lunga
NL NM
9 0 1 2 3 5 6 7 8
9 8 7 6 5 4

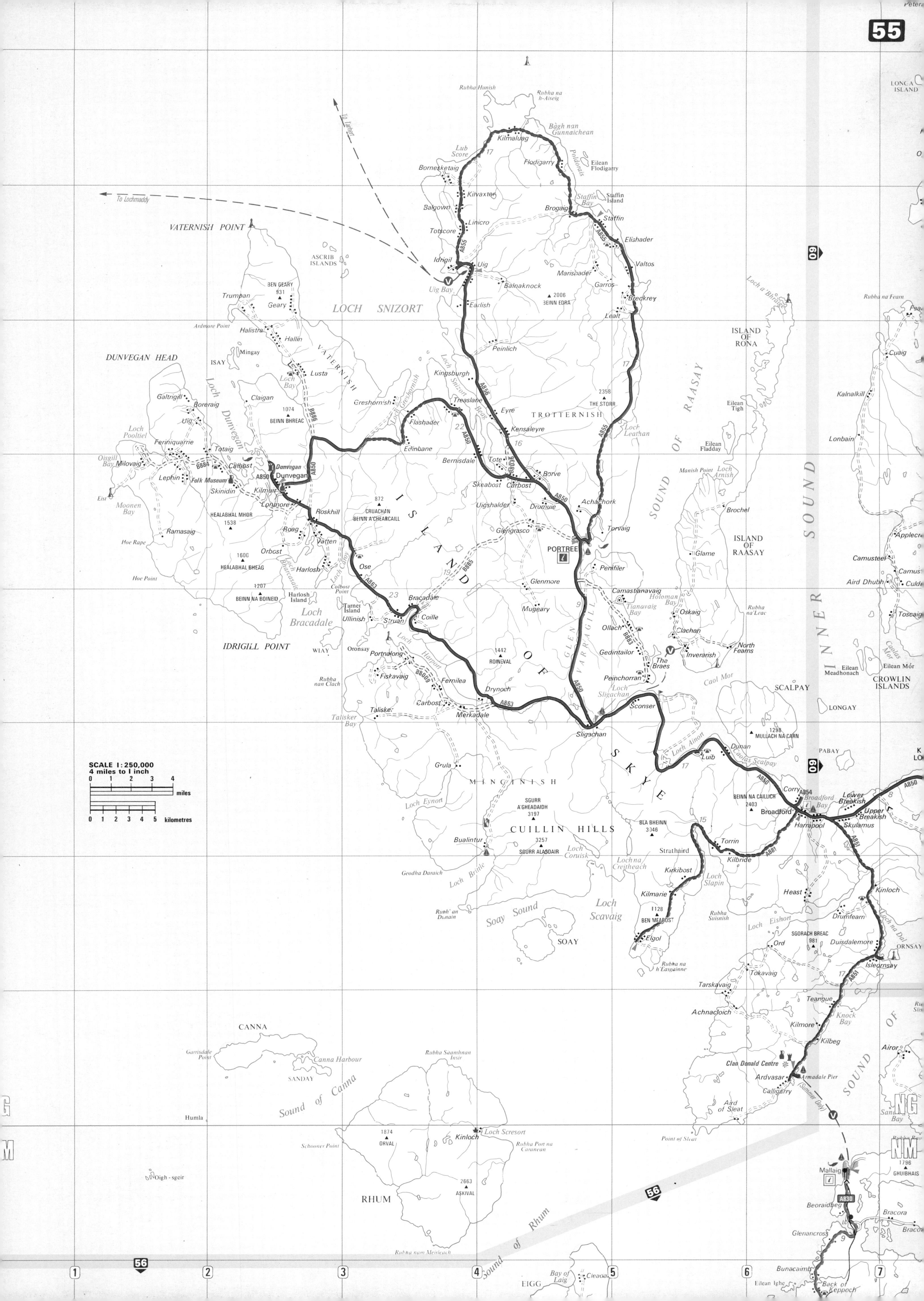
Rubha Hunish
Rubha na h-Aiseig
Kilmaluag
Bàgh nan Gunnaichean
Lub Score
Flodigarry
Poldorais
Eilean Flodigarry
Borneskeitaig
Kilvaxter
Staffin Bay
Staffin Island
Balgown
Brogaig
Staffin
To Lochmaddy
To Tarbert
VATERNISH POINT
Linicro
Totscore
Elishader
ASCRIB ISLANDS
Idrigil
Uig
Valtos
Uig Bay
Marishader
Garros
Balnaknock
Trumpan
BEN GEARY 931
Geary
2006 BEINN EDRA
Breckrey
LOCH SNIZORT
Earlish
Lealt
Loch a' Bhràige
Rubha na Fearn
Ardmore Point
Halistra
ISLAND OF RONA
Hallin
Peinlich
Cuaig
Mingay
DUNVEGAN HEAD
ISAY
VATERNISH
Lusta
Loch Bay
Kingsburgh
Loch Snizort Beag
SOUND OF RAASAY
Galtrigill
Claigan
A856
Kalnalkill
Boreraig
Loch Dunvegan
2358 THE STORR
Eilean Tigh
Uig
B886
1074 BEINN BHREAC
Greshornish
Loch Greshornish
Treaslane
Eyre
TROTTERNISH
Loch Pooltiel
Flashader
Kensaleyre
A855
Loch Leathan
Lonbain
Feriniquarrie
Edinbane
A850
Eilean Fladday
Oisgill Bay
Milovaig
Totaig
B884
Colbost
Bernisdale
Tote
B8036
Manish Point
Loch Arnish
A850
Dunvegan
Borve
Lephin
Folk Museum
Skinidin
Kilmuir
Skeabost
Carbost
INNER SOUND
Eist
Moonen Bay
Lonmore
Uigshalder
Drumuie
Achachork
Brochel
HEALABHAL MHOR 1538
Roskhill
872 CRUACHAN BEINN A'CHEARCAILL
ISLAND OF SKYE
Glengrasco
Torvaig
Hoe Rape
Ramasaig
Roag
Vatten
PORTREE
ISLAND OF RAASAY
Applecross
Orbost
1600 HEALABHAL BHEAG
Loch Caroy
Ose
B885
Glame
Camusteel
Loch Bracadale
Harlosh
Penifiler
Camusterach
Hoe Point
Colbost Point
A863
Glenmore
Aird Dhubh
Culduie
1207 BEINN NA BOINEID
Harlosh Island
Tarner Island
Bracadale
Camastianavaig
Holoman Bay
Tianavaig Bay
Rubha na' Leac
Ullinish
Struan
Coille
Mugeary
Oskaig
Toscaig
Loch Bracadale
GLEN VARRAGILL
Ollach
B883
Clachan
IDRIGILL POINT
WIAY
Oronsay
Loch Harport
1442 ROINEVAL
Gedintailor
The Braes
Inverarish
North Fearns
Portnalong
Fiskavaig
B8009
Fernilea
Caolas Mòr
Eilean Meadhonach
Eilean Mòr
CROWLIN ISLANDS
Rubha nan Clach
Drynoch
Peinchorran
Caol Mòr
SCALPAY
Loch Sligachan
Carbost
A863
Sconser
LONGAY
Talisker
Merkadale
Talisker Bay
Sligachan
1298 MULLACH NA CARN
Loch Ainort
Dunan
Caolas Scalpay
PABAY
Luib
SCALE 1:250,000
4 miles to 1 inch
0 1 2 3 4 miles
0 1 2 3 4 5 kilometres
Grula
MINGINISH
Corry
A850
BEINN NA CAILLICH 2403
Broadford Bay
Lower Breakish
Upper Breakish
SGURR A'GHEADAIDH 3197
Broadford
Harrapool
Skulamus
Loch Eynort
CUILLIN HILLS
BLA BHEINN 3046
Bualintur
3257 SGURR ALASDAIR
Loch Coruisk
Strathaird
Torrin
Kilbride
A881
A851
Geodha Daraich
Loch Brittle
Loch na Creitheach
Kirkibost
Loch Slapin
Kinloch
Kilmarie
Heast
Rubh' an Dùnain
Soay Sound
Loch Scavaig
1128 BEN MEABOST
Rubha Suisnish
Loch Eishort
Drumfearn
Loch na Dal
SOAY
Elgol
SGORACH BREAC 981
Ord
Duisdalemore
ORNSAY
Rubha na h'Easgainne
Isleornsay
Tokavaig
Tarskavaig
Teangue
Achnacloich
Knock Bay
CANNA
Kilmore
Kilbeg
Garrisdale Point
Canna Harbour
Rubha Saamhnan Insir
Clan Donald Centre
Airor
SANDAY
Ardvasar
Armadale Pier
Calligarry
(Summer Only)
SOUND OF SLEAT
Sound of Canna
Aird of Sleat
Humla
1874 ORVAL
Loch Scresort
Kinloch
Point of Sleat
Schooner Point
Rubha Port na Caranean
Mallaig
NG
NM
1796 GHUIBHAIS
Oigh-sgeir
2663 ASKIVAL
RHUM
A830
Beoraidbeg
Bracora
Sound of Rhum
Glenancross
Rubha nam Meirleach
Bay of Laig
Cleadale
Bunacaimb
EIGG
Eilean Ighe
Back of Keppoch
56
1
2
3
4
5
6
7

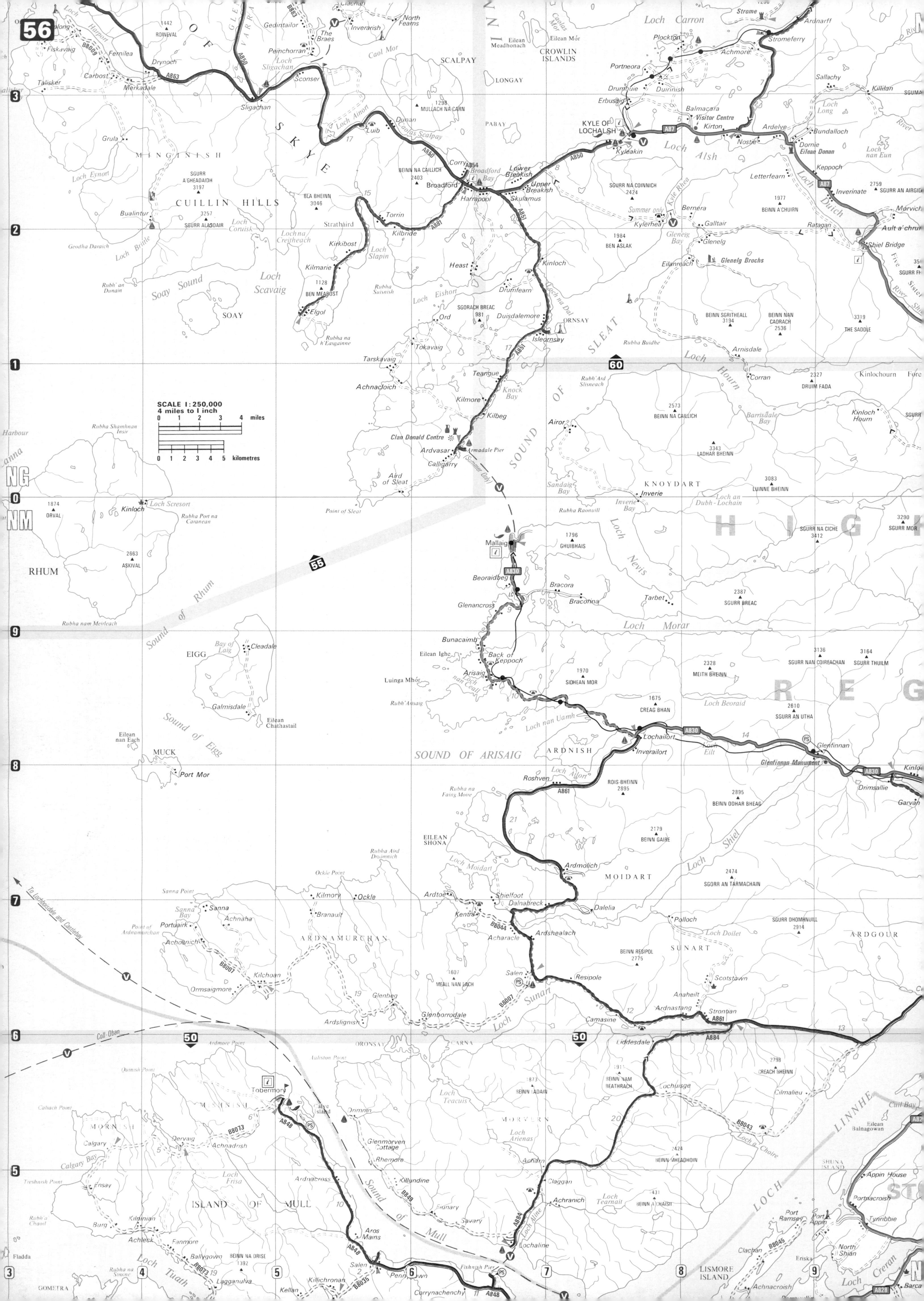

Fiskavaig
Harport
Fernilea
B8009
1442
ROINEVAL
Drynoch
Carbost
Talisker
Merkadale
A863
Sligachan
A850
Gedintailor
Peinchorran
The Braes
Inverarish
North Fearns
Caol Mor
Loch Sligachan
Sconser
SCALPAY
1298
MULLACH NA CARN
Loch Ainort
Luib
Duisdale
Caolas Scalpay
17
Grula
MINGINISH
SKYE
Loch Eynort
SGURR A'GHEADAIDH
3197
CUILLIN HILLS
3257
SGURR ALASDAIR
Bualintur
Loch Coruisk
Loch Brittle
Geodha Daraich
Rubh' an Dunain
Soay Sound
SOAY
BLA BHEINN
3046
Lochna Creitheach
Strathaird
Kirkibost
Kilmarie
Torrin
Kilbride
A881
Loch Slapin
Loch Scavaig
1128
BEN MEABOST
Elgol
Rubha na h'Easgainne
Rubha Suisnish
BEINN NA CAILLICH
2403
Broadford
Broadford Bay
Corry
A854
A850
Harrapool
Lower Breakish
Upper Breakish
Skulamus
A851
PABAY
LONGAY
Eilean Meadhonach
Eilean Mór
CROWLIN ISLANDS
Caolas Mòr
Loch Carron
Strome
Plockton
Ardnarff
Stromeferry
Achmore
Portneora
Drumbuie
Duirinish
Erbusaig
KYLE OF LOCHALSH
Kyleakin
Balmacara
Visitor Centre
Kirton
A87
Nostie
Ardelve
Loch Alsh
Dornie
Eilean Donan
Bundalloch
Sallachy
Killilan
Loch Long
River
Loch nan Eun
Keppoch
Letterfearn
Loch Duich
A87
Inverinate
2759
SGURR AN AIRGID
Morvich
Ault a' chruinn
Shiel Bridge
Five Sisters
River Shiel
SGURR NA COINNICH
2424
Kyle Rhea
Summer only
Kylerhea
Bernera
Galltair
Glenelg Bay
Glenelg
1977
BEINN A' CHUIRN
Ratagan
1984
BEN ASLAK
Eilanreach
Glenelg Brochs
Heast
Loch Eishort
SGORACH BREAC
981
Drumfearn
Loch na Dal
Duisdalemore
Ord
ORNSAY
Isleornsay
Tokavaig
Tarskavaig
Achnacloich
Teangue
Knock Bay
Kilmore
Kilbeg
Clan Donald Centre
Armadale Pier
Ardvasar
Calligarry
(Summer Only)
Aird of Sleat
Point of Sleat
SOUND OF SLEAT
Rubha Buidhe
BEINN SGRITHEALL
3194
BEINN NAN CAORACH
2536
3319
THE SADDLE
Arnisdale
Loch Hourn
Corran
2327
DRUIM FADA
Kinlochourn
Rubh' Ard Slisneach
2573
BEINN NA CAILLICH
Barrisdale Bay
Kinloch Hourn
Airor
3343
LADHAR BHEINN
KNOYDART
Inverie
Inverie Bay
Sandaig Bay
3083
LUINNE BHEINN
Loch an Dubh - Lochain
Rubha Raonuill
SCALE 1:250,000
4 miles to 1 inch
miles
kilometres
Harbour
Rubha Shamhnan Insir
NG
NM
1874
ORVAL
Kinloch
Loch Scresort
Rubha Port na Caranean
RHUM
2663
ASKIVAL
Rubha nam Meirleach
55
Sound of Rhum
Mallaig
A830
Beoraidbeg
1796
GHUIBHAIS
Loch Nevis
Bracora
Bracorina
Glenancross
Tarbet
2387
SGURR BREAC
Loch Morar
HIGHLAND REGION
SGURR NA CICHE
3412
3290
SGURR MOR
EIGG
Bay of Laig
Cleadale
Bunacaimb
Eilean Ighe
Back of Keppoch
Arisaig
Loch nan Ceall
Luinga Mhór
Rubh' Arisaig
1970
SIDHEAN MOR
2328
MEITH BHEINN
3136
SGURR NAN COIREACHAN
3164
SGURR THUILM
Galmisdale
Eilean Chathastail
Sound of Eigg
Eilean nan Each
MUCK
Port Mor
SOUND OF ARISAIG
1675
CREAG BHAN
Loch Beoraid
2610
SGURR AN UTHA
Loch nan Uamh
ARDNISH
Lochailort
Inverailort
A830
Loch Eilt
Glenfinnan
Glenfinnan Monument
A830
Kinlocheil
Drimsallie
Garvan
Roshven
Loch Ailort
A861
ROIS-BHEINN
2895
2895
BEINN ODHAR BHEAG
Rubha na Faing Moire
21
EILEAN SHONA
2179
BEINN GAIRE
Loch Shiel
Rubha Aird Druimnich
Loch Moidart
Ardmolich
MOIDART
2474
SGORR AN TARMACHAIN
Ockle Point
Sanna Point
Sanna Bay
Sanna
Kilmory
Ockle
Ardtoe
Shielfoot
Dalnabreck
Dalelia
Achnaha
Branault
Kentra
Polloch
SGURR DHOMHNUILL
2914
ARDGOUR
Point of Ardnamurchan
Portuairk
ARDNAMURCHAN
B8044
Acharacle
Ardshealach
Loch Doilet
Achosnich
BEINN RESIPOL
2775
SUNART
To Lochboisdale and Castlebay
B8007
Kilchoan
1607
MEALL NAN EACH
Salen
Resipole
Scotstown
Ormsaigmore
Glenbeg
B8007
Loch Sunart
Anaheilt
Ardnastang
Strontian
A861
Ardslignish
Glenborrodale
Camasine
Coll-Oban
50
Ardmore Point
ORONSAY
CARNA
50
Liddesdale
A884
13
Quinish Point
Auliston Point
1911
BEINN NAM BEATHRACH
2798
CREACH BHEINN
Tobermory
1873
BEINN IADAIN
Lochuisge
Cilmalieu
Caliach Point
MORNISH
MISHNISH
Calve Island
Drimnin
Loch Teacuis
MORVERN
LINNHE
Cuil Bay
Eilean Balnagowan
B8073
Dervaig
Achnadrish
Glenmorven Cottage
Rhemore
Loch Arienas
20
B8043
Loch a' Choire
Calgary
Calgary Bay
Treshnish Point
Loch Frisa
Killundine
Sound of Mull
Acharn
BEINN MHEADHOIN
2424
SHUNA ISLAND
Appin House
Ensay
Arnabost
B849
Claggan
431
BEINN A' CHAISIL
Loch Tearnait
Achranich
Portnacroish
ISLAND OF MULL
10
Fiunary
A884
Savary
Loch Aline
LOCH
Port Ramsay
Port Appin
Tynribbie
Rubh' a' Chaoil
Kilninian
Burg
Aros Mains
Lochaline
Achleck
Fanmore
Ballygown
BEINN NA DRISE
1392
A848
Salen
Fishnish Pier
B8045
Clachan
Eriska
North Shian
Fladda
Loch Tuath
B8073
Rubha na Sròine
Lagganulva
Pennygown
LISMORE ISLAND
Achnacroish
Loch Creran
GOMETRA
Kellan
Killichronan
B8035
Corrynachenchy
A848
A828
Barcaldine
3
4
5
6
7
8
9

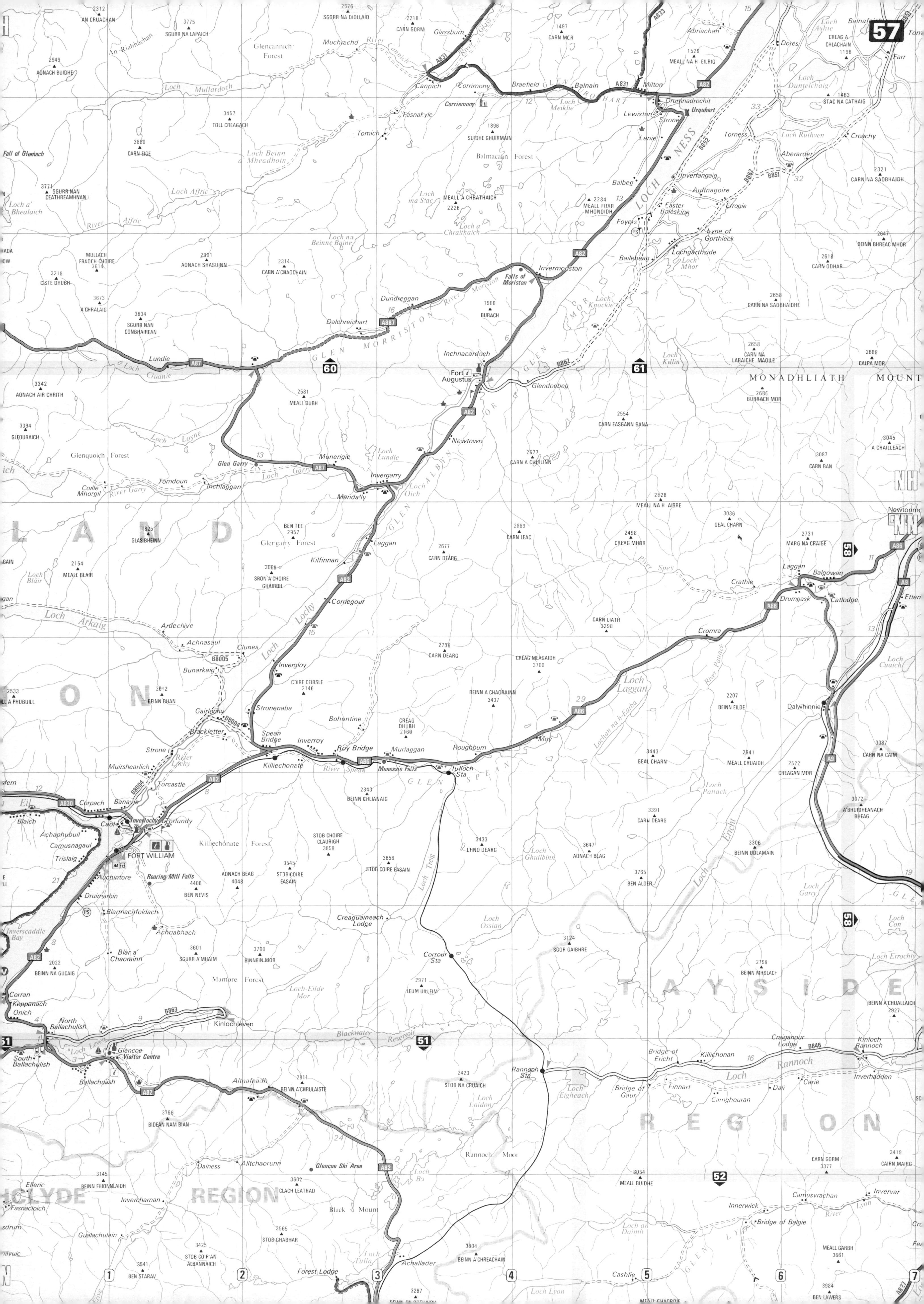
AN CRUACHAN
SGURR NA LAPAICH
SGORR NA DIOLLAID
CARN GORM
Glassburn
CARN MOR
Abriachan
MEALL NA H-EILRIG
Dores
CREAG A CHLACHAIN
Balnafoich
Farr
An Riabhachan
Glencannich Forest
Muchrachd
River Cannich
River Glass
AONACH BUIDHE
Loch Mullardoch
Cannich
Cormony
Braefield
Balnain
GLEN URQUHART
Milton
Drumnadrochit
Urquhart
Corriemony
Loch Meiklie
Lewiston
Strone
Loch Duntelchaig
STAC NA CATHAIG
TOLL CREAGACH
Fasnakyle
Tomich
SUIDHE GHUIRMAIN
Lenie
LOCH NESS
Torness
Loch Ruthven
Croachy
CARN EIGE
Fall of Glomach
Loch Beinn a' Mheadhoin
Balmacaan Forest
Aberarder
SGURR NAN CEATHREAMHNAN
Loch Affric
Loch ma Stac
MEALL A' CHRATHAICH
MEALL FUAR MHONAIDH
Balbeg
Inverfarigaig
Aultnagoire
Errogie
CARN NA SAOBHAIDH
Loch a' Bhealaich
River Affric
Loch a Chraithaich
Foyers
Easter Boleskine
Loch na Beinne Baine
Lyne of Gorthleck
BEINN BHREAC MHOR
MULLACH FRAOCH CHOIRE
AONACH SHASUINN
CARN A' CHAOCHAIN
Lochgarthside
Bailebeag
Loch Mhor
CARN ODHAR
CISTE DHUBH
Invermoriston
Falls of Moriston
BURACH
Loch Knockie
A' CHRALAIG
Dundreggan
River Moriston
CARN NA SAOBHAIDHE
SGURR NAN CONBHAIREAN
Dalchreichart
GLEN MORRISTON
GLEN MOR
Lundie
Loch Cluanie
Inchnacardoch
Fort Augustus
Glendoebeg
Loch Killin
CARN NA LARAICHE MAOILE
CALPA MOR
MONADHLIATH MOUNT
AONACH AIR CHRITH
MEALL DUBH
BURRACH MOR
GLEOURAICH
Loch Loyne
Newtown
CARN EASGANN BANA
Glenquoich Forest
Glen Garry
Munerigie
Loch Lundie
CARN A' CHUILINN
A' CHAILLEACH
CARN BAN
Tomdoun
Inchlaggan
Loch Garry
Invergarry
Loch Oich
Corrie Mhorgil
River Garry
Mandally
GLEN ALBYN
MEALL NA H-AISRE
NH
Newtonmore
BEN TEE
Glengarry Forest
CARN LEAC
GEAL CHARN
LAND
GLAS BHEINN
Laggan
CARN DEARG
CREAG MHOR
MARG NA CRAIGE
Kilfinnan
River Spey
MEALL BLAIR
Loch Blair
SRON A' CHOIRE GHAIRBH
Laggan
Balgowan
Crathie
Drumgask
Catlodge
Corriegour
Loch Arkaig
Loch Lochy
Ardechive
CARN LIATH
Cromra
Achnasaul
Clunes
CARN DEARG
CREAG MEAGAIDH
Bunarkaig
Invergloy
COIRE CEIRSLE
Loch Laggan
River Pattack
Loch Cuaich
A' PHUBUILL
BEINN BHAN
BEINN A' CHAORAINN
BEINN EILDE
Stronenaba
Gairlochy
Bohuntine
CREAG DHUBH
Dalwhinnie
Brackletter
Spean Bridge
Inverroy
Roy Bridge
Murlaggan
Roughburn
Moy
Lochan na h-Earba
Strone
River Lochy
Killiechonate
River Spean
Monessie Falls
Tulloch Sta
GLEN SPEAN
GEAL CHARN
MEALL CRUAIDH
CREAGAN MOR
CARN NA CAIM
Muirshearlich
Torcastle
Corpach
Banavie
Loch Eil
BEINN CHLIANAIG
Loch Pattack
A' BHUIDHEANACH BHEAG
Blaich
Caol
Inverlochy
Torlundy
Achaphubuil
Camusnagaul
Killiechonate Forest
STOB CHOIRE CLAURIGH
CARN DEARG
Trislaig
FORT WILLIAM
CHNO DEARG
Loch Ghuilbinn
AONACH BEAG
BEINN UDLAMAIN
Roaring Mill Falls
STOB COIRE EASAIN
STOB COIRE EASAIN
Loch Treig
Loch Ericht
Auchintore
BEN NEVIS
BEN ALDER
Loch Garry
Drumarbin
Blarmachfoldach
Creaguaineach Lodge
Loch Ossian
Loch Con
Inverscaddle Bay
Achriabhach
Corrour Sta
SGOR GAIBHRE
Loch Errochty
Blàr a' Chaorainn
SGURR A' MHAIM
BINNEIN MOR
BEINN NA GUCAIG
Mamore Forest
Loch Eilde Mor
LEUM UILLEIM
TAYSIDE
BEINN MHOLACH
BEINN A' CHUALLAICH
Corran
Keppanach
Onich
North Ballachulish
Kinlochleven
Blackwater Reservoir
Loch Leven
Glencoe
Visitor Centre
South Ballachulish
Craiganour Lodge
Kinloch Rannoch
Bridge of Ericht
Killichonan
Loch Rannoch
Inverhadden
Ballachulish
Altnafeadh
BEINN A' CHRULAISTE
Rannoch Sta
STOB NA CRUAICH
Loch Eigheach
Bridge of Gaur
Finnart
Carie
Dall
Camghouran
Loch Laidon
BIDEAN NAM BIAN
REGION
Rannoch Moor
CARN GORM
CAIRN MAIRG
Dalness
Alltchaorunn
Glencoe Ski Area
Loch Ba
BEINN FHIONNLAIDH
CLACH LEATHAD
MEALL BUIDHE
Camusvrachan
Invervar
HCLYDE REGION
Fasnacloich
Inverchaoran
Black Mount
Innerwick
Bridge of Balgie
River Lyon
Loch an Daimh
Gualachulain
STOB GHABHAR
STOB COIR' AN ALBANNAICH
Loch Tulla
BEINN A' CHREACHAIN
Achallader
MEALL GARBH
BEN STARAV
Forest Lodge
Cashlie
GLEN LYON
Loch Lyon
BEN LAWERS
A82
A87
A887
A831
A833
A86
A9
A830
B862
B852
B851
B8005
B8004
B863
B846
60
61
58
51
52
1
2
3
4
5
6
7

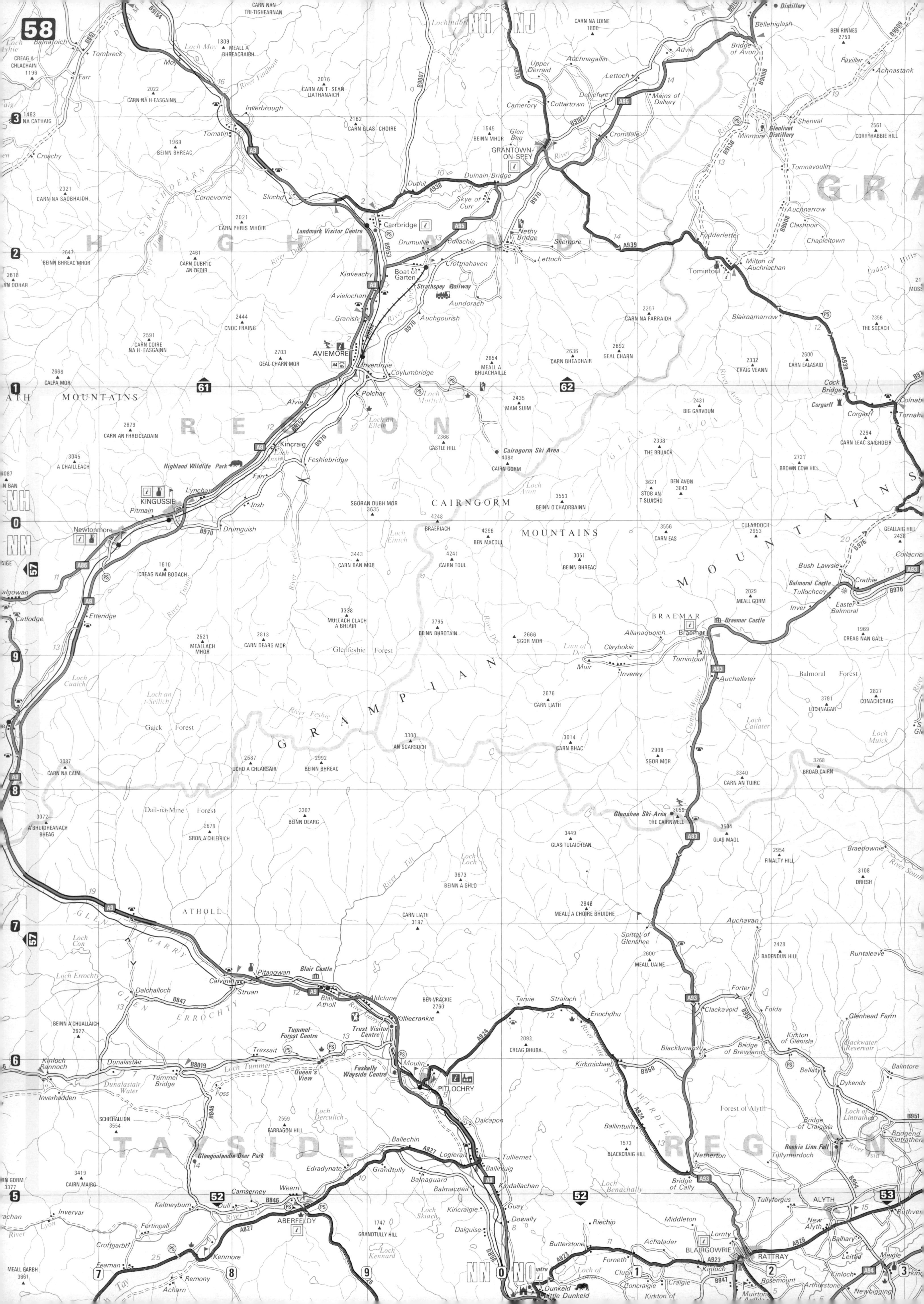
HIGHLAND REGION
GRAMPIAN REGION
TAYSIDE REGION
MONADHLIATH MOUNTAINS
CAIRNGORM MOUNTAINS
GRAMPIAN MOUNTAINS
NH
NJ
NN
NO
61
62
57
52
53
Moy
Tomatin
Inverbrough
Slochd
Carrbridge
Landmark Visitor Centre
Dulnain Bridge
GRANTOWN-ON-SPEY
Cromdale
Advie
Bridge of Avon
Nethy Bridge
Boat of Garten
Strathspey Railway
AVIEMORE
Inverdruie
Coylumbridge
Kincraig
Highland Wildlife Park
Feshiebridge
KINGUSSIE
Newtonmore
Glenlivet Distillery
Tomnavoulin
Tomintoul
Cock Bridge
Corgarff
Cairngorm Ski Area
CAIRN GORM 4084
BRAERIACH 4248
BEN MACDUI 4296
CAIRN TOUL 4241
BRAEMAR
Braemar Castle
Balmoral Castle
Crathie
Inverey
Linn of Dee
LOCHNAGAR 3791
Glenshee Ski Area
THE CAIRNWELL 3059
GLAS MAOL 3504
Spittal of Glenshee
Blair Castle
Blair Atholl
Calvine
Killiecrankie
Trust Visitor Centre
Tummel Forest Centre
Queen's View
Faskally Wayside Centre
PITLOCHRY
Moulin
Kinloch Rannoch
Tummel Bridge
SCHIEHALLION 3554
Glengoulandie Deer Park
ABERFELDY
Weem
Kenmore
Fortingall
Logierait
Ballinluig
Dunkeld
Little Dunkeld
Bridge of Cally
BLAIRGOWRIE
RATTRAY
ALYTH
Reekie Linn Fall
Kirkmichael
Enochdhu
A9
A93
A95
A939
A924
A923
A827
A86
B970
B9152
B846
B8019
B950

NJ
STRATHBOGIE
THE SCALP
Succoth
Tillathrowie
Tomnaven
Inverharroch
Cabrach
Milton of Lesmore
Milton of Noth
Rhynie
Wheeddlemont
Druminnor Castle
Clatt
Kennethmont
Ardlair
Duncanston
Leith Hall
KNOCKANDY HILL
Cults
Crofts of Shanquhar
Kirkstile
Crofts of Blackburn
Coynachie
Culdrain
Clashindarroch
Baillieward
Slioch
Denend
Agricultural Museum
Thomastown
Newtongarry Croft
Wells of Ythan
Redhill
Fisherford
Rothienorman
Rothiebrisbane
Kirkton of Culsalmond
Colpy
Cairnhill
Rothmaise
Newseat
Tocher
Folla Rule
Largie
Wrangham
Kirkton of Rayne
Meikle Wartle
Old Rayne
Aulton
Insch
Ardoyne
Westhall
Durno
Daviot
Whiteford
Oyne
Pittodrie
Pitcaple
Leslie
Auchleven
Kirkton
B9002
MPIAN
REGION
GARIOCH
THE BUCK
Lumsden
Correen Hills
Coldwells Croft
Muckletown
BENNACHIE
Inveramsay
Burgh Muir
Balhalgardy
INVERURIE
Port Elphinstone
Bograxie
Burnhervie
Keig
Tullynessle
Montgarrie
Bridge of Alford
Alford
Whitehouse
Mossat
Kildrummy
Rinmore
Belnacraig
Glenbuchat
Milltown
Auchintoul
CREAG AN EUNAN
Glenkindie
Towie
Milltown of Towie
Sinnahard
Heugh-head
Boultenstone
Hillockhead
Milton of Cushnie
Leochel-Cushnie
Craigievar Castle
Muir of Fowlis
Ley
Kintocher
PRESSENDYE
Easter Davoch
Migvie
Coynach
Douneside
Craskins
Tarland
Logie Coldstone
MORVEN
Coull
Milton of Auchinhove
Auchlossan
Lumphanan
Tornaveen
Drumlasie
Torphins
Mid Beltie
HILL OF FARE
Milltown of Campfield
Slug of Dess Falls
Ordie
Dinnet
Aboyne
Birsemore
Kincardine O'Neil
Backhill of Trustach
Potarch
Birse
Maryweli
Bridge of Canny
Milton of Tullich
Glascorn
BALLATER
BLACK CRAIG
CARNFERG
TOM'S CAIRN
Tillygarmond
Percie
Dromhead
CAIRN LEUCHAN
CLACHAN YELL
Ballochan
Water of Tanar
PETER HILL
Water of Aven
MOUNT KEEN
HILL OF CAT
HILL OF SAUGHS
MOUNT BATTOCK
Auchronie
Tarfside
The Retreat
Mid Cairncross
Loch Lee
GLEN ESK
River North Esk
CRUYS
WEST KNOCK
BEN TIRRAN
HILL OF WIRREN
Auchmull
FINBRACKS
Wheen
Rottal
Rorandle
Pitfichie
Pitmunie
Monymusk
Grantlodge
Kemnay
Craigearn
Kirkton
Tillyfourie
Ordhead
Sauchen
Lauchintilly
Castle Fraser
Achath
Corsindae
Bankhead
Corners
Echt
Dunecht
Loch of Skene
Lyne of Skene
Garlogie
South Kirkton
Landerberry
Cullerlie
Redhill
Hardgate
Drum Castle
Hirn
Myrebird
Brathens
East Mains
Upper Lochton
Tillyfourie
BANCHORY
Auchattie
Bridge of Feugh
Strachan
Crathes Castle
The Neuk
Crathes
Kirkton of Durris
Crossroads
Lochton
MONGOUR
KERLOCH
LEACHIE HILL
Bridge of Dye
CAIRN O'MOUNT
Milton of Dillavaird
Glenbervie
Auchenblae
Glensaugh
East Cairnbeg
Fasque
Thaneston
Fettercairn
Dalbog
Meikle Strath
Mains of Thorton
Gannachy
Edzell
Bainfield
West Water
Dunlappie
Sauchieburn
Luthermuir
Bridgend
Tillyarblet
Inchbare
Glenmoy
Redheugh
Auchnacree
Kirkton of Menmuir
Tigerton
Mains of Balhall
Newtonmill
Keithock
Ogil
Little Brechin
Trinity
West Muir
Fern
Horiehaugh
Glenquiech
Newmill of Inshewan
Dykehead
Careston
BRECHIN
Cortachy
Memus
Tannadice
Netherton
River S Esk
Murthill
Shielhill
Inverquharity
Finavon
Oathlaw
Northmuir
KIRRIEMUIR
HILL OF FINAVON
Aberlemno
Pitkennedy
Turin
Dubton
Lunanhead
Reswallie
Mains of Ballindarg
FORFAR
Burnside
Dunnichen
Letham
Pitmuies
Kingsmuir
Drumgley
Glamis Castle
Glamis
Douglastown
Lownie Moor
Kirkton
Thornton
Craichie
Tulloes
Foffarty
Whigstreet
Mosston
Gateside
Kirkbuddo
Greystone
Redford
Colliston
Carmyllie
Vigeans
Auchmithie
Guthrie
Friockheim
Glasterlaw
Balgavies
Kinnell
Inverkeilor
Boysack
Chapelton
Cauldcots
Leysmill
Marywell
South Mains
Redcastle
Lunan
Lunan Bay
Braehead
Boddin
Fishtown of Usan
Ferryden
Kirkton of Craig
Westerton
Farnell
Carcary
Bonnyton
Meryton
Barnhead
Middle Drums
Bolshan
Montrose Basin
MONTROSE
Scurdie Ness
Dun
Kirkhill
Hillside
Muirton of Ballochy
Logie Pert
Pert
Logie
Craigo
Marykirk
Morphie
Lochside
St Cyrus
Milton Ness
Johnshaven
Benholm
Gourdon
Bervie Bay
INVERBERVIE
Kinneff
Allardice
Arbuthnott
Tulloch
LAURENCEKIRK
Fordoun
Brownmuir
Parkneuk
Roadside of Kinneff
Catterline
Todhead Point
Crawton
Mondynes
Pitforthie
Barras
Fiddes
Drumlithie
Glaslaw
Dunnottar
STONEHAVEN
Kirktown of Fetteresso
HILL OF TRUSTA
Mergie
Rickarton
New Mains of Ury
Garron Point
Mowtie
Union Cottage
Craiggiecat
Bridge of Muchalls
Muchalls Castle
Muchalls
Doonie Point
Cookney
Netherley
Borrowfield
Upper Burnhaugh
Newtonhill
Downies
Cammachmore
Muirskie
Denside
Woodlands
Portlethen
Findon
Hillside
Hare Ness
Auchlunies
Kirkton of Maryculter
Charlestown
Cove Bay
Souter Head
Nigg
Banchory-Devenick
Cults
Bieldside
Milltimber
Peterculter
Park
Mains of Drum
Craigton
Nether Contlaw
Easter Ord
Bentnoul
Carnie
Elrick
Kirkton of Skene
Westhill
Kingswells
Mannofield
Blacktop
Ruthrieston
Torry
ABERDEEN
Old Aberdeen
Kittybrewster
Northfield
Mastrick
Bucksburn
Bridge of Don
Bankhead
Craibstone
Stoneywood
Dyce
ABERDEEN
Blackburn
Clinterty
East Auchronie
Overton
Denmore
Mundurno
Blackdog
Milton of Potterton
Belhelvie
Whitecairns
Kinmundy
Cothall
Hatton of Fintray
Wester Fintray
Balbithan
Kintore
Cottown
Leylodge
Clovenstone
Kinmuck
Balbithan
Nether Crimond
Whiterashes
Straloch
Newmachar
Tillygreig
Attack
Pettymuk
Tillycorthie
Minnes
Foveran
Newburgh
Drums
Delfrigs
Craigie
Causeyend
Balmedie
Hattoncrook
Hillbrae
Kirktown of Bourtie
Mill of Kingoodie
Udny Green
Cairnbrogie
Pitmedden
Tolquhon Castle
Auquhorthies
Craigdam
Tarves
FORMARTINE
OLDMELDRUM
Fingask
Jackstown
Cross of Jackston
Balgove
St Katherines
Cromblet
Petty
Fyvie
Woodhead
Haddo
Methlick
Collynie
Barthol Chapel
Earlsford
Wedderlairs
Ythsie
Kinharrachie
Esslemont
Quilquox
Drumwhindle
Arthrath
Ythanbank
Hilton
Bromfield
ELLON
Artrochie
Auchmacoy
Kirkton of Logie Buchan
Meikle Tarty
Tipperty
Collieston
Cultercullen
Toll of Birness
Birness
Leask
Coldwells
Murtack
Inverebrie
Schivas
R Ythan
To Lerwick
NK
NP
SCALE 1:250,000
4 miles to 1 inch
0 1 2 3 4 miles
0 1 2 3 4 5 kilometres
NO 0 NP
4
5
6
7
8
9
63
53

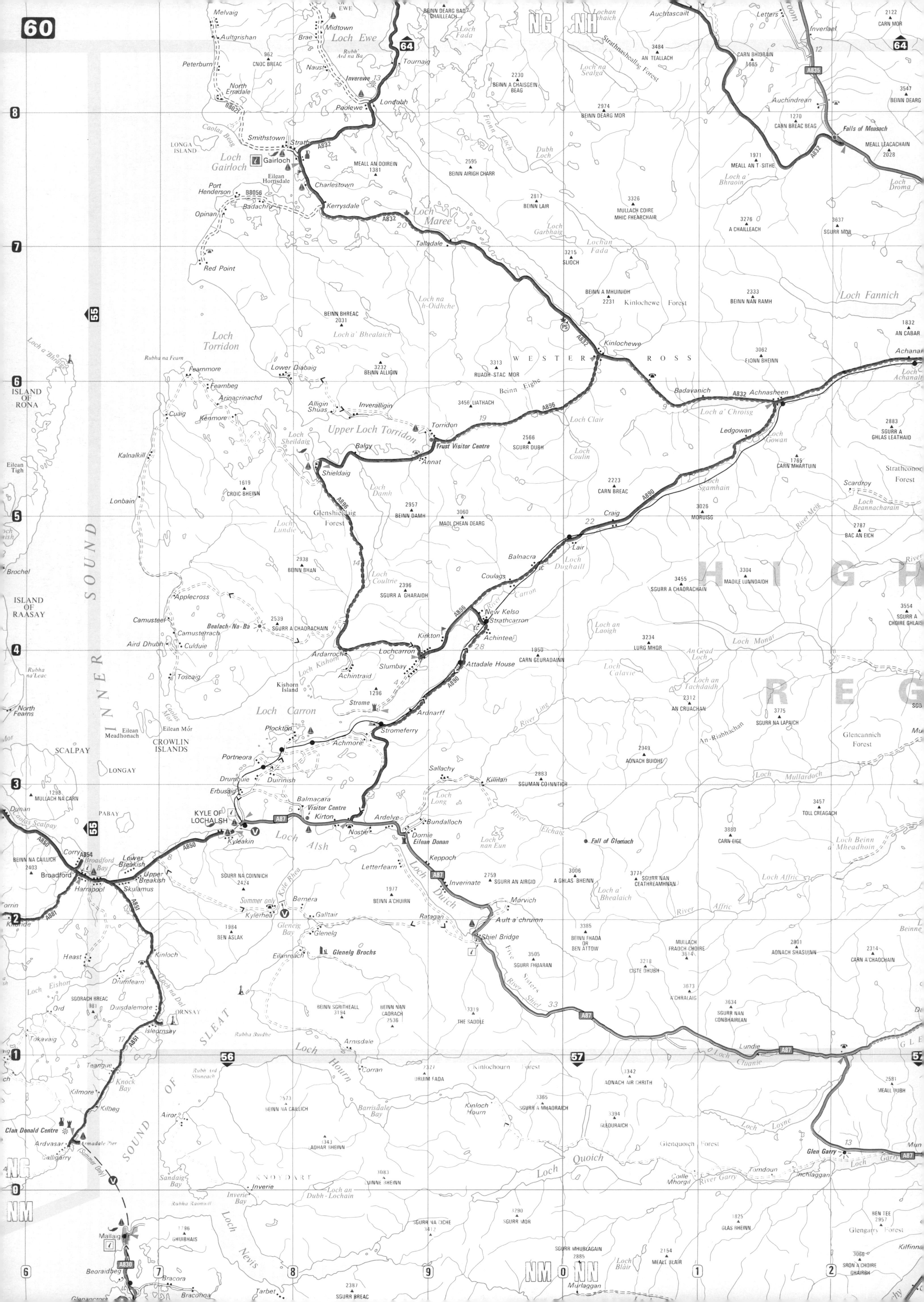

NG
NH
NM
NN
64
55
56
57
Melvaig
Aultgrishan
Peterburn
962 CNOC BREAC
North Erradale
B8021
Midtown
Loch Ewe
Brae
Naust
Rubh' Ard na Ba
Inverewe
Tournaig
Poolewe
Londubh
BEINN DEARG BAD CHAILLEACH
Loch Fada
Lochan Fhaich
Auchtascailt
Letters
Inverlael
2122 CARN MOR
3484 AN TEALLACH
Strathnashealag Forest
Loch na Sealga
2230 BEINN A' CHAISGEIN BEAG
CARN BHIORAIN 1665
A835
3547 BEINN DEARG
Auchindrean
1270 CARN BREAC BEAG
Falls of Measach
MEALL LEACACHAIN 2028
1971 MEALL AN T-SITHE
A832
Loch a' Bhraoin
Loch Droma
2974 BEINN DEARG MOR
Fionn Loch
Dubh Loch
2595 BEINN AIRIGH CHARR
Caolas Beag
LONGA ISLAND
Smithstown
Strath
Loch Gairloch
Gairloch
A832
Eilean Horrisdale
Charlestown
MEALL AN DOIREIN 1381
Port Henderson
B8056
Badachro
Opinan
Kerrysdale
Loch Maree
20
Talladale
2817 BEINN LAIR
3326 MULLACH COIRE MHIC FHEARCHAIR
3276 A CHAILLEACH
3637 SGURR MOR
Loch Garbhaig
Lochan Fada
3215 SLIOCH
Red Point
Loch na h-Oidhche
BEINN A' MHUINIDH 2231
Kinlochewe Forest
2333 BEINN NAN RAMH
Loch Fannich
1832 AN CABAR
BEINN BHREAC 2031
Loch a' Bhealaich
Loch Torridon
Loch a' Bhraige
Rubha na Fearn
Fearnmore
Fearnbeg
Arinacrinachd
Lower Diabaig
3232 BEINN ALLIGIN
3313 RUADH-STAC MOR
WESTER ROSS
Kinlochewe
3062 FIONN BHEINN
Achanalt
ISLAND OF RONA
Cuaig
Kenmore
Alligin Shuas
Inveralligin
3456 LIATHACH
Beinn Eighe
A896
Badavanich
A832
Achnasheen
Loch a' Chroisg
9
Loch Achanalt
Upper Loch Torridon
Torridon
19
Loch Clair
Ledgowan
Loch Gowan
2883 SGURR A' GHLAS LEATHAID
Loch Sheildaig
Balgy
Trust Visitor Centre
Annat
2566 SGURR DUBH
Loch Coulin
Kalnalkill
Eilean Tigh
Shieldaig
1765 CARN MHARTUIN
Strathconon Forest
1619 CROIC BHEINN
Loch Damh
2223 CARN BREAC
Loch Sgamhain
Scardroy
Lonbain
A896
Glenshieldaig Forest
2957 BEINN DAMH
3060 MAOL CHEAN DEARG
A890
22
Craig
3026 MORUISG
Loch Beannacharain
2787 BAC AN EICH
Loch Lundie
River Meig
INNER SOUND
Brochel
2938 BEINN BHAN
14
Lair
Loch Dughaill
Balnacra
Loch Coultrie
Coulags
3304 MAOILE LUNNDAIDH
HIGHLAND REGION
3455 SGURR A' CHAORACHAIN
2396 SGURR A' GHARAIDH
River Carron
ISLAND OF RAASAY
Applecross
New Kelso
Strathcarron
3554 SGURR A' CHOIRE GHLAIS
Camusteel
Camusterrach
Bealach-Na-Ba
2539 SGURR A' CHAORACHAIN
Kirkton
Achintee
Loch an Laoigh
Aird Dhubh
Culduie
Lochcarron
28
1950 CARN GEURADAINN
3234 LURG MHOR
An Gead Loch
Loch Monar
Rubha na' Leac
Ardarroch
Loch Kishorn
Slumbay
Attadale House
Loch Calavie
Toscaig
Achintraid
4
A890
Loch an Tachdaidh
2312 AN CRUACHAN
North Fearns
Kishorn Island
1296
Strome
Loch Carron
Ardnarff
River Ling
3775 SGURR NA LAPAICH
Caolas Mor
Eilean Meadhonach
Eilean Mor
Stromeferry
An Riabhachan
Glencannich Forest
CROWLIN ISLANDS
Plockton
Achmore
SCALPAY
Portneora
2349 AONACH BUIDHE
LONGAY
Drumbuie
Duirinish
7
Sallachy
Killilan
2883 SGUMAN COINNTICH
Loch Mullardoch
1298 MULLACH NA CARN
Erbusaig
Balmacara
Visitor Centre
Loch Long
3457 TOLL CREAGACH
Dunan
Caolas Scalpay
PABAY
KYLE OF LOCHALSH
A87
Kirton
Ardelve
Bundalloch
River Elchaig
A850
Kyleakin
Loch Alsh
Nostie
Dornie
Eilean Donan
Loch nan Eun
Fall of Glomach
3880 CARN EIGE
Loch Beinn a' Mheadhoin
Corry
A854
Broadford Bay
Lower Breakish
A850
BEINN NA CAILLICH 2403
Broadford
Harrapool
Upper Breakish
Skulamus
SGURR NA COINNICH 2424
Letterfearn
Keppoch
A87
Loch Duich
Inverinate
2759 SGURR AN AIRGID
3006 A' GHLAS BHEINN
3771 SGURR NAN CEATHREAMHNAN
Loch Affric
A851
Kyle Rhea
Summer only
1977 BEINN A' CHUIRN
Loch a' Bhealaich
River Affric
A881
Kylerhea
Bernera
Galltair
Ratagan
Morvich
Ault a' chruinn
1984 BEN ASLAK
Glenelg Bay
Glenelg
Shiel Bridge
3385 BEINN FHADA OR BEN ATTOW
MULLACH FRAOCH-CHOIRE 3614
2801 AONACH SHASUINN
2314 CARN A' CHAOCHAIN
Heast
Kinloch
Eilanreach
Glenelg Brochs
3505 SGURR FHUARAN
Five Sisters
3218 CISTE DHUBH
Loch Eishort
Drumfearn
Loch na Dal
3673 A' CHRALAIG
SGORACH BREAC 981
Ord
Duisdalemore
ORNSAY
BEINN SGRITHEALL 3194
BEINN NAN CAORACH 2536
3319 THE SADDLE
River Shiel
33
A87
3634 SGURR NAN CONBHAIREAN
Tokavaig
Isleornsay
SOUND OF SLEAT
Rubha Bhaidhe
A851
17
Loch Hourn
Arnisdale
Lundie
A87
Loch Cluanie
Teangue
Knock Bay
Corran
2321 DRUIM FADA
Kinlochourn Forest
3342 AONACH AIR CHRITH
Kilmore
Kilbeg
Airor
2573 BEINN NA CAILLICH
Barrisdale Bay
Kinloch Hourn
3385 SGURR A' MHAORAICH
3394 GLEOURAICH
Loch Loyne
2581 MEALL DUBH
Clan Donald Centre
Ardvasar
Armadale Pier
Calligarry
Summer Only
1343 ADHAR BHEINN
Glenquoich Forest
13
Glen Garry
A87
Loch Quoich
KNOYDART
3083 LUINNE BHEINN
Coille Mhorgil
River Garry
Tomdoun
Inchlaggan
Loch Garry
Sandaig Bay
Inverie
Rubha Raonuill
Inverie Bay
Loch an Dubh-Lochain
Loch Nevis
1796 GHUIBHAIS
SGURR NA CICHE 3412
1290 SGURR MOR
1825 GLAS BHEINN
BEN TEE 2957
Glengarry Forest
Mallaig
A830
Beoraidbeg
Bracora
Braconna
Tarbet
2387 SGURR BREAC
SGURR MHURLAGAIN 2885
Loch Blair
Murlaggan
2154 MEALL BLAIR
3066 SRON A' CHOIRE GHAIRBH
Kilfinnan

EASTER ROSS
DORNOCH FIRTH
Tarbat Ness
Portmahomack
TAIN
Edderton
Easter Fearn
Struie Hill
Cambuscurrie Bay
Fendom
Inver
Rockfield
Arboll
Hill of Fearn
Hilton of Cadboll
Balintore
Shandwick
Nigg Bay
Nigg
Chapelhill
Port an Righ
Milton
Kilmuir
Barbaraville
Balintraid
Saltburn
INVERGORDON
Alness
Evanton
Rosskeen
Dalmore
Balnapaling
CROMARTY
Sutors of Cromarty
Castlecraig
Blue Head
MORAY FIRTH
CROMARTY FIRTH
Udale Bay
Cromarty Bay
Newton
Balblair
Resolis
Jemimaville
Cullicudden
Brae
Culbo
Shoretown
Findon Mains
Culbokie
Killen
Rosemarkie
FORTROSE
Avoch
Chanonry Point
Fort George
Waiteness Head
NAIRN
Tradespark
Auldearn
Culbin Forest
Kintessack
Brodie Castle
Dyke
Milton
Cooper
Campbelltown or Ardersier
Gollanfield
Clephanton
Cawdor
Culcharry
Piperhill
Righoul
Urchany
Littlemill
Redburn
Ferness
Kirkton of Barevan
Easter Galcantray
Croy
Tornagrain
Newton
Cantraywood
Cartraydoune
Clunas
Clava Cairns
Balloch
Smithton
Culloden
Easter Muckovie
Urchal
Castle Stuart
Fisherton
MORAY FIRTH
North Kessock
Charlestown
Artafallie
Kilmuir
Bogallan
Munlochy
Tore
Suddie
Knockbain
Belmaduthy
Duncanston
Easter Kinkell
BLACK ISLE
Redcastle
Kilcoy
Balvaird
Milton
Beauly Firth
Bunchrew
Leachkin
INVERNESS
Dochgarroch
Daviot
Essich
Balnafoich
Tombreck
Farr
Dores
Loch Ashie
Loch Duntelchaig
Abriachan
Lochend
Lairgmore
Moy
Loch Moy
Inverbrough
Tomatin
Slochd
Corrievorrie
STRATHDEARN
Croachy
Loch Ruthven
Aberarder
Torness
Inverfarigaig
Aultnagoire
Errogie
Easter Boleskine
Foyers
Lyne of Gorthleck
Lochgarthside
Loch Mhor
Bailebeag
LOCH NESS
Strone
Lenie
Lewiston
Drumnadrochit
Urquhart
Milton
Balnain
Braefield
GLEN URQUHART
Corrimony
Cannich
Fasnakyle
Balmacaan Forest
Balbeg
Invermoriston
Falls of Moriston
River Moriston
Inchnacardoch
Fort Augustus
Glendoebeg
Newtown
Loch Oich
GLEN ALBIN
Loch Killin
MONADHLIATH MOUNTAINS
Carrbridge
Landmark Visitor Centre
Dulnain Bridge
Duthil
Skye of Curr
Drumuillie
Cullachie
Croftnahaven
Boat of Garten
Strathspey Railway
Kinveachy
Avielochan
Aundorach
Granish
Auchgourish
AVIEMORE
Inverdruie
Coylumbridge
Polchar
Loch Morlich
Alvie
Kincraig
Loch Insh
Feshiebridge
Highland Wildlife Park
Lynchat
KINGUSSIE
Pitmain
Insh
Drumguish
Newtonmore
Laggan
Balgowan
Crathie
Drumgask
Catlodge
Etteridge
Loch an Eilein
Loch Einich
River Spey
River Findhorn
River Nairn
River Dulnain
DINGWALL
Strathpeffer
Maryburgh
Conon Bridge
Alcaig
Conntown
Jamestown
Contin
Marybank
Urray
Muir of Ord
Corry of Ardnagrask
Ardnagrask
Tomich
Rheindown
Ruilick
Priory
Beauly
Kirkhill
Drumchardine
Easter Moniack
Moniack Castle Highland Winery
Balchraggan
Kilmorack
Crask of Aigas
Culburnie
Kiltarlity
Camault Muir
Eskadale
Mains
Struy
Crinaglack
Leishmore
Glassburn
Loch Bruicheach
Orrin Falls
Orrin Reservoir
STRATHCONON
Loch Achonachie
Loch Achilty
Loch Ussie
Gower
Auchterneed
Bottacks
Falls of Rogie
Heights of Brae
Mountgerald
Ardullie
Swordale
Redburn
Garve
Loch Garve
Gorstan
Corriemoille
Corriemoille Forest
Loch Luichart
Fall of Conon
Little Scatwell
Loch Meig
Garbat
Strathvaich Forest
Glencalvie Forest
Crom Loch
Loch Vaich
Loch a' Chaorainn
Loch Morie
Loch Glass
Boath
Braeantra
Wester Lealty
Achandunie
Easter Ardross
Dalnavie
Stittenham
Stonyfield
Rhicullen
Balnaguisich
Achnagarron
Wester Lonvine
Tullich Muir
Ballchraggan
Scotsburn
Lamington
East Lamington
Newfield
Logie Hill
Cuthill
Wilk
Loch Eye
Rhynie
Tullich
Arkerville
INVERNESS (DALCROSS)
Corriemony
Fall of Conon
CARN BAN
CARN BHRAIN
BEINN THARSUINN
CARN CHUINNEAG
CNOC MUIGH-BHLARAIDH
CARN CAS NAN GABHAR
CNOC AN T-SABHAIL
MEALL A' GHRIANAIN
BEINN NAN EUN
CARN NAN CON RUADHA
MEALL MOR
CNOC CEISLEIN
BEN WYVIS
CARN NA DUBH CHOILLE
LITTLE WYVIS
CLOCH MHOR
SGURR MARCASAIDH
CARN NA CAINNICH
MEALLAN BUIDHE
BEINN A' BHA'ACH ARD
CARN GORM
CARN MOR
AN LEACAINN
MEALL NA H-EILRIG
CREAG A' CHLACHAIN
STAC NA CATHAIG
SADDLE HILL
CARN SGUMAIN
HILL OF AITNOCH
CARN NAN TRI TIGHEARNAN
MEALL A' BHREACRAIBH
CARN AN T-SEAN LIATHANAICH
CARN NA H-EASGAINN
CARN GLAS-CHOIRE
BEINN BHREAC
CARN NA SAOBHAIDH
CARN PHRIS MHOIR
BEINN BHREAC MHOR
CARN DUBH 'IC AN DEOIR
CARN ODHAR
CNOC FRAING
CARN COIRE NA H-EASGAINN
GEAL-CHARN MOR
CARN NA SAOBHAIDHE
CARN NA LARAICHE MAOILE
CALPA MOR
BURBACH MOR
SUIDHE GHUIRMAIN
MEALL A' CHRATHAICH
MEALL FUAR MHONAIDH
BURACH
CARN EASGANN BANA
CARN AN FHREICEADAIN
A' CHAILLEACH
CARN BAN
CARN A' CHUILINN
MEALL NA H-AISRE
GEAL CHARN
CARN LEAC
CREAG MHOR
MARG NA CRAIGE
CARN DEARG
CREAG NAM BODACH
SGORAN DUBH MOR
BRAERIACH
CARN BAN MOR
CAIRN TOUL
CASTLE HILL
MULLACH CLACH A' BHLAIR
A9
A82
A831
A832
A833
A834
A835
A836
A862
A95
A96
A939
A938
A86
B851
B852
B862
B861
B9006
B9091
B9090
B9101
B9161
B9163
B9160
B9169
B9175
B9165
B817
B970
B9152
B9153
B9154
B9039
B9092
B9007
65
62
57
58
4
5
6
7
8
9
NH
NN

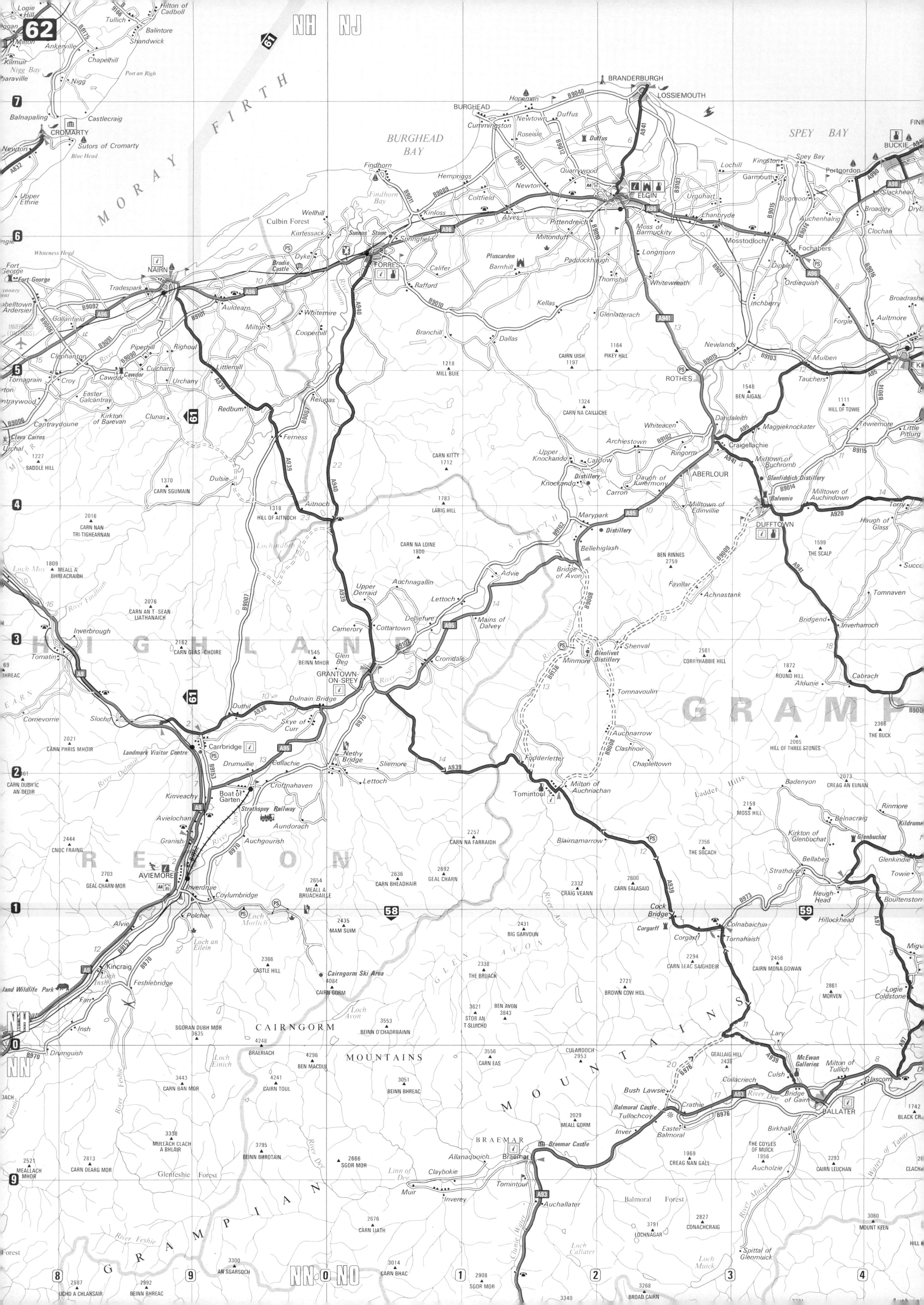

62
61
NH NJ
MORAY FIRTH
BURGHEAD BAY
SPEY BAY
Logie Hill
Hilton of Cadboll
Tullich
Balintore
Shandwick
Milton
Ankerville
Kilmuir
Nigg Bay
Chapelhill
Port an Righ
Nigg
Balnapaling
Castlecraig
CROMARTY
Sutors of Cromarty
Blue Head
Newton
A832
Upper Ethrie
Whiteness Head
Fort George
Ardersier
NAIRN
Tradespark
Auldearn
Gollanfield
INVERNESS (DALCROSS)
Clephanton
Croy
Cawdor
Culchary
Piperhill
Righoul
Urchany
Easter Galcantray
Kirkton of Barevan
Clunas
Cantraydoune
Clava Cairns
1227 SADDLE HILL
1370 CARN SGUMAIN
Dulsie
Littlemill
Redburn
Ferness
Relugas
Milton
Whitemire
Coopershill
Brodie Castle
Dyke
Kintessack
Culbin Forest
Wellhill
Findhorn
Findhorn Bay
Suenos Stone
Springfield
FORRES
Califer
Rafford
Kinloss
Hempriggs
Coltfield
Alves
Burghead
Cummingston
Hopeman
Duffus
Newtown
Roseisle
Quarrywood
Newton
ELGIN
Pittendreich
Miltonduff
Pluscarden
Barnhill
Paddockhaugh
Thomshill
Kellas
Glenlatterach
Moss of Barmuckity
Longmorn
Whitewreath
BRANDERBURGH
LOSSIEMOUTH
Lochill
Kingston
Spey Bay
Garmouth
Urquhart
Lhanbryde
Bogmoor
Mosstodloch
Fochabers
Dipple
Ordiequish
Inchberry
Portgordon
BUCKIE
Slackhead
Broadley
Clochan
Auchenhalrig
Broadrashes
Aultmore
Forgie
Newlands
Mulben
Tauchers
ROTHES
1546 BEN AIGAN
1111 HILL OF TOWIE
Towiemore
Little Pitlurg
Maggieknockater
Dandaleith
Craigellachie
Midtown of Buchromb
Glenfiddich Distillery
Balvenie
Milltown of Auchindown
DUFFTOWN
Haugh of Glass
1599 THE SCALP
Tomnaven
Bridgend
Inverharroch
Cabrach
1872 ROUND HILL
Aldunie
2366 THE BUCK
2065 HILL OF THREE STONES
Badenyon
2073 CREAG AN EUNAN
Rinmore
Kildrummy
Belnacraig
Kirkton of Glenbuchat
Glenbuchat
Glenkindie
Bellabeg
Strathdon
Towie
Heugh-Head
Boultenstone
Hillockhead
1164 PIKEY HILL
CARN UISH 1197
1218 MILL BUIE
Branchill
Dallas
1324 CARN NA CAILLICHE
Whiteacen
Archiestown
Upper Knockando
Cardow
Ringorm
ABERLOUR
Knockando
Daugh of Kinermony
Carron
Milltown of Edinvillie
Marypark
Distillery
Bellehiglash
Bridge of Avon
BEN RINNES 2759
Favillar
Achnastank
CARN KITTY 1712
1783 LARIG HILL
CARN NA LOINE 1800
1318 HILL OF AITNOCH
Aitnoch
Lochindorb
2016 CARN NAN TRI-TIGHEARNAN
Loch Moy
1809 MEALL A' BHREACRAIBH
2076 CARN AN T-SEAN LIATHANAICH
Upper Derraid
Auchnagallin
Lettoch
Advie
Mains of Dalvey
Dellefure
Cottartown
Camerory
Inverbrough
HIGHLAND
2162 CARN GLAS-CHOIRE
1545 BEINN MHOR
Glen Beg
GRANTOWN-ON-SPEY
Cromdale
Shenval
Glenlivet Distillery
Minmore
2561 CORRYHABBIE HILL
Tomatin
Tomnavoulin
GRAMP
Dulnain Bridge
Duthil
Slochd
Corrievorrie
Skye of Curr
Carrbridge
Landmark Visitor Centre
2021 CARN PHRIS MHOIR
CARN DUBH'IC AN DEOIR
Drumuillie
Cullachie
Nethy Bridge
Sliemore
Lettoch
Auchnarrow
Clashnoir
Chapeltown
Fodderletter
Tomintoul
Milton of Auchriachan
Ladder Hills
2159 MOSS HILL
Kinveachy
Boat of Garten
Croftnahaven
Strathspey Railway
Aundorach
Avielochan
Granish
Auchgourish
REGION
2444 CNOC FRAING
2257 CARN NA FARRAIDH
Blairnamarrow
2356 THE SOCACH
AVIEMORE
2703 GEAL-CHARN MOR
Inverdruie
Coylumbridge
2654 MEALL A' BHUACHAILLE
2636 CARN BHEADHAIR
2692 GEAL CHARN
2332 CRAIG VEANN
2600 CARN EALASAID
Alvie
Polchar
Loch Morlich
Loch an Eilein
2435 MAM SUIM
58
2431 BIG GARVOUN
Cock Bridge
Corgarff
Colnabaichin
Tornahaish
59
Kincraig
Insh
Feshiebridge
Highland Wildlife Park
Cairngorm Ski Area
4084 CAIRN GORM
2366 CASTLE HILL
2338 THE BRUACH
GLEN AVON
2294 CARN LEAC SAIGHDEIR
2456 CAIRN MONA GOWAN
Migvie
Logie Coldstone
2861 MORVEN
2721 BROWN COW HILL
3621 STOB AN T-SLUICHD
BEN AVON 3843
Feshie
Insh
Drumguish
Loch Avon
3553 BEINN A' CHAORRAINN
SGORAN DUBH MOR 3635
CAIRNGORM
4248 BRAERIACH
4296 BEN MACDUI
MOUNTAINS
3556 CARN EAS
CULARDOCH 2953
Lary
GEALLAIG HILL 2438
McEwan Galleries
Milton of Tullich
Culsh
Glascorrie
Loch Einich
3443 CARN BAN MOR
4241 CAIRN TOUL
3051 BEINN BHREAC
Bush Lawsie
Collacriech
Crathie
Balmoral Castle
Tullochcoy
Bridge of Gairn
BALLATER
1742 BLACK CRAIG
River Dee
MOUNTAINS
2029 MEALL GORM
Easter Balmoral
Inver
Birkhall
3338 MULLACH CLACH A BHLAIR
3795 BEINN BHROTAIN
BRAEMAR
Braemar Castle
Allanaquoich
Braemar
Claybokie
Linn of Dee
2666 SGOR MOR
1969 CREAG NAN GALL
THE COYLES OF MUICK 1956
Aucholzie
2293 CAIRN LEUCHAN
Water of Tanar
2521 MEALL A' MHOR
2813 CARN DEARG MOR
Glenfeshie Forest
Muir
Inverey
Tomintoul
Auchallater
Balmoral Forest
GRAMPIAN
2676 CARN LIATH
3791 LOCHNAGAR
2827 CONACHCRAIG
3080 MOUNT KEEN
River Feshie
Clunie Water
Loch Callater
Loch Muick
Spittal of Glenmuick
River Muick
3300 AN SGARSOCH
3014 CARN BHAC
2908 SGOR MOR
3268 BROAD CAIRN
3340
2587 CARN A' CHLARSAIR
2992 BEINN BHREAC
NN NO
8 9 0 1 2 3 4
7 6 5 4 3 2 1 0 9
A9 A95 A96 A939 A940 A941 A93 A920 A97 A98 A938 B9007 B9008 B9009 B9102 B9103 B970 B976

NJ
NK
KNOCKIE
CULLEN
Cullen Bay
Logie Head
Redhythe Point
Sandend Bay
Sandend
PORTSOY
Knock Head
Boyndie Bay
Whitehills
MACDUFF
BANFF
Duff
Head of Garness
Gamrie Bay
Crovie
Gardenstown
Troup Head
Pennan
ROSEHEARTY
Quarry Head
Egypt
Sandhaven
Kinnaird Head
FRASERBURGH
Fraserburgh Bay
Cairnbulg Point
Inverallochy
St. Combs
Inzie Head
Pitsligo
Peathill
Percyhorner
Memsie
Rathen
Mid Ardlaw
Boyndlie
New Aberdour
Dubford
Longmanhill
Silverford
Greenskairs
Gamrie
Cushnie
Minnonie
Netherbrae
Glasslaw
Ladysford
Craigmaud
Hillhead of Auchentumb
Crofts of Savoch
Loch of Strathbeg
Rattray Head
Crimond
Blackhill
Logie
Strichen
New Leeds
New Pitsligo
New Byth
Bonnykelly
Ironside
Balthangie
Cuminestown
Garmond
Muiryfold
TURRIFF
Kirkton
Fintry
Milltown of Craigston
Gorrachie
Keilhill
Muirden
Fattahead
The Pole of Itlaw
Oldtown of Ord
Cornhill
Middle Witchyburn
Finnygaud
ABERCHIRDER
Cranna
Bognie
Carnousie
Clunie
Marnoch
Lootcherbrae
Knock
Drumnagorrach
Bracobrae
Sillyearn
Gordonstown
KNOCK HILL 1412
Crannach
Toux
Berryhillock
Milton
Fordyce
Lintmill
Boyndie
Wester Culbeuchly Crofts
Farmtown
Rothiemay
Yonder Bognie
Bogniebrae
Hillbrae
Auchininna
Inverkeithny
Corse of Kinnoir
Cairnie
Fotrie
Crofts of Inverthernie
Birkenhills
Darra
Colp
Howe of Teuchar
Muirtack
Maryhill
Slacks of Cairnbanno
Fedderate
Culsh
New Deer
Maud
Drum
Deer Abbey
Old Deer
Mintlaw
Longside
Flushing
Inverugie
Torterston
PETERHEAD
Burnhaven
Sandford Bay
Buchan Ness
Boddam
St Fergus
Scotstown Head
Kirkton
Kirktown
Rora
Backfolds
Leys
Denhead
Fetterangus
Toux
Dunshillock
Stuartfield
Backhill of Clackriach
Bulwark
Crichie
Dumuir
Nethermuir
Kinnadie
Skelmuir
Annochie
Inverquhomery
Millbreck
Clola
Nether Kinmundy
Little Dens
Hillhead of Cocklaw
Kinharrachie
Smallburn
Sandfordhill
Blackhill
Teuchan
Stonegate Crofts
Colowells
Hatton
Cruden Bay
Chapel Hill
Bay of Cruden
Whinnyfold
Bogbrae
Toll of Birness
Birness
Auchleuchries
Muirtack
Arthrath
Milton of Coldwells
Fortree
Inkhorn
Auchnagatt
Barrack
Cairnorrie
Crofts of Meikle Ardo
Kirkton
Lethenty
Gourdas
Steinmanhill
Kirktown of Auchterless
Balgaveny
Aucharnie
Corse
Drumblade
HUNTLY
Huntly
Brideswell
Slioch
Logie Newton
Wells of Ythan
Badenscoth
Gordonstown
Rothiebrisbane
Fyvie
Woodhead
Backhill
Monkshill
Cottown
Brownhill
Ardo
Crofts of Haddo
Methlick
Skelmonae
Quilquox
Drumwhindle
Collynie
Haddo
R. Ythan
Ythanbank
Inverebrie
Hilton
Bromfield
ELLON
Leask
Artrochie
Auchmacoy
Collieston
Kirkton of Logie Buchan
Meikle Tarty
Tipperty
Newburgh
Foveran
Drums
Delfrigs
Esslemont
Ythsie
Kinharrachie
Tarves
FORMARTINE
Wedderlairs
Earlsford
Barthol Chapel
Balgove
Petty
Crombie
St Katherines
Cross of Jackston
Jackston
Folla Rule
Newseat
Rothienorman
Redhill
Fisherford
Agricultural Museum
Thomastown
Crofts of Shanquhar
Denend
Kirkstile
Newtongarry Croft
Crofts of Blackburn
Culdrain
KNOCKANDY HILL 1425
Largie
Colpy
Kirkton of Culsalmond
Cairnhill
Rothmaise
Tocher
Wrangham
Kirkton of Rayne
Meikle Wartle
Durno
Daviot
Craigdam
Auquhorthies
Tolquhon Castle
Pitmedden
Cairnbrogie
OLDMELDRUM
Fingask
Old Rayne
Insch
Auton
Ardlair
Leith Hall
Kennethmont
Cults
Milton of Noth
Rhynie
Druminnor Castle
Duncanston
Clatt
Cottown
Ardoyne
Westhall
Whiteford
Kirkton
Oyne
Pittodrie
Pitcaple
Balhalgardy
Kirktown of Bourtie
Mill of Kingoodie
Udny Green
Aftleck
Culterculien
Pettymuk
Minnes
Tillycorthie
Tillygreig
Leslie
Auchleven
GARIOCH
1733 BENNACHIE
Inveramsay
Burgh Muir
INVERURIE
Hillbrae
Hattoncrook
Whiterashes
Nether Crimond
Straloch
Craigie
Causeyend
Coldwells Croft
Correen Hills
Muckletown
Tullynessle
Keig
Montgarrie
Bridge of Alford
Alford
Auchintoul
Whitehouse
Rorandle
River Don
Pitfichie
Bograxie
Burnhervie
Port Elphinstone
Kinmuck
Balbithan
Newmachar
Kinmundy
Whitecairns
Belhelvie
Balmedie
Grantlodge
Clovenstone
KINTORE
Wester Fintray
Hatton of Fintray
Cothall
Milton of Potterton
Blackdog
Monymusk
Kemnay
Cottown
Pitmunie
Craigearn
Lauchintilly
Castle Fraser
Leylodge
Overton
Dyce
Blackburn
Mundurno
Denmore
Bridge of Don
Kirkton
Tillyfourie
Ordhead
Sauchen
Achath
Lyne of Skene
Clinterty
Stoneywood
Craibstone
Bankhead
East Auchronie
Dunecht
Bucksburn
Northfield
Mastrick
Kittybrewster
Old Aberdeen
ABERDEEN
To Lerwick
Ley
Milton of Cushnie
Muir of Fowlis
Leochel-Cushnie
Craigievar Castle
Kintocher
Corsindae
Bankhead
Comers
Loch of Skene
Kirkton of Skene
Westhill
Elrick
Tornaveen
Echt
Garlogie
Kingswells
Mannofield
Craskins
Lumphanan
Drumlasie
HILL OF FARE 1545
South Kirkton
Landerberry
Carnie
Cullerlie
Easter Ord
Blacktop
Nether Contlaw
Bieldside
Cults
Ruthrieston
Torry
Nigg
Coull
Milton of Auchinhove
Auchlossan
Torphins
Redhill
Benthoul
Craigton
Banchory Devenick
Girdle Ness
Souter Head
Cove Bay
Slug of Dess Falls
Mid Beltie
Milltown of Campfield
Hirn
Drum Castle
Mains of Drum
Park
Culter
Peterculter
Milltimber
Charlestown
Hare Ness
Aboyne
Kincardine O'Neil
Birsemore
Backhill of Trustach
Brathens
East Mains
Upper Lochton
The Neuk
Crathes Castle
Myrebird
Kirkton of Maryculter
Auchlunies
Findon
Portlethen
Hillside
Birse
Marywell
Potarch
Bridge of Canny
BANCHORY
Auchattie
Crathes
Kirkton of Durris
Woodlands
Muirskie
Denside
Cammachmore
Downies
Bridge of Feugh
Upper Burnhaugh
Netherley
Newtonhill
Crossroads
Cookney
Muchalls Castle
Muchalls
Bridge of Muchalls
Borrowfield
Craiggiecat
Doonie Point
1724 CARNFERG
1017 TOM'S CAIRN
Tillygarmond
Dromhead
Percie
Strachan
Lochton
Ballochan
1232 MONGOUR
Union Cottage
2025 PETER HILL
Water of Aven
1754 KERLOCH
Mergie
Rickarton
Mowtie
New Mains of Ury
Garron Point
1052 HILL OF RUSTA
LEACHIE HILL 1289
Bridge of Dye
Kirktown of Fetteresso
STONEHAVEN
Glaslaw
Dunnottar
2554 MOUNT BATTOCK
Milton of Dillavaird
Drumlithie
A98
A95
A97
A96
A920
A947
A948
A952
A950
A981
A92
A90
A944
A93
A980
A957
A94
A975
A956
B9139
B9022
B9025
B9121
B9023
B9018
B9117
B9024
B9001
B9031
B9032
B9033
B9093
B9105
B9027
B9170
B9106
B9029
B9030
B9005
B992
B9002
B9000
B999
B993
B979
B977
B973
B994
B9126
B9119
B9075
B9094
B976
B974
B9077
B979
59
NO
NP
5
6
7
8
9
1
SCALE 1:250,000
4 miles to 1 inch
0 1 2 3 4 miles
0 1 2 3 4 5 kilometres

NB
NC
OUTER HEBRIDES
SCALE
0
5
10 miles
0
5
10
15 kilometres
Butt of Lewis
Europie
Port of Ness
Skigersta
NESS
Cellar Head
Black House
Brue
Barvas
Bragar
Shawbost
Carloway
Dun Carloway Broch
Ista Chaolais
BEINN MHOLACH 955
MUIRNEAG 813
New Tolsta
Tolsta Head
North Tolsta
Back
ISLE OF LEWIS
Newmarket
STORNOWAY
Tiumpan Head
Portnaguran
Aird
Eye Peninsula
Garrabost
Bayble
Chicken Head
Knock
Flannan Isles
Gallan Head
W Loch Roag
Valtos
Breaclete
Bernera
Timsgarry
Ardroil
Miavaig
Callanish
Garynahine
Achmore
Grimshader
Crossbost
Cromore
Balallan
Laxay
Kershader
Gravir
Loch Odhairn
Kebock Hd
Lemreway
PARK
1874 BEINN MHOR
Loch Shell
Loch Bhrollum
Islivig
Aird Brenish
Brenish
Mealasta I
Loch Suainaval
Grunavat
Loch Resort
Loch Langavat
Arivruaich
Scarp
Hushinish
Hushinish Pt
2227 TIRGA MOR
Forest of Harris
Ardvourlie
Seaforth
Gasker
Amhuinnsuidhe
CLISHAM 2622
Taransay Glorigs
Taransay
West Loch Tarbert
Ardhasig
Tarbert
Cearnach
Scalpay
Sound of Shiant
Shiant Islands
Sound of Taransay
Toe Head
HARRIS
Loch Tarbert
Grosebay
Shillay
Pabbay
Sound of Pabbay
Northton
Ensay
Leverburgh
Manish
Finsbay
Berneray
Rodel
Renish Point
Killegray
Boreray
Borve
Sound of Harris
Haskeir
Griminish Pt
Vallay
Newton
Sollas
Tigharry
NORTH UIST
Lochmaddy
Causamul
Bayhead
Deasker
Clachan
SOUTH LEE 920
Lochportain
EAVAL 1139
Baleshare
Monach Islands
Sound of Monach
Carinish
BENBECULA
Balivanich
Ronay
Grimsdale
BENBECULA
Creagorry
Balgarva
Ardvachar Pt
Wiay
Bagh nam Faoileann
Stilligarry
Howmore
HECLA 1988
Usinish
Verran I
Stoneybridge
BEINN MHOR 2033
Rubha Ardvule
SOUTH UIST
Loch Eynort
Stuley
Daliburgh
Lochboisdale
Loch Boisdale
Kilbride
Sound of Barra
Eriskay
Fiaray
Scurrival Pt
BARRA
Greian Head
Fuday
Stack Islands
Gighay
Hellisay
BARRA
HEAVAL 1260
Borve
Bruernish Pt
Kisimul
Ersary
Castlebay
Vatersay
Muldoanich
Flodday
Sandray
Lingay
Pabbay
Rosinish
Mingulay
Berneray
Barra Hd
THE MINCH
THE LITTLE MINCH
THE HEBRIDES
SEA OF THE HEBRIDES
To Ullapool
To Uig
To Oban
Lochmaddy-Tarbert
To Stornoway
NA
NB
NF
NG
NL
HANDA ISLAND
Scourie Bay
Badcall Bay
OLDANY ISLAND
Eddrachillis
Point of Stoer
Culkein Drumbeg
Drumbeg
Culkein
Clashnessie Bay
Achnacarnin
Clashmore
Clashnessie
Cluas Deas
Nedd
Balchladich
Rienachachait
Stoer
Clachtoll
Loch Beannach
Rhicarn
Achmelvich
Baddidarach
Lochinver
Soyea Island
Loch Inver
Strathan
Inverkirkaig
Rubha Coigeach
Rubha na Breige
Enard Bay
Eilean Mor
Fionn Loch
Reiff
Brae of Achnahaird
Altandhu
Eilean Mullagrach
Isle Ristol
Polbain
Loch Osgaig
Loch Sionascaig
Inverpolly Forest
Glas-leac Mor
SUMMER ISLES
Achiltibuie
Tanera Beg
Badentarbat Bay
Tanera Mor
Polglass
Loch Lurgainn
CUL BEAG 2523
Glas-leac Beag
HORSE ISLAND
Horse Sound
Achduart
Achnahaird
Culnacraig
COIGACH
PRIEST ISLAND
Eilean Dubh
Strathkanaird
ISLE MARTIN
Leac Dhonn
Greenstone Point
Cailleach Head
Ardmair
Rubha Beag
Annat Bay
Morefield
Static Point
GRUINARD ISLAND
Badluchrach
2082 BEINN GHOBHLACH
ULLAPOOL
Little Loch Broom
Achgarve
Mungasdale
Dundonnell
Mellon Charles
Laide
Gruinard Bay
Badrallach
Rubha Reidh
Cove
Ormiscaig
Coast
Inchina
Badcaul
Ardessie
Eilean Darach
Ardindrean
972 AN CUAIDH
Aultbea
Tighnafiline
Little Gruinard
ISLE OF EWE
897 BEINN DEARG BAD CHAILLEACH
Lochan Gaineamhaich
Auchtascailt
Melvaig
Midtown
Loch Fada
Aultgrishan
Brae
Loch Ewe
Strathnasheallag
3484 AN TEALLACH
962 CNOC BREAC
Rubh' Ard na Ba
Tournaig
Poolewe
CARN BHIORAIDH
A857
A858
A859
A866
B895
B897
B8060
B8011
B887
A865
B893
A867
B892
B888
A888
A837
B869
A832
A835
B8057
55
60
NG
NH

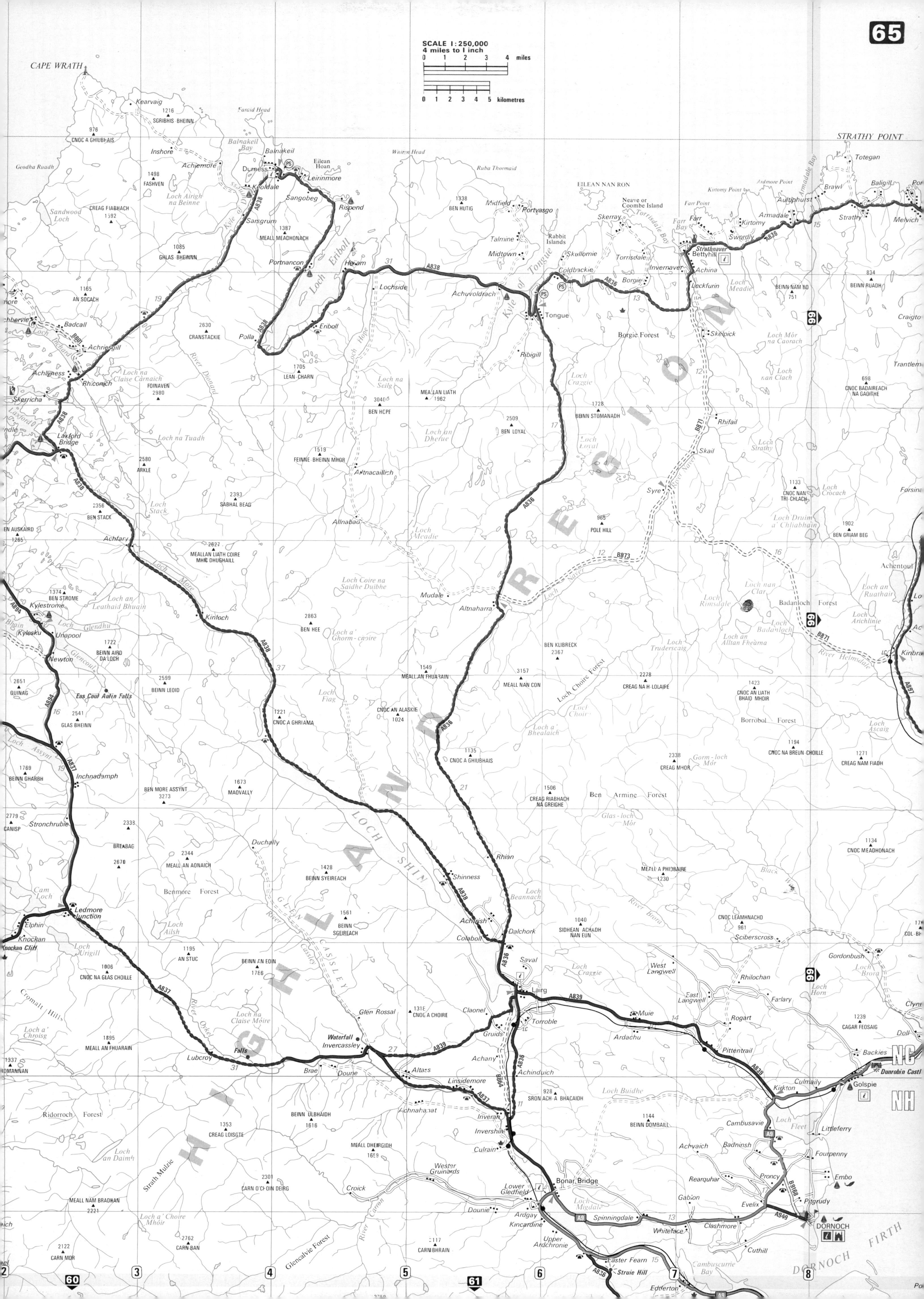
SCALE 1:250,000
4 miles to 1 inch
0 1 2 3 4 miles
0 1 2 3 4 5 kilometres
CAPE WRATH
Kearvaig
1216
SGRIBHIS BHEINN
976
CNOC A GHIUBHAIS
Faraid Head
Balnakeil Bay
Balnakeil
Inshore
Geodha Ruadh
Achiemore
Durness
Eilean Hoan
Leirinmore
1498
FASHVEN
Keoldale
Loch Airigh na Beinne
Sangobeg
Rispond
Sandwood Loch
CREAG FIABHACH
1592
Kyle of Durness
Sarsgrum
1387
MEALL MEADHONACH
1085
GHLAS BHEINN
Portnancon
Loch Eriboll
Heilam
1165
AN SOCACH
Badcall
Achriesgill
Kinlochbervie
Loch Inchard
B801
2630
CRANSTACKIE
Polla
Eriboll
A838
Achlyness
Rhiconich
Loch na Claise Carnaich
FOINAVEN
2980
River Dionard
1705
LEAN CHARN
Skerricha
Laxford Bridge
Loch na Tuadh
2580
ARKLE
Loch Stack
2356
BEN STACK
2393
SABHAL BEAG
Achfary
2627
MEALLAN LIATH COIRE MHIC DHUGHAILL
Loch More
1374
BEN STROME
Kylestrome
Loch an Leathaid Bhuain
Kylesku
Unapool
Loch Glendhu
Newton
Kinloch
1722
BEINN AIRD DA LOCH
2651
QUINAG
Eas Coul Aulin Falls
2599
BEINN LEOID
2541
GLAS BHEINN
A894
Loch Assynt
1769
BEINN GHARBH
Inchnadamph
A837
BEN MORE ASSYNT
3273
1673
MAOVALLY
2779
CANISP
Stronchrubie
2338
BREABAG
2670
2344
MEALL AN AONAICH
Duchally
Benmore Forest
Cam Loch
Ledmore Junction
Elphin
Knockan
Knockan Cliff
Loch Ailsh
Loch Urigill
1195
AN STUC
1806
CNOC NA GLAS CHOILLE
Cromalt Hills
Loch a' Chroisg
1895
MEALL AN FHUARAIN
1337
Ridorroch Forest
1353
CREAG LOISGTE
Loch an Daimh
Strath Mulzie
MEALL NAM BRADHAN
2221
Loch a' Choire Mhoir
2762
CARN BAN
2122
CARN MOR
River Oykel
Loch na Claise Moire
Lubcroy
Falls
Waterfall
Invercassley
2301
CARN O'CHOIN DEIRG
Glencalvie Forest
River Carron
Croick
2117
CARN BHRAIN
Whiten Head
Ruba Thormaid
1338
BEN HUTIG
Midfield
Portvasgo
Talmine
Midtown
Rabbit Islands
Lochside
A838
Achuvoldrach
Kyle of Tongue
Tongue
Loch Hope
Ribigill
Loch na Seilg
3040
BEN HOPE
MEALLAN LIATH
1962
2509
BEN LOYAL
Loch an Dherue
1519
FEINNE BHEINN MHOR
Altnacaillich
Allnabad
Loch Meadie
Loch Coire na Saidhe Duibhe
Mudale
Altnaharra
2863
BEN HEE
Loch a' Ghorm-choire
1549
MEALL AN FHUARAIN
Loch Fiag
CNOC AN ALASKIE
1024
1221
CNOC A GHRIAMA
1135
CNOC A GHIUBHAIS
A836
LOCH SHIN
Glen Cassley
River Cassley
1428
BEINN SYEIREACH
Shinness
1561
BEINN SGEIREACH
Achfrish
Colaboll
BEINN AN EOIN
1786
1318
CNOC A CHOIRE
Glen Rossal
Rhian
Dalchork
Saval
Lairg
Claonel
Gruids
Achany
Altass
Brae
Doune
Linsidemore
Achnahanat
Invershin
Inveran
Culrain
BEINN ULBHAIDH
1616
MEALL DHEIRGIDH
1659
Wester Gruinards
Lower Gledfield
Ardgay
Kincardine
Dounie
Upper Ardchronie
Bonar Bridge
Loch Migdale
Spinningdale
A9
Easter Fearn
Struie Hill
Edderton
EILEAN NAN RON
Neave or Coombe Island
Skerray
Torrisdale Bay
Skullomie
Coldbackie
Torrisdale
Invernaver
Borgie
Borgie Forest
Farr Point
Farr Bay
Farr
Kirtomy Point
Kirtomy
Swordly
Strathnaver
Bettyhill
Achina
Armadale
Armadale Bay
Ardmore Point
STRATHY POINT
Totegan
Brawl
Baligill
Aultiphurst
Strathy
Melvich
Leckfurin
Loch Meadie
BEINN NAM BO
751
834
BEINN RUADH
Skelpick
Loch Mor na Caorach
Loch nan Clach
Trantlemore
698
CNOC BADAIREACH NA GAOITHE
Loch Craggie
1728
BEINN STUMANADH
Loch Loyal
Rhifail
B871
Skail
Loch Strathy
River Naver
Syre
1133
CNOC NAN TRI-CHLACH
Loch Crocach
Loch Druim a' Chliabhain
1902
BEN GRIAM BEG
965
POLE HILL
B873
Loch Naver
Achentoul
Loch nan Clar
Loch Rimsdale
Badanloch Forest
Loch an Ruathair
Loch Badanloch
Loch Arichlinie
Loch an Alltan Fhearna
River Helmsdale
Kinbrace
BEN KLIBRECK
2367
Loch Truderscaig
3157
MEALL NAN CON
Loch Choire Forest
2278
CREAG NA H-IOLAIRE
1423
CNOC AN LIATH BHAID MHOIR
Loch Choire
Loch a' Bhealaich
Borrobol Forest
Loch Ascaig
1194
CNOC NA BREUN-CHOILLE
1271
CREAG NAM FIADH
2338
CREAG MHOR
Gorm-loch Mor
1506
CREAG RIABHACH NA GREIGHE
Ben Armine Forest
Glas-loch Mor
1134
CNOC MEADHONACH
MEALL A PHIOBAIRE
1230
Black Water
River Brora
Loch Beannach
1040
SIDHEAN ACHADH NAN EUN
CNOC LEAMHNACHD
961
Sciberscross
Gordonbush
Loch Craggie
West Langwell
East Langwell
Rhilochan
Loch Brora
Loch Horn
Fairy
A839
Muie
Torroble
Rogart
Ardachu
1239
CAGAR FEOSAIG
Pittentrail
Backies
Dunrobin Castle
Golspie
Kirkton
Culmaily
Achinduich
928
SRON ACH A' BHACAIDH
Loch Buidhe
1144
BEINN DOMBAILL
Cambusavie
Loch Fleet
Littleferry
Achvaich
Badninish
Fourpenny
Embo
Rearquhar
Proncy
Gablon
Evelix
B9168
Pitgrudy
DORNOCH
Clashmore
Whiteface
Cuthill
Cambuscurrie Bay
DORNOCH FIRTH
HIGHLAND REGION
NC
NH
2
3
4
5
6
7
8
60
61
69

NC
ND
To Stromness
DUNNET HEAD
Langaton Point
Nethertown
ISLAND OF STROMA
Uppertown
St John's Point
Boars of Duncansby
Briga Head
Scarfskerry
Ham
Castle of Mey
Mey
Brough
St John's Loch
Rattar
Gills Bay
Huna
The Thirl
Dunnet
A836
Barrock
Gills
Canisbay
John o'Groats
West Dunnet
DUNNET BAY
Inkstack
Loch Heilen
Brabstermire
Skirza
Brims Ness
Spear Head
Crosskirk
Scrabster
Thurso Bay
Clardon Head
Tofts
Freswick Bay
7
STRATHY POINT
Totegan
Atomic Energy Authority Exhibition
Buldoo
Bridge of Forss
Clardon
Murkle
Castlehill
Greenland
Slickly
Freswick
Ness Head
Armadale Bay
Ardmore Point
Brawl
Baligill
Portskerra
Melvich Bay
Red Point
Sandside Bay
Achreamie
THURSO
Castletown
Tain
Alterwall
Aultiphurst
Armadale
Bighouse
Isauld
Dounreay
Cnoc Freicadain
Newlands of Geise
Geise
A882
Weydale
Reaster
Auckengill
Kirtomy
Strathy
Melvich
A836
Reay
Shebster
Westfield
Hilliclay
Durran
B876
Bowermadden
Sortat
Nybster
A836
15
Golval
Achingills
Bower
Lythe
Howe
Brough Head
795 BEINN RATHA
Lieurary
B874
Sordale
Bowertower
16
17
Keiss
6
834 BEINN RUADH
BEINN NAM BO 751
Broubster
B870
Calder Mains
Roadside
Knockdee
Loch Scarmclate
Halcro
Hastigrow
Tang Head
Loch Calder
Kirk
Mireland
Loch of Wester
A897
Loch na Seilge
Halkirk
A882
B874
North Watten
B870
Westerloch
Achiemore
Shurrery
65
Craigtown
Brawlbin
Loch Scye
Lynegar
Loch Watten
B876
Killimster
SINCLAIR'S BAY
Loch Mòr na Caorach
Scotscalder Sta
Harpsdale
Loch Shurrery
A895
Spital
Watten
Reiss
Castles Girnigoe & Sinclair
Noss Head
Dalhalvaig
953 BEINN NAM BAD MOR
Dorrery
Olgrinmore
Winless
Sealky Head
Loch nan Clach
Trantlemore
Trantelbeg
CNOC AN FHUARAIN BHAIN 797
524 BLAR DEARG
B870
Backlass
Loch of Toftingall
Bilbster
Wick River
B874
A9
Ackergill
Staxigoe
698 CNOC BADAIREACH NA GAOITHE
Loch Tuim Ghlais
Loch Caluim
Mybster
Westerdale
Acharole
Strath
A882
Milton
WICK
Wick Bay
5
23
665 CNOC PREAS A MHADAIDH
Forsinain
Badibster
Newton
Loch Hempriggs
Castle of Old Wick
Whiterow
Loch Strathy
Halladale River
21
918 SLETILL HILL
Altnabreac Sta
Strathmore Lodge
446 BEINN CHAITEAG
Tannach
Helman Head
Loch More
1133 CNOC NAN TRI-CHLACH
Loch Crocach
Forsinard
Loch Ruard
Thrumster
Camster
A9
Sarclet
Achavanich
Loch of Yarrows
Loch Druim a' Chliabhain
1902 BEN GRIAM BEG
Loch Sand
Loch Rangag
Camster
17
Ulbster
4
16
Dalnawillan Lodge
741 COIRE NA BEINN
A895
Whaligoe
1144 BEN ALISKY
Crofts of Benachielt
Roster
Bruan
Achentoul
Forest
881 CNOCAN CONACHREAG
Halberry Head
Loch nan Clar
Loch an Ruathair
West Clyth
Clyth
Lochside
Houstry
Swiney
Badanloch
Forest
Loch Arichlinie
Forse
Lybster
65
Loch Badanloch
Achentoul
Knockfin Heights
CNOC LOCH MHADAIDH 1040
Latheron
Smerral
Loch an Fhearna
B871
Kinbrace
River Helmsdale
A9
Janetstown
Berriedale Water
3
1423 CNOC AN LIATH-BHAID MHOIR
1434 CNOC COIRE AN FEARNA
2313 MORVEN
Braemore
Dunbeath
A897
1699 CNOC AN EIREANNAICH
Knockally
Ramscraigs
Borrobol
Forest
Loch Ascaig
2055 SCARABEN
Wag
Langwell
Forest
Borgue
HIGHLAND REGION
1194 CNOC NA BREUN-CHOILLE
1271 CREAG NAM FIADH
Learable Hill
1819 CREAG SCALABSDALE
Newport
20
STRATH OF KILDONAN
Kildonan Lodge
1315 CNOC NA MAOILE
Berriedale
17
Kildonan
1365 BEINN DUBHAIN
Boch-ailean
Ousdale
2
A897
Kilphedir
Torrish
A9
1134 CNOC MEADHONACH
Ord Point
West Helmsdale
Black Water
2060 BEINN DHORAIN
Helmsdale
Gartymore
Portgower
LEAMHNACHD 961
1765 COL-BHEINNN
Lothmore
Scibercross
Lothbeg
1
Gordonbush
Loch Brora
21
Lothbeg Point
Rhilochan
65
Loch Horn
A9
West Clyne
Farlary
Clynelish
1239 CAGAR FEOSAIG
Rogart
Doll
Brora
NC
Backies
0
A839
Dunrobin Castle
NH
Culmaily
Kirkton
Golspie
Pambusavie
Loch Fleet
Littleferry
A9
Fourpenny
Proncy
B9168
Embo
Evelix
Pitgrudy
9
A949
DORNOCH
DORNOCH FIRTH
Tarbat Ness
Cuthill
Wilkhaven
8
9
61
Portmahomack
NH
0
NJ
1
2
62
3
4

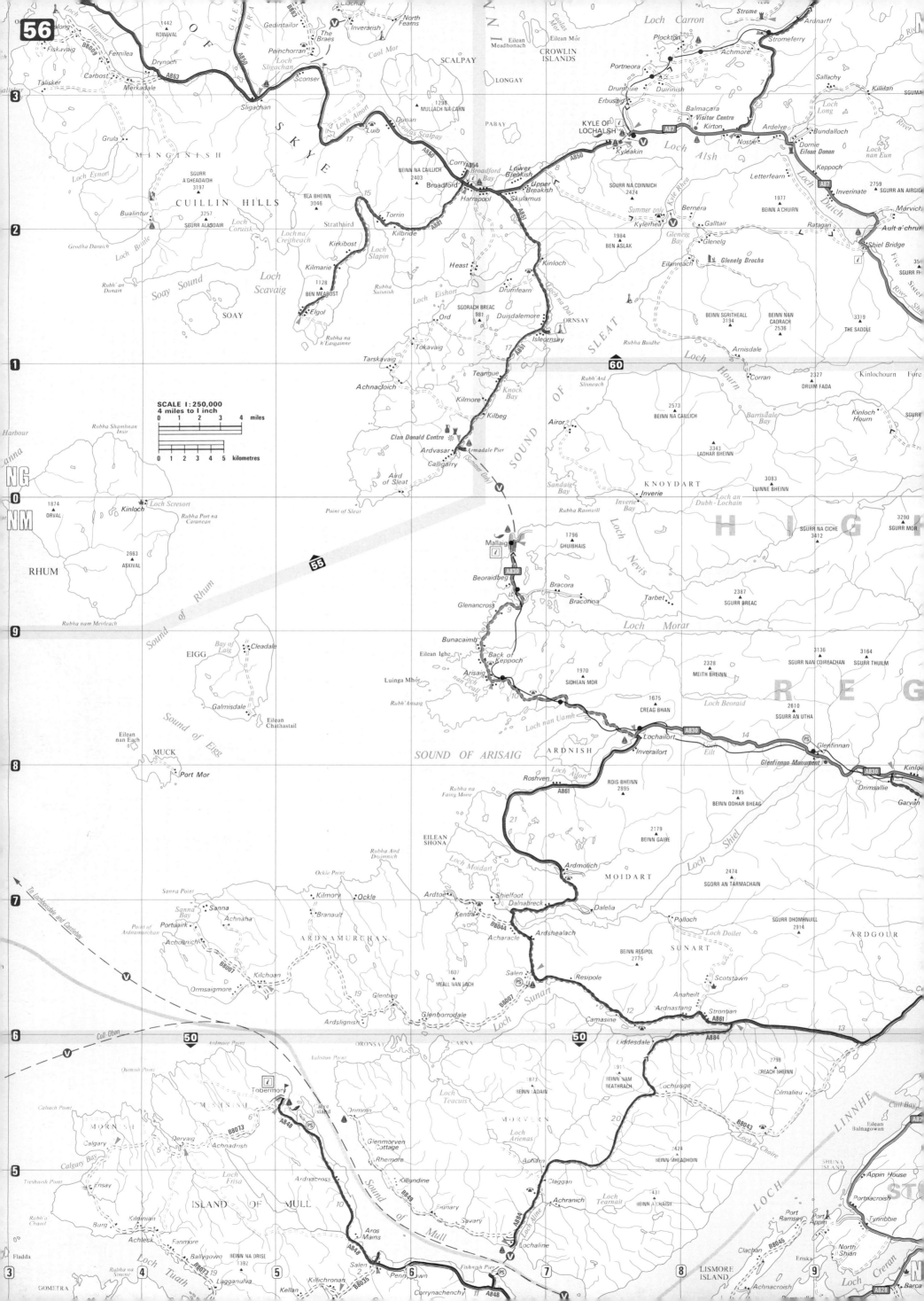

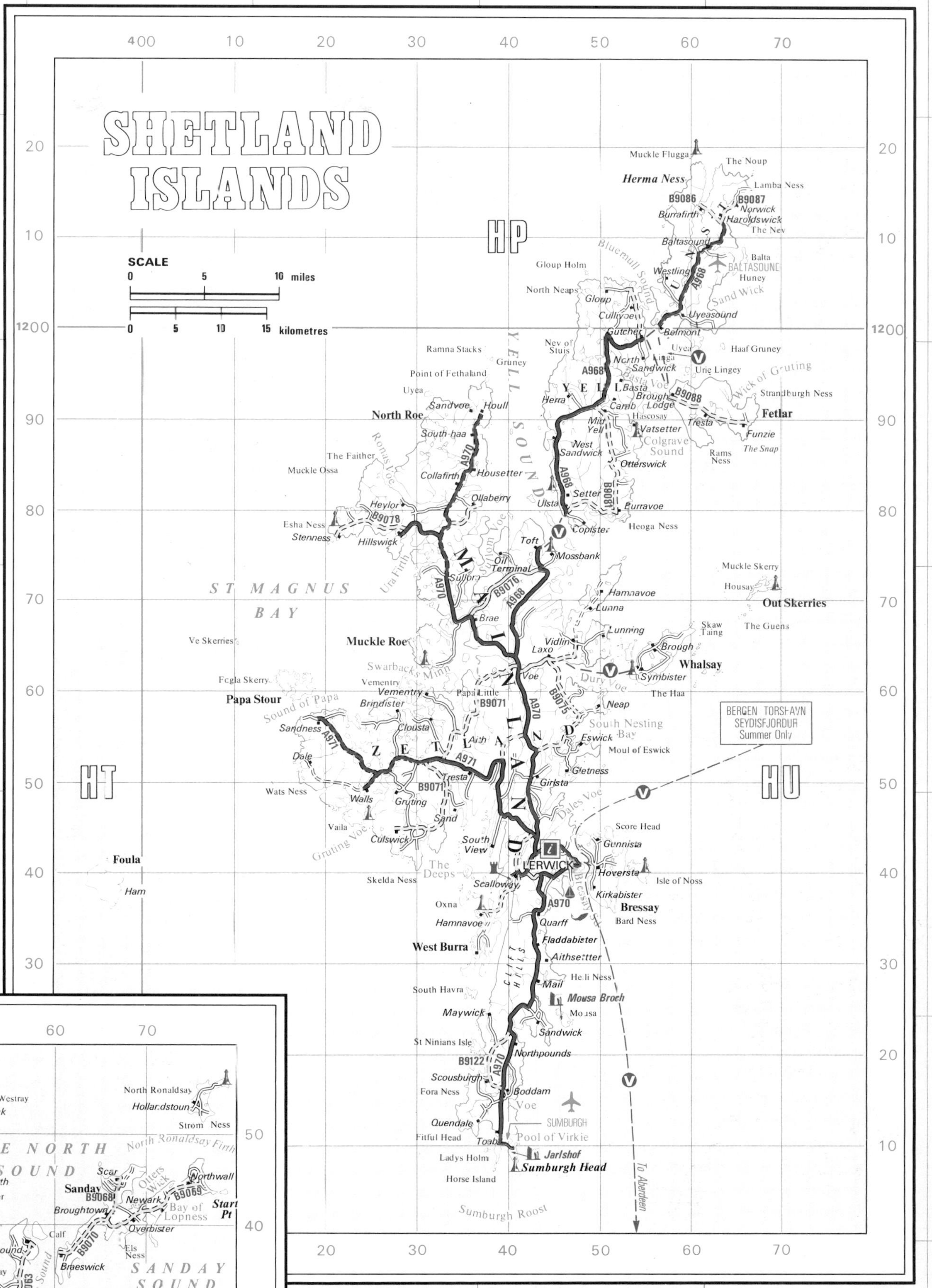
SHETLAND ISLANDS
SCALE
0 5 10 miles
0 5 10 15 kilometres
HP
HT
HU
Muckle Flugga
Herma Ness
The Noup
Lamba Ness
B9086
B9087
Burrafirth
Norwick
Haroldswick
The Nev
Baltasound
Balta
BALTASOUND
Huney
Westing
UNST
A968
Uyeasound
Bluemull Sound
Gloup Holm
North Neaps
Gloup
Cullivoe
Gutcher
Belmont
Uyea
Haaf Gruney
Une Lingey
Wick of Gruting
Strandburgh Ness
Fetlar
Funzie
The Snap
Rams Ness
Ness of Sound
Ramna Stacks
Gruney
Point of Fethaland
Uyea
North Roe
Sandvoe
Houll
South-haa
The Faither
Muckle Ossa
Ronas Voe
Collafirth
Housetter
Ollaberry
Heylor
B9078
Esha Ness
Stenness
Hillswick
YELL SOUND
YELL
North Sandwick
A968
Herra
Basta Voe
Brough Lodge
B9088
Tresta
Mid Yell
Hascosay
Vatsetter
Colgrave Sound
West Sandwick
Otterswick
Setter
B9081
Burravoe
Ulsta
Toft
Copister
Heoga Ness
Mossbank
Oil Terminal
Sullom Voe
B9076
A970
Ura Firth
MAINLAND
Brae
ST MAGNUS BAY
Ve Skerries
Muckle Roe
Hamnavoe
Luana
Lunning
Muckle Skerry
Housay
Out Skerries
The Guens
Skaw Taing
Brough
Whalsay
Symbister
The Haa
Vidlin
Laxo
Dury Voe
Voe
Swarbacks Minn
Foula Skerry
Vementry
Papa Stour
Sound of Papa
Brindister
Papa Little
B9071
B9075
Neap
South Nesting Bay
BERGEN TORSHAVN SEYDISFJORDUR Summer Only
Sandness
A971
Clousta
Aith
Eswick
Moul of Eswick
Dale
ZETLAND
A971
Gletness
Girlsta
Wats Ness
Walls
Gruting
B9071
Tresta
Dales Voe
Vaila
Gruting Voe
Culswick
Sand
Score Head
Gunnista
Foula
Ham
Skelda Ness
The Deeps
South View
LERWICK
Scalloway
Hoversta
Isle of Noss
Kirkabister
Bressay
Bard Ness
Oxna
Hamnavoe
A970
Quarff
West Burra
Fladdabister
Aithsetter
Helli Ness
CLIFT HILLS
South Havra
Mail
Mousa Broch
Mousa
Maywick
Sandwick
St Ninians Isle
Northpounds
B9122
Scousburgh
Fora Ness
Boddam
Voe
SUMBURGH
Pool of Virkie
Quendale
Fitful Head
Toab
Jarlshof
Ladys Holm
Sumburgh Head
Horse Island
Sumburgh Roost
To Aberdeen

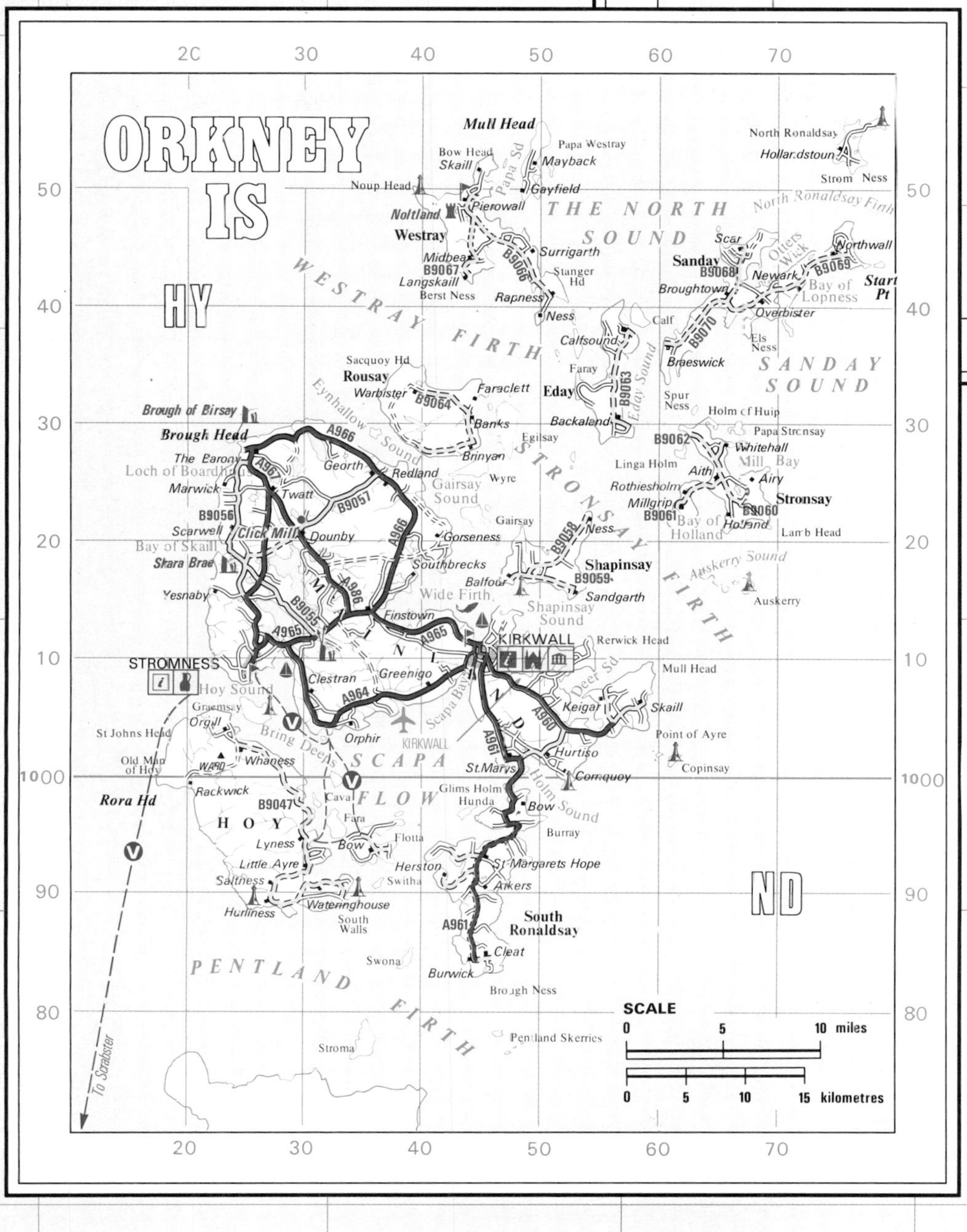
ORKNEY IS
HY
ND
Mull Head
Papa Westray
Bow Head
Skaill
Mayback
North Ronaldsay
Hollandstoun
Strom Ness
Noup Head
Gayfield
Noltland
Pierowall
Westray
THE NORTH SOUND
North Ronaldsay Firth
Scar
Northwall
Sanday
B9068
Newark
Start Pt
Midbea
B9067
Langskaill
Berst Ness
Surrigarth
Stanger Hd
Rapness
Ness
Broughtown
Bay of Lopness
Overbister
WESTRAY FIRTH
Calf
Calfsound
B9070
Els Ness
Sacquoy Hd
Faray
Backaland
Breswick
SANDAY SOUND
Rousay
Warbister
B9064
Faraclett
Eday
Eday Sound
B9063
Spur Ness
Brough of Birsay
Brough Head
Eynhallow Sound
Banks
Backaland
Holm of Huip
Papa Stronsay
The Barony
A966
Georth
Egilsay
B9062
Whitehall
Mill Bay
Loch of Boardhouse
Redland
Brinyan
Wyre
Linga Holm
Aith
Airy
Stronsay
Marwick
Twatt
B9057
Gairsay Sound
Rothiesholm
Millgrip
B9060
Holland
Lamb Head
B9056
Scarwell
Click Mill
Dounby
Gairsay
B9058
Ness
Bay of Skaill
Skara Brae
Gorseness
Southbrecks
Shapinsay
B9059
Balfour
Sandgarth
Auskerry Sound
Auskerry
Yesnaby
Wide Firth
Shapinsay Sound
STRONSAY FIRTH
Finstown
A965
KIRKWALL
Rerwick Head
STROMNESS
B9055
MAINLAND
Clestran
Greenigo
A964
A960
Deer Sd
Mull Head
Hoy Sound
Graemsay
Orgill
A961
Keigar
Skaill
St Johns Head
Orphir
KIRKWALL
Scapa Bay
Hurtiso
Point of Ayre
Old Man of Hoy
Ward
Whaness
Bring Deeps
SCAPA FLOW
St Marys
Cornquoy
Copinsay
Rackwick
Caval
Glims Holm
Hunda
Rora Hd
B9047
Fara
Bow
Holm Sound
Burray
HOY
Lyness
Flotta
Little Ayre
Herston
St Margarets Hope
Saltness
Switha
Ankers
Hurliness
Wateringhouse
South Walls
A961
South Ronaldsay
Swona
Cleat
PENTLAND FIRTH
Burwick
Brough Ness
Stroma
Pentland Skerries
SCALE
0 5 10 miles
0 5 10 15 kilometres
To Scrabster

NE
NK

Abbeydorney G2
Abbeyfeale G2
Abbeyleix G4
Adamstown G4
Adare G2
Adrigole H2
Ahascragh F3
Ahoghill D5
Allihies H1
Anascaul H1
Annalong E5
Annestown H4
Antrim D5
Ardagh G2
Ardara D3
Ardcath F5
Ardee E4
Ardfert G2
Ardfinnan G3
Ardglass E5
Ardgroom H1
Arklow G5
Arless G4
Armagh D4
Armoy C5
Arthurstown H4
Arvagh E4
Ashbourne F4
Ashford F5
Askeaton G2
Athboy E4
Athea G2
Athenry F3
Athleague F3
Athlone F3
Athy F4
Augher D4
Aughnacloy D4
Aughrim G5
Avoca G5

Bailieborough E4
Balbriggan F5
Balla E2
Ballacolla G4
Ballaghaderreen E3
Ballina G3
Ballina E2
Ballinafad E3
Ballinagh E4
Ballinakill G4
Ballinalee E3
Ballinamallard D4
Ballinamore F3
Ballinamore E3
Ballinascarty H2
Ballinasloe F3
Ballindine E2
Ballineen H2
Ballingarry G3
Ballingarry G2
Ballingeary H2
(Beal Atha an Ghaorfthaidh)
Ballinhassig H3
Ballinlough E3
Ballinrobe E2
Ballinspittle H2
Ballintober E3
Ballintra D3
Ballivor F4
Ballon G4
Ballybaun F3
Ballybay E4
Ballybofey D3
Ballybunion G2
Ballycanew G5
Ballycarry D5
Ballycastle D2
Ballycastle C5
Ballyclare D5
Ballyconneely F1
Ballycotton H3
Ballycumber F3
Ballydehob J2
Ballydesmond H2
Ballyduff H3
Ballyduff G2
Ballyfarnan E3
Ballygalley D5
Ballygar F3
Ballygawley D4
Ballygowan D5
Ballyhaise E4
Ballyhale G4
Ballyhaunis E3
Ballyhean E2
Ballyheige G1
Ballyjamesduff E4
Ballykeeran F3
Ballylanders G3
Ballylongford G2
Ballylooby G3
Ballylynan G4
Ballymahon F3
Ballymakeery H2
Ballymaloe H3
Ballymena D5
Ballymoe E3
Ballymoney C4
Ballymore F3
Ballymore Eustace F4
Ballymote E3
Ballynahinch D5
Ballynure D5
Ballyragget G4
Ballyroan G4
Ballyronan D4
Ballysadare E3
Ballyshannon D3
Ballyvaughan F2
Ballywalter D5
Balrothery F5
Baltimore J2
Baltinglass G4
Banagher F3
Banbridge D5
Bandon H2
Bangor D5
Bangor Erris E2
Bansha G3
Banteer H2
Bantry H2
Barryporeen H3
Beaufort H2
Belcoo D3
Belfast D5
Belgooly H3
Bellaghy D4
Belleek D3
Belmullet D2
(Beal an Mhuirhead)
Belturbet E4
Benburb D4
Bennetsbridge G4
Beragh D4
Birr F3
Blacklion D3
Blackwater G5
Blarney H3
Blessington F4
Boherbue H2
Borris G4
Borris-in-Ossory G3
Borrisokane F3
Borrisoleigh G3
Boyle E3
Bracknagh F4
Bray F5
Bridgetown H4
Brittas F4
Broadford G3
Broadford G2
Broughshane D5
Bruff G3
Bruree G3
Bunclody G4
Buncrana C4
Bundoran D3
Bunnahowen D2
Bunnyconnellan E2
Bushmills C4
Butler's Bridge E4
Buttevant H2

Cadamstown F3
Caherconlish G3
Caherdaniel H1
Cahir G3
Cahirciveen H1
Caledon D4
Callan G4
Caltra F3
Camolin G4
Camp G1
Cappagh White G3
Cappamore G3
Cappoquin H3
Carlanstown E4
Calingford E5
Carlow G4
Carndonagh C4
Carnew G4
Carnlough C5
Carracastle E3
Carrick D3
(An Charraig)
Carrickfergus D5
Carrickmacross E4
Carrickmore D4
Carrick-on-Shannon E3
Carrick -on-Suir G4
Carrigahorig F3
Carrigaline H3
Carrigallen E3
Carriganimmy H2
Carrigans C4
Carrigtohill H3
Carrowkeel C4
Carryduff D5
Cashel G3
Castlebar E2
Castlebellingham E5
Castleblayney E4
Castlebridge G4
Castlecomer G4
Castle Cove H1
Castlederg D4
Castledermot G4
Castleisland G2
Castlemaine H2
Castlemartyr H3
Castleplunkett E3
Castlepollard E4
Castlerea E3
Castlerock C4
Castleshane E4
Castletown F4
Castletownbere H1
Castletownroche H3
Castletownshend J2
Castlewellan E5
Causeway G2
Cavan E4
Ceanannus Mor (Kells) E4
Celbridge F4
Charlestown E3
Clady D4
Clane F4
Clara F3
Clarecastle G2
Claremorris E2
Clarinbridge F2
Clashmore H3
Claudy C4
Cliffony D3
Clogan F3
Clogh G4
Clogheen H3
Clogher D4
Clohamon G4
Clonakilty H2
Clonard F4
Clonaslee F4
Clonbulloge F4
Clonbur (An Fhairche) E2
Clondalkin F4
Clones E4
Clonmany C4
Clonmel G3
Clonmellon E4
Clonmore G3
Clonony F3
Clonoulty G3
Clonroche G4
Clontibret E4
Cloonbannin H2
Cloondara E3
Cloonkeen H2
Cloonlara G3
Clough D5
Cloughjordan F3
Cloyne H3
Coagh D4
Coalisland D4
Cobh H3
Coleraine C4
Collinstown E4
Collon E4
Collooney E3
Comber D5
Conna H3
Cookstown D4
Coole E4
Cooraclare G2
Cootehill E4
Cork H3
Cork Airport H3
Cornamona F2
Corofin F2
Courtmacsherry H2
Courtown Harbour G5
Craigaven D5
Craughwell F3
Creggs E3
Cresslough C3
Croagh G2
Crolly (Croithli) C3
Crookedwood E4
Crookhaven J1
Crookstown H2
Croom G2
Crossakeel E4
Cross Barry H2
Crosshaven H3
Crossmaglen E4
Crossmolina E2
Crumlin D5
Crusheen F2
Culdaff C4
Culleybackey D5
Curracloe G4
Curraghboy F3
Curry E3

Daingean F4
Delvin E4
Derrygonnelly D3
Derrylin E4
Dervock C4
Dingle (An Daingean) H1
Doagh D5
Donaghadee D5
Donaghmore G3
Donegal D3
Doneraile H3
Doonbeg G2
Douglad H3
Downpatrick D5
Dowra E3
Draperstown D4
Drimoleague H2
Dripsey H2
Drogheda E5
Droichead Nua F4
(Newbridge)
Dromahair D3
Dromcolliher G2
Dromore D5
Dromore D4
Dromore West D2
Drum E4
Drumconrath E4
Drumkeeran E3
Drumlish E3
Drumod E3
Drumquin D4
Drumshanbo E3
Drumsna E3
Duagh G2
Dublin F5
Duleek E4
Dunboyne F4
Duncormick H4
Dundalk E5
Dunderrow H2
Dundrum E5
Dunfanaghy C3
Dungannon D4
Dungarvan H3
Dungarvan G4
Dungiven C4
Dungloe C3
Dungourney H3
Dunkineely D3
Dun Laoghaire F5
Dunlavin F4
Dunleer E4
Dunloy C5
Dunmanway H2
Dunmore E3
Dunmore East H4
Dunmurry D5
Dunshauglin F4
Durrow G4
Durrus H2

Eaky D2
Edenderry F4
Edgeworthstown E3
Eglinton C4
Elphin E3
Emyvale D4
Enfield F4
Ennis G2
Enniscorthy G4
Enniscrone D2
Enniskean H2
Enniskillen D4
Ennistymon F2
Eyrecourt F3

Farnaght E3
Farranfore H2
Feakle F3
Fenagh E3
Fermoy H3
Ferns G4
Fethard H4
Fethard G3
Finnea E4
Fintona D4
Fivemiletown D4
Fontstown F4
Foulkesmills G4
Foxford E2
Foynes G2
Freemount G2
Frenchpark E3
Freshford G4
Fuerty E3

Galbally G3
Galway F2
Garrison D3
Garvagh C4
Geashill F4
Gilford D5
Glandore J2
Glanmire H3
Glanworth H3
Glaslough D4
Glassan F3
Glenamaddy E3
Glenarm C5
Glenavy D5
Glenbeigh H1
Glencolumbkille D3
(Gleann Cholm Cille)
Glendalough F5
Glenealy G5
Glenfarne D3
Glengarriff H2
Glenmore G4
Glenties D3
Glenville H3
Glin G2
Glinsk F2
(Glinsce)
Golden G3
Goleen J1
Goresbridge G4
Gorey G5
Gort F2
Gortin D4
Gowran G4
Graiguenamanagh G4
Grallagh E3
Granard E4
Grange D3
Greencastle E5
Greyabbey D5
Greystones F5
Gulladuff D4

Hacketstown G4
Headford F2
Herbertstown G3
Hillsborough D5
Hilltown E5
Hospital G3
Holycross G3
Holywood D5
Howth F5

Inch H1
Inchigeelagh H2
Inishannon H2

Johnstown G3

Kanturk H2
Keadue E3
Keady E4
Keel E1
Keenagh E3
Kells D5
Kenmare H2
Kesh D3
Kilbeggan F4
Kilberry E4
Kilbrittain H2
Kilcar D3
(Cill Charthaigh)
Kilcock F4
Kilcolgan F2
Kilconnell F3
Kilconnell F2
Kilcoole F5
Kilcormac F3
Kilcullen F4
Kilcurry E4
Kildare F4
Kildavin G4
Kildorrery H3
Kildress D4
Kilfenora F2
Kilfinnane G3
Kilgarvan H2
Kilkee G2
Kilkeel E5
Kilkelly E2
Kilkenny G4
Kilkieran F2
(Cill Ciarain)
Kilkinlea G2
Kill H4
Killadysert G2
Killala D2
Killaloe G3
Killarney H2
Killashandra E4
Killashee E3
Killeagh H3
Killeigh F4
Killenaule G3
Killimer G2
Killimor F3
Killiney F5
Killinick H4
Killorglin H1
Killough E5
Killucan F4
Killybegs D3
Killyleagh D5
Kilmacanoge F5
Kilmacrenan C3
Kilmacthomas H4
Kilmaganny G4
Kilmaine E2
Kilmallock G3
Kilmanagh G4
Kilmanahan G3
Kilmeaden H4
Kilmeage F4
Kilmeedy G2
Kilmichael H2
Kilmore Quay H4
Kilnaleck E4
Kilrea C4
Kilrush G2
Kilsheelan G3
Kiltealy G4
Kiltegan G4
Kiltimagh E2
Kiltoom F3
Kingscourt E4
Kinlough D3
Kinnegad F4
Kinnitty F3
Kinsale H3
Kinvarra F2
Kircubbin D5
Knock E2
Knockcroghery E3
Knocklofty G3
Knockmahon H4
Knocktopher G4

Lahinch F2
Lanesborough E3
Laragh F5
Lauragh H1
Laurencetown F3
Leap J2
Leenene E2
Leighlinbridge G4
Leitrim E3
Leixlip F4
Lemybrien H3
Letterfrack E2
Letterkenny C3
Lifford D4
Limavady C4
Limerick G3
Lisbellaw D4
Lisburn D5
Liscarroll G2
Lisdoonvarna F2
Lismore H3
Lisnaskea D4
Lisryan E4
Listowel G2
Loghill G2
Londonderry C4
Longford E3
Loughbrickland D5
Loughgall D4
Loughglinn E3
Loughrea F3
Louisburgh E2
Lucan F4
Lurgan D5
Lusk F5

Macroom H2
Maghera E5
Maghera D4
Magherafelt D4
Maguiresbridge D4
Malahide F5
Malin C4
Malin More D3
Mallow H2
Manorhamilton D3
Markethill D4
Maynooth F4
Maze D5
Middletown D4
Midleton H3
Milford C4
Millstreet H2
Milltown H2
Milltown Malbay G2
Mitchelstown H3
Moate F3
Mohill E3
Molls Cap H2
Monaghan E4
Monasterevin F4
Moneygall G3
Moneymore D4
Monivea F3
Mooncoin H4
Moorfields D5
Mount Bellew F3
Mount Charles D3
Mountmellick F4
Mountrath F4
Mountshannon F3
Mourne Abbey H3
Moville C4
Moy D4
Moylett E4
Moynalty E4
Moyvore F3
Muckross H2
Muff C4
Muine Bheag G4
Mullabohy E4
Mullagh F4
Mullinavat G4
Mullingar F4
Myshall G4

Naas F4
Nad H2
Naul F5
Navan E4
Neale E2
Nenagh G3
Newbliss E4
Newcastle E5
Newcastle West G2
Newinn G3
Newmarket H2
Newmarket-on-Fergus G2
Newport G3
Newport E2
New Ross G4
Newry E5
Newtown G4
Newtownabbey D5
Newtownards D5
Newtown Butler E4
Newtown Forbes E3
Newtownhamilton E4
Newtown Mount Kennedy F5
Newtownstewart D4
Nobber E4

Oilgate G4
Oldcastle E4
Omagh D4
Omeath E5
Oola G3
Oranmore F2
Oughterard F2
Ovens H2

Pallasgreen G3
Parknasilla H1
Partry E2
Passage East H4
Passage West H3
Patrickswell G2
Paulstown G4
Pettigo D3
Plumbridge D4
Pomeroy D4
Portadown D4
Portaferry D5
Portarlington F4
Portavogie D5
Portglenone D4
Port Laoise F4
Portmarnock F5
Portrane F5
Portroe G3
Portrush C4
Portstewart C4
Portumna F3
Poyntzpass D5

Raharney F4
Randalstown D5
Rasharkin C4
Rathangen F4
Rathcoole F4
Rathcormack H3
Rathdowney G3
Rathdrum G5
Rathfriland E5
Rathkeale G2
Rath Luric G2
(Charleville)
Rathmelton C4
Rathmolyon F4
Rathmore H2
Rathmullan C4
Rathnew F5
Rathowen E4
Rathvilty G4
Ratoath F4
Ray C4
Ring H3
(An Rinn)
Ringaskiddy H3
Riverstown F3
Rockcorry E4
Roosky E3
Rosapenna C3
Rosebercon G4
Roscommon E3
Roscrea F3
Ross Carberry J2
Rosscor D3
Rosses Point D3
Rosslare Harbour H4
Rosslea E4
Rostrevor E5
Roundstone F2
Roundwood F5
Rush F5

St Johnstown C4
Saintfield D5
Sallins F4
Scarriff G3
Scartaglen H2
Scarva D5
Schull J2
Scramoge E3
Scribbagh D3
Seskinore D4
Shanagolden G2
Shannon Airport G2
Shannonbridge F3
Shercock E4
Shillelagh G4
Shinrone F3
Shrule F2
Silvermines G3
Sion Mills D4
Sixmilebridge G2
Skerries F5
Skibbereen J2
Slane E4
Sligo D3
Smithborough E4
Sneem H1
Spiddal F2
(An Spideal)
Sporthouse Cross Roads H4
Stewartstown D4
Stonyford G4
Strabane D4
Stradbally F4
Stradone E4
Strandhill D3
Strangford D5
Stranorlar D3
Stratford F4
Strokestown E3
Summerhill F4
Swanlinbar E3
Swatragh D4
Swinford E2
Swords F5

Taghmon G4
Tagoat H4
Tahilla H1
Tallaght F5
Tallow H3
Tallowbridge H3
Tandragee D5
Tang F3
Tarbert G2
Templemore G3
Templepatrick D5
Templetouhy G3
Termonfeckin E5
Thomas Street F3
Thomastown G4
Thurles G3
Timahoe F4
Timoleague H2
Tinahely G4
Tipperary G3
Tobercurry E3
Tobermore D4
Togher F3
Toomyvara G3
Toormore J1
Tralee G2
Tramore H4
Trim F4
Tuam F2
Tuamgraney G3
Tulla G2
Tullamore F4
Tullow G4
Tulsk E3
Turlough E2
Tyholland D4
Tyrrellspass F4

Urlingford G3

Virginia E4
Waddington H4
Warrenpoint E5
Waterford H4
Watergrasshill H3
Waterville H1
Westport E2
Wexford G4
Whitegate H3
Whitehead D5
Wicklow F5
Woodenbridge G5
Woodford F3

Youghal H3

LEGEND

- Motorway with number
- Primary route
- Main road
- Trunk road (Republic of Ireland)
- Secondary road
- Other road
- Road numbers
- Distance in miles between symbols
- International Boundary
- Customs (0900-1700)

Scale: 16 miles to 1 inch (approx)

miles: 0 10 20 30
kilometres: 0 10 20 30 40

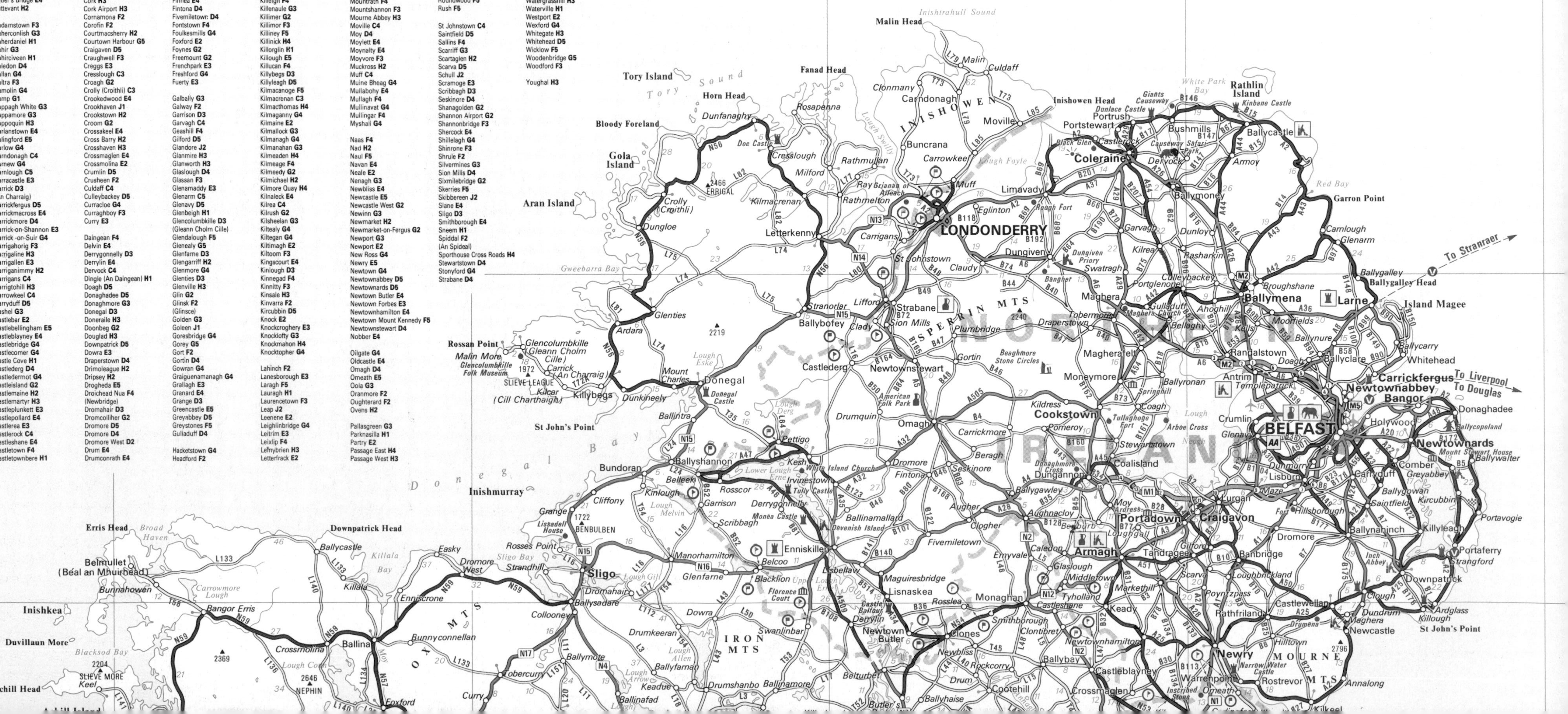

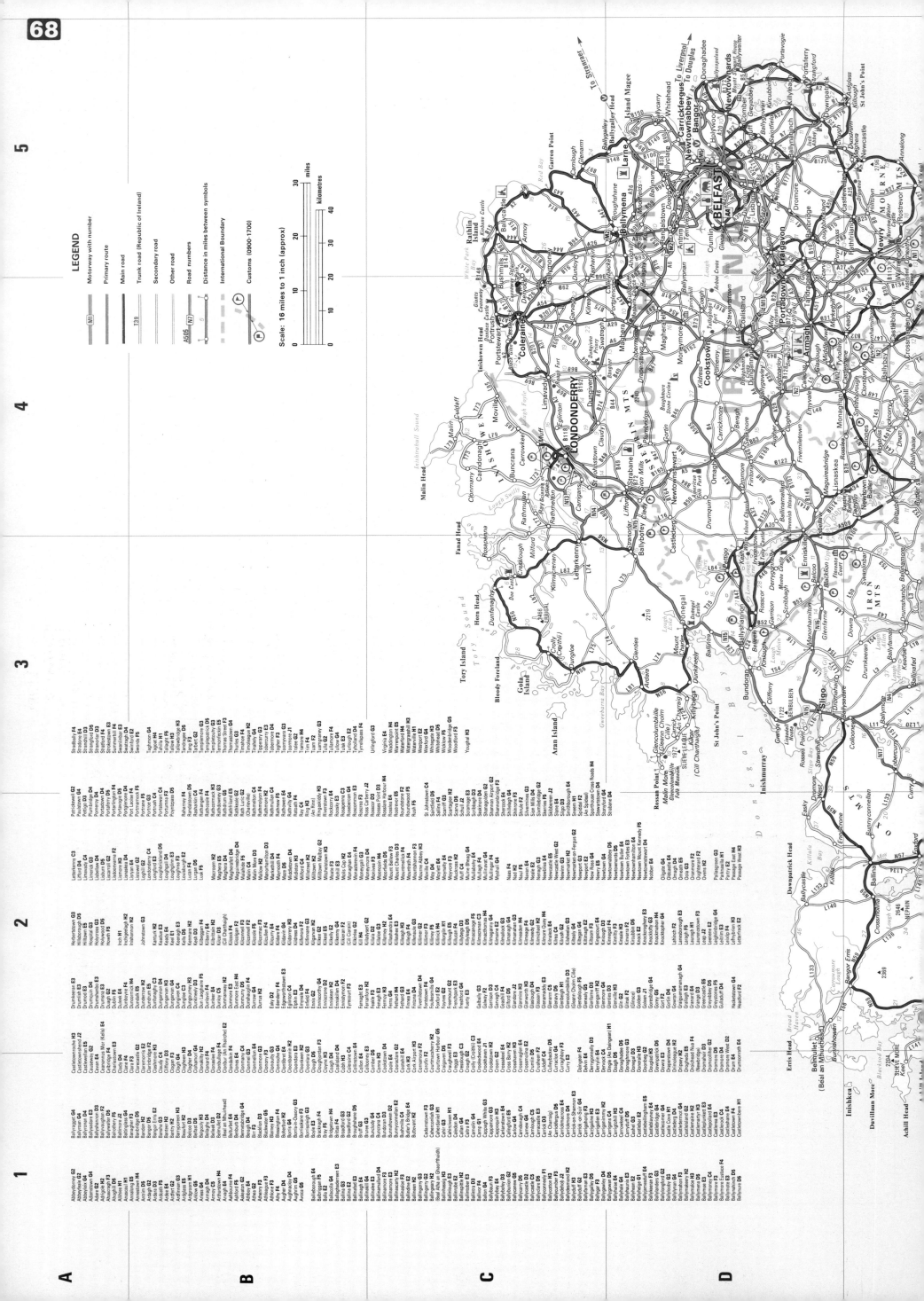

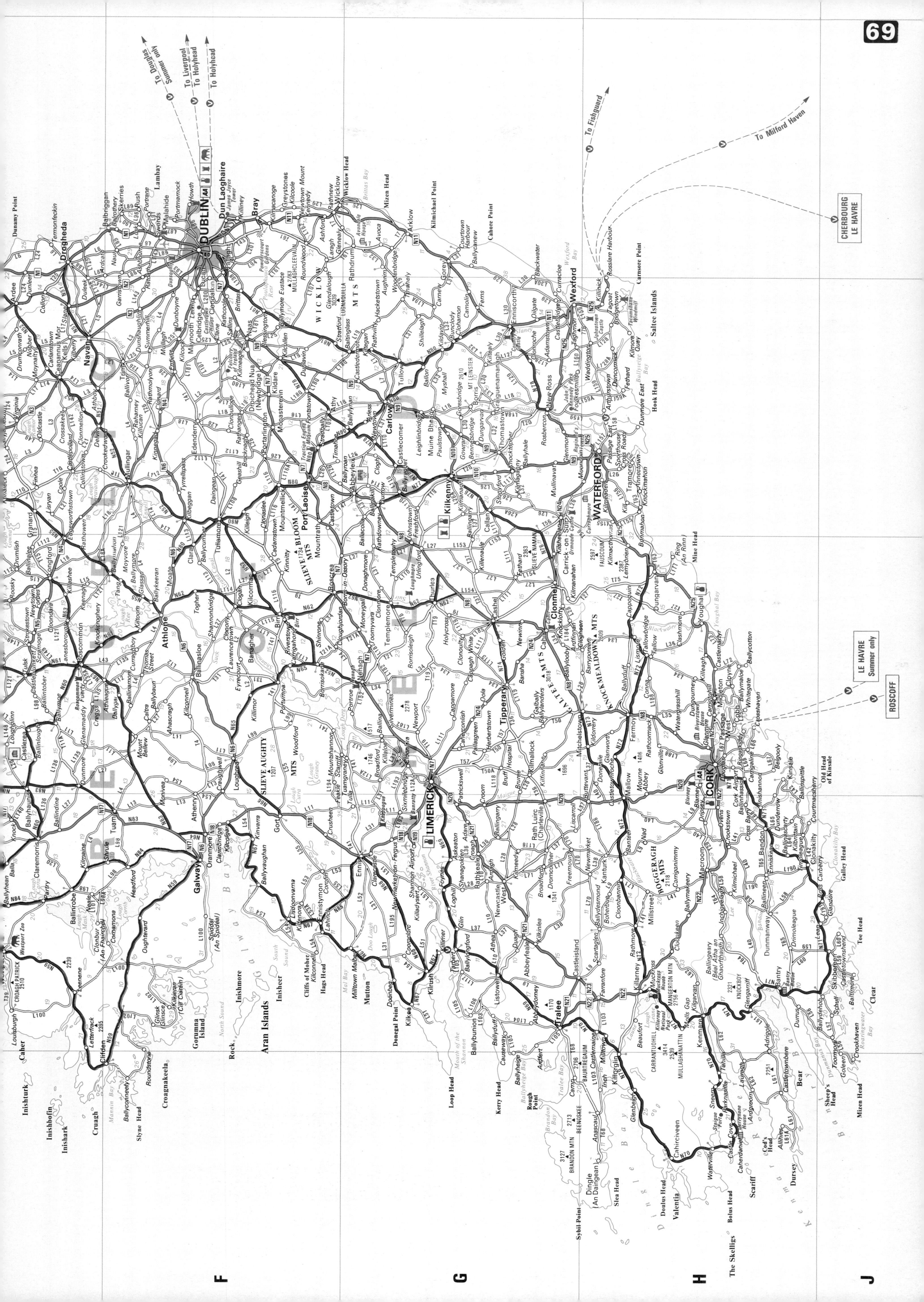
To Douglas Summer only
To Liverpool
To Holyhead
To Holyhead
To Fishguard
To Milford Haven
CHERBOURG LE HAVRE
LE HAVRE Summer only
ROSCOFF
DUBLIN
Dun Laoghaire
Drogheda
Navan
Mullingar
Athlone
Longford
Galway
Tuam
Roscommon
Port Laoise
Kilkenny
Carlow
Wexford
WATERFORD
Clonmel
Tipperary
LIMERICK
CORK
Tralee
Killarney
Ennis
WICKLOW MTS
SLIEVE BLOOM MTS
SLIEVE AUGHTY MTS
GALTEE MTS
KNOCKMEALDOWN MTS
BOGGERAGH MTS
Aran Islands
Inishmore
Inisheer
Loop Head
Kerry Head
Mizen Head
Carnsore Point
Hook Head
Saltee Islands
Valentia
The Skelligs
F
G
H
J

# Index to Atlas

To locate a place in the atlas, first look up the name of the town or village required in the index. Turn to the page number indicated in bold type and find the location using the last four numbers. Taking Hythe (Kent)........*11* TR 1635 as our example: take the first figure of the reference, 1, this refers to the number along the bottom of the page. The second figure, 6, tells you the distance to move in tenths to the right of this numbered line. A vertical line through this point is the first half of the reference. The third figure, 3, refers to the number on the lefthand side of the page. Finally, the fourth figure, 5, indicates the distance to move in tenths above this numbered line. A horizontal line drawn through this point to intersect with the first line gives the precise location of the place in question.







## B

# C

# D



# E

# F



# G

# H

# I



# J



# K

# L

# M



# N

# O



# P

# T

## U



## V



## W